ISSUES IN EDUCATION

ISSUES IN EDUCATION

G. Pankajam

ISBN : 978-81-212-1217-5

Price: ₹ 970

First Published 2014

Published by

Gyan Publishing House
23, Main Ansari Road, Darya Ganj
New Delhi-110002
Phones : 23282060, 23261060
Fax : 011-23285914
E-mail: books@gyanbooks.com
Website: www.gyanbooks.com

Laser Typesetting: Gyan Prints, Delhi
Printed at: G. Print Process, Delhi

Cataloging in Publication Data--DK
Courtesy: D.K. Agencies (P) Ltd. <docinfo@dkagencies.com>

Pankajam, G.
Issues in education / by G. Pankajam.
p. cm.
Includes bibliographical references (p.) and index.
ISBN 9788121212175

1. Education, Higher--India. 2. Education and state--India. 3. Women--India--Social conditions. 4. Women in development--Government policy--India. 5. Teachers--Training of--India. I. Title.

DDC 378.54 23

Contents

Preface

To achieve a knowledge-based society and for expansion of quality education for all, we have to provide accessibility and affordability. The glimpses into the educational system in India provided in the foregoing chapters show how the system affordability ways of imparting literacy and practical knowledge to the masses. Higher education is no more the monopoly of the rich. The emergence of a global economy due to increased trade, investment and mobility of people to learn and work across borders to earn has forced nations to adapt their systems of education at all levels to the changed global realities. Higher education has received a lot of attention in India over the past few years. The Government of India has increased funding significantly during the Twelfth Five-Year-Plan and issue of access and equity are central to higher education, at the same time ensuring quality in education is a much needed move for the growing education industry in India.

Higher education is critical to India's aspirations of emerging as a major player in the global knowledge economy. **Expansion,** Excellence and Equity are the three major considerations to improve and educate the masses in India. This alone will lead to the expansion of knowledge and **Employability. To attain these we have to create an** enabling research environment. This would involve creating adequate means of research funding and practical application of research. The need of the hour is also to create a conducive environment and attract high quality faculty by providing incentives to retain them. Efforts should also be taken to improve education technology for enhancing the teaching-learning experience to ensure better outcomes.

The author has been concerned about these issues while delivering convocation addresses and giving inaugural, valedictory and Key note address in National and State level conferences, seminars and workshops on important issues in education starting from non formal education early childhood education, school education, teacher education, women's education and tertiary education and how the present systems of education offered ways of imparting quality literacy and practical knowledge to the masses. Her involvement in the process of Accreditation of higher education institutions in the country has also made her deliver lectures on quality in education, how to measure the quality and their bench marks as we have to develop its robust quality assurance system not only in higher education but also at the school level which lays the foundation for future learning.

Being in a Gandhian Institution and working for the upliftment of masses through Gandhian principles of education and build a nonviolent society as a student of Basic Education—'Nai Talim' she has incorporated these issues also as part of this book. The author wished to spread her ideas and hence compiled all these papers to publish in a book form and it emerged as *"Issues in Education"*.

G. PANKAJAM

Acknowledgements

I would like to thank all those institutions and heads of these institutions who had invited me to deliver convocation addresses, inaugural, key note and valedictory addresses on different occations. Talking and interacting with children, students, teachers, women and the public inspired me and made me think and analyse the different issues in education. They also served as critics.

I am also thankful to my niece Dr Devaki Nadimuthu, Assistant Professor in Education in Gandhi Gram Rural Institute (Deemed University), for going through the manuscripts of the papers and for giving suggestions. I thank my nephew Mr. G. Nadimuthu for his help in typing and compiling.

I thank Ms. P. Kalaiselvi for her help in arranging the papers in order and in compiling the papers.

I express my sincere thanks to Gyan Publishing House, New Delhi, for publishing this book entitled "Issues in Education" in a very short-time on receipt of the manuscripts.

I will be highly thankful to the readers if they could send their comments and suggestions for further improvement while bringing out the revised edition of the book.

G. PANKAJAM

1

Towards a Meaningful Higher Education

India has made considerable economic progress since its Independence. Most noticeable are the expansion and diversification of production both in industry and agriculture. New technologies introduced in many industries. Industrial investment took place in a variety of new industries. Modern management system and were introduced. New classes of entrepreneurs have come up. But there is serious concern at this juncture. The proportion of our population, in the relevant age group, that enters the world of higher education is just about 7 per cent only, though we aim at 15 per cent by 2015. The opportunities for higher education in terms of the number of places in universities are simply not adequate in relation to our needs. Large segments of our population do not have access to higher education.

According to National Knowledge Commission (NKC) "It is important to recognise that there is a quiet crisis in higher education in India which runs deep. The time has come to address this crisis in a systematic and forthright manner. NKC's recommendations constitute an important beginning; the changes suggested would make a real difference. There is more to be done, and NKC will continue to think about next steps, but it emphasizes the urgency of the situation, because India's future depends on it." Higher education is important, for it provides the cutting edge. And universities and colleges are the life-blood of higher education As per NKC it is a clear, that higher education needs a systematic overall, so that we could educate much larger numbers without diluting academic standards. This will also increase the gross ratio increment in enrolment.

Crisis in Higher Education System

Deprivation of Educations

The Indian academics are disturbed by the educational deprivation and "Exclusion of a vast majority of the people from the process of education is a most disturbing aspect of educational and social planning." While the present education system has succeeded in establishing a measure of cohesion among elites across class, caste and regional boundaries, it has promoted increasing differentiation between the highly educated, the not-so-highly educated and not educated within each community and region. It characterizes this class of elites. Government's pervasive involvement in higher education and academic research, show that the real beneficiaries are middle and upper-income students and the rest of society especially the poor are exploited and denied the benefits. The reality is that these beneficiaries are the intellectual followers of the west rather than intellectual leaders of our country.

There have been significant changes in the field of higher education during the last three decades. The phenomenal growth in the number of colleges and universities, the high enrolment and turn over of degree holders, the increase in the teacher salaries, and six-fold increase in the higher education budget provide some indicators of the progress made. On the other side of the balance sheet is the high percentage of drop out, the ever-growing educated unemployed, the drain of skilled manpower and the continuing chorus of concern about the lowering standards of teaching.

Irrelevant Education

The productive capacity of the system has gone up but the relevance of the product has gone down. The cause of the irrelevance of product is rooted in the system itself. The system lays greater emphasis on quantitative expansion rather than on qualitative change. The present education system is alien in our own land through an improvement on the one set by the British. It is not conceived as a process of socialisation to one's own culture and ethos. The standard is not set by Indian scholars keeping in view the Indian intellectual traditions and the needs of Indian societies. The standards are dictated by the developed countries. Therefore, the acceptance or rejection of our standard of education is by the U.K. or U.S. Higher education Institutions, Universities and colleges should spread not only knowledge and skills but also values of humanity and virtues. Besides spurring the nation's technological and economics advancement higher education has to fulfillment the aspiration of the youth, who are with full of energy and looking for proper direction. Another deficiency wc see in higher education institutions is the dearth of talent for academic and research positions in institutions of higher education.

Lowering of Standard

There is no comprehensive and uniform approach to the question of standards of education. Standards are constantly lowered for specific regions, castes and subjects while at the same time favour of the minorities as a convenient handle to beat the opponents espousing the cause of the majority. Unfortunately, it is not understood that the relationship between the majority and the minority is not one of opposition, but one of interdependence. Therefore, the standards of higher education need not be lowered in competition with one another.

Urbanised

Another major cause of irrelevance of Indian higher education is that most of our institutions of higher learning are urban based. The population of India is overwhelmingly rural. But institutions of higher learning are not only located in urban centres, they create urbanised individuals who are far removed from the rural ethos and have become aliens in their own land.

Brain Drain

We observe and even proud of brain drain, turning India into exporters of highest quality and skilled human resources to other parts of the globe. A look at the major components of the Indian population and their vocational interest and the course structure on the Indian universities is enough to prove the irrelevance of higher education. 90 per cent of the total population of India is engaged in or dependent on agriculture. But the conventional universities have little to do with agriculture. There is also greater reluctance on the part of funding agencies to support on agriculture-related research where such interests exist in conventional universities.

Medium of Instruction

One more crisis is medium of education which has a major role in maintaining the standard as well as lowering the quality of education in India. The elite are in favour of English as the medium which they consider a status symbol. Today the national consensus is in favour of a switchover to regional language media which is expected not only to increase the access to education, but also establish a viable relation between tradition and change. The lukewarm attitude of the academics towards the changeover has resulted in half-hearted teaching of both English and the regional languages and consequently lowering of the general standard of education. The grudging switchover of only 52 per cent of universities to the regional language media, the total confusion arising from the un preparedness in not being able to evolve suitable methods and materials, are examples of lack of firm leadership in this area. An understanding of and command over the English language is a most important determinant of access to higher education, employment possibilities and social opportunities.

Isolated Researches

There is very little socially relevant and inter disciplinary study in the universities and in other Higher Education Institutions Social sciences like Psychology, Anthropology, Sociology, Linguistics, Political Science and other Science subjects study problems relating to their own in an isolated manner, but interdisciplinary study for the wholesome development is almost nonexistent. Interdisciplinary Research is a substantive and practical guide to the most effective avenues for collaborative and integrative research in the social, behavioural, and bio-medical sciences. Inter disciplinary studies will enable the science and technology students aware of the various issues concerning man and society and sensitize them to the broader social, cultural, economic, ethical and humane issues involved in social change and social interactions.

Poor Student Support Services

Owing to transformation of economy and society, the 21st century would depend, insignificant part, on the spread and the quality of education among our people, particularly in higher education. The objectives of reform and change in our higher education system must be expansion, excellence and inclusion. In the increasing global competition for the best students— our most important stakeholder of education, the quality and attractiveness of an institution does no longer depend only on its academic, teaching and research standards: services to students have come to play an important role in the quality assessment–and thus competitiveness of institutions. Student support services have direct bearing on the quality of education provided in the institutions. It will reduce the drop out rate and enable successful completion of their studies.

International Cooperation in Higher Education

Knowledge and exploration generation is a borderless enterprise, but our academic institutions lack meaningful international connections. The international mobility of students and the teachers has considerably gained ground as a major policy all over the globe last 2 decades. Universities and other higher education institutions operate in an increasingly international environment. Internationalisation of higher education, once a marginal concern, has gained and moved to centre. It has become "mainstreamed" and is now regarded as part and parcel of "higher education policy". Education anywhere in the globe should move towards improving cultural and economic development of the country, for national integration and for realising the ideals of a society of common citizenship and culture, and strengthening the integrity of the people. Continuous effort to be taken to expand educational opportunity; a sustained and intensive effort to raise the quality of education at all stages; by emphasising on the development of science and technology; and the cultivation of moral and social values. The educational system must produce young men and women of character and ability committed to national service and development. Only then education will be able to play its vital role in promoting national progress, creating a sense of national integration. We have to take a proactive strategy towards providing and getting more meaningful and quality higher education for all irrespective of their socio economic status. Neither the social status nor the poverty be the causes for not having an access to higher education. Attempts should be taken to expand provision towards universal access, promoting coherence and co-ordination, raising the quality of provision, improving the quality of training adequate funds and investment, developing appropriate pedagogies and engaging families and communities.

The Future Ahead

Knowledge Economy

With the advent of changes in the world scenario like Globalisation, Liberalisation and WTO etc., many changes have taken place in the education system in the country like knowledge economy that has been added in to the education system. The teachers have become knowledge workers. Economy has been attached to the gains of educational system. Knowledge generation is attached to economic outputs. The poverty can no more remain as a factor and avoid getting education. There are good governmental systems that are providing good quality education to the children free of charge. Private enterprise in school and higher education has changed the entire policy planning structure of education in the country.

Education is among the fastest growing service sectors of the economy. It is one of the important public attributes of social and human development. Hence, it has been accorded an honored place in the Indian society. Prior to independence, the growth of institutions of higher education in India was very slow and diversification in the areas of the studies was very limited. With the passing of the resolution on Scientific Policy under the leadership of Jawaharlal Nehru, the development of science, technology and scientific research received special emphasis. Education being a powerful instrument of social, economic and political change, its broad principles and objectives are related to the long term national goals.

Identification of Talent

For the cultivation of excellence and talents among the youth it is necessary that education system is revamped, talent in diverse fields are identified at an early age and maximum stimulus, encouragement and opportunity are given to complete with global arena. These efforts will revitalise India in different dimensions and the dream of the youth will become a reality. The higher education system must provide for accountability to society and create accountability within. An expansion of higher education which provides students with choices and creates competition between institutions is going to be vital in enhancing accountability and quality in higher education system. Only when India takes interest in innovation to increase its capacity succeed in global competition. It should permeate into all sectors to move towards a balanced inclusive and sustainable development and growth, of people at the bottom of the society.

Work-Experience and Vocational Education

The educational institutions and the stakeholders of education like community should come closer through suitable programmes of mutual interests, services and support. Work-experience and national service including participation in meaningful and challenging programmes of community and national reconstruction should accordingly become an integral part of education especially at the tertiary level to enable a competent wok force to emerge and participate in nation building programme. Vocational Education to play an effective-role in the changing national context and for India to enjoy the fruits there is an urgent need to redefine the curriculum for imparting vocational education to make them flexible, contemporary, relevant, inclusive and creative. Students should be permitted multiple entry and exit options in the vocational education stream. Links should be established between the vocational education stream as well as academic stream at higher education level. Schemes for life-long skill up-gradation in various trades and soft skill development through short training programmes should be introduced by allocating more resources. There should be a provision for generating a cadre of multi-skilled persons to take up any jobs besides being a professional.

Education for Agriculture and Industry

India wants to stick to stand on agriculture and encourage the farmers as well as small scale and agro based industries in our country to provide employment opportunities to over growing population. Special emphasis should therefore be placed on the development of education for agriculture and industry. Our education system should cultivate the work culture among the youth. Our universities are not producing the educated workforce. There is little relationship between what they learn in the class rooms and the work force needed on the field. He need to train/educate our young population on employable skills so that we will have more number of people who will work and be productive in future rather than dependent population and be a burden to the nation.

Science Education and Research

With a view to accelerating the growth of the national economy, science education and research should receive high priority. Science and mathematics should be an integral part of general education till the end of the school stage. Special attention should be given to provide postgraduate courses and to the improvement of standards and quality of training and research at the higher education level. Centres of advanced study in different parts of the country should be strengthened and a small number of 'cluster of centres' aiming at the highest possible standards in research and training should be established and encouraged to take up higher level researches that will be of boost to scientists. India has to allocate adequate fund for research and innovation in different discipline with the private partnership. But it is hardly 0.9 per cent of GDP is being spent on (R&D) research and development in India. Emphasis on expansion, excellence and access in the Higher Education system with a focus on reforms in, leveraging information and communication technology (ICT) to create dedicated research and education networks, and the need for making our professional education streams more responsive to national realities as well as global competitive challenges.

Part-time Education and Correspondence Courses

Part-time education and correspondence courses should be developed on a large scale at the higher education level to provide HE to all at any time, at anywhere. Such facilities should also be developed for secondary school students, for teachers and for agricultural, industrial and other workers who could not enter the portal of higher education institutions through Community colleges. Such facilities will smoothen transition from school to work, promote the cause of education and provide opportunities to the large number of people who have the desire to have higher education, further but cannot do on a full-time basis. NKC recommendations on distance education focus on creating a national ICT infrastructure, developing web based common open resources, establishing a credit bank and providing a national testing service. The greatest challenge lies in providing training for potential entrants in the unorganised/informal sector, which accounts for the largest proportion of employment. Here comes the role of community colleges which are coming in a big way.

Increasing Budgets Allocation

The reconstruction of education on the basis of bench marks suggested will need additional outlay. The costs of government support for universities are negligible today. To set up new institutions based on norms, upgrade and reform existing institutions and ensure accreditation to provide benchmarks for quality increase public spending and diversify sources of financing. The expansion of our system of higher education is not possible without enhanced levels of financing. This must necessarily come from both public and private sources It is stated in the XIth Plan document there is proposal to allocate Rs. 2.5 trillion, a four-fold increase in the allocation for education over the Xth Plan, make the share of education in the total plan will accordingly increase from 7.7 per cent to 19 per cent. At least 6 per cent of the national income should be invested on higher education.

We have to establish many more universities including 50 National Universities as suggested by NKC, so that there can be a massive expansion of opportunities, through 1500 universities nationwide, that would enable

India to attain a gross enrolment ratio of at least 15 per cent by 2015. The focus would have to be on new universities, along with the promotion of clusters of affiliated colleges as universities. While increasing the number of Universities we should also reform existing universities and upgrade to the world class universities. Only when our system is strong and robust the world will respect us and be willing to work with us.

Human Resources

In terms of human resources needed for providing quality higher education there is need for human resources-faculty, teachers, with adequate potential and commitment. We are moving towards an age of ICT—the digital world and in the midst of the information age. As a result, the concept of a classroom as learning environment with chalk, blackboard, duster, textbook, homework, examinations, grades etc. will change and new strategies of teaching and learning should emerge. Teachers should be well equipped with knowledge skill and commitment to the profession, to make universities/departments as the centres of excellence. Higher education in India must be made affordable for all irrespective of their socio economic status. HE institutions must be brought closer to their door steps by innovative techniques and knowledge sharing.

Conclusion

Reforming academic structure and institutions anywhere is a long term process. A comprehensive action plan is to be evolved on the basis of the requirement with a participatory approach—government and public sectors contributing to the growth and development of education in India. It should be need based with a future vision, especially at the higher education level, so that education could become a powerful instrument of social change and penetrate into every walk of life at the micro and macro level in a democratic country like India. As Rusk says "Democratic institutions cannot exist without education, for democracy functions only when the people are informed and aware, thirsting for knowledge and are exchanging ideas… And in the underdeveloped economies, education itself, stimulates development by demonstrating that tomorrow need not be the same as yesterday that change can take place, that the outlook is hopeful."

Human Resources

2

Quest for Excellence in Higher Education

Be careful to leave your sons well instructed rather than rich, for the hopes of the instructed are better than the wealth of the ignorant.

Knowledge explosion, increase in use of information and communication technology has led high competition in every walk of life. This has led to drastic changes in various dimensions in higher education system in India. At the same time there is demand for accountability and for creating what is the best to the society to make higher education more meaningful and need based. As a result, higher education has made a significant contribution to economic development, social progress and political democracy in independent India. But there is serious cause for concern at this juncture. The proportion of our population, in the relevant age group, that enters the world of higher education is about seven per cent only where as it is much higher in developed countries. The opportunities for higher education in terms of the number of places seals in universities are simply not adequate in relation to our needs and the population. Large segments of our population just do not have access to higher education. What is more, the quality of higher education in most of our higher education institutions is a great concern. The higher education system must now concentrate not only on establishing more number of higher education institution but also quality and accountability to society.

There is a clear, view that higher education needs a systematic overhaul, so that India can educate much larger numbers of its vibrant youth according to their choice without diluting academic standards. This is essential because the transformation of economy and society in the 21st century would depend, in significant part, on the spread and the quality of education among our people, particularly in the sphere of higher education. It is only an inclusive and powerful society that can provide strong foundations for a knowledge society.

For quality in higher education we should think of paradigm that builds efficiency that is integrated into institutional structures. To measure the quality in different dimensions of education the following criteria should be taken into consideration. Curricular aspects, Teaching — Learning and Evaluation, Research, Consultancy, Extension, Infrastructure, Learning, Resources, Student support and Progression, Governance and leadership and Innovative practices. These are the Bench marks, which have been evolved by (NAAC) National Assessment and Accreditation Council of India. Tools are also being developed to measure quality or benchmark, the progress and success of these efforts, taken by higher education institutions.

Among the improvement strategies and techniques such as Total Quality Management (TQM), Continuous Quality Improvement (CQI), Process Re-engineering (PR) and Benchmarking have emerged as a useful, easily understood, and effective step to face the competitive world.

Bench Marking

The Strategy of bench marking is important both conceptually and practically, and is being used for improving administrative processes as well as instructional models in colleges and universities by examining processes and models at other schools and adapting their techniques and approaches (Chaffee & Sherr 1992; Clark 1993). As Kempner 1993 says "Benchmarking is an ongoing, systematic process for measuring and comparing the work processes of one organisation to those of another, by bringing an external focus to internal activities, functions, or operations". Bench marking should therefore, be integrated into the fundamental operations in the institutions to measure its progress.

Bench marking is a positive process, and provides objective measurements for base lining (setting the initial values), goal-setting and improvement tracking, which can lead to dramatic innovations (Shafer & Coate 1992). In addition, quality strategies and reengineering efforts are enhanced by bench marking because it can identify areas that could benefit most from TQM and make it possible to improve operations. Bench marking helps to identify institutional strengths and its weaknesses and to decide the Best practices to be adopted to improve the quality of educational practices in all dimensions. Steven M. Bragg defines a "Best Practice as any improvement over existing systems". SACUBO (Southern Association of College and University Business Officers) defines it as "creating better, more efficient and customer friendly business practice". Quality assurance, or a quality management system, is a method of ensuring a consistent standard of deliverables or outputs. A quality assurance process is at the heart of producing a professional and consistent product or service.

Quality has no end it is an ever extending ongoing process of goal sitting and practices. The better you are, the better you need to be. The management of the quality process is infinite, and marked only by milestones, never by completion! Quality assurance refers to both customers as well as other interested parties (stakeholders) are convinced of the fact that the requirements pertaining to products are met so that external confidence is achieved.

Measures to be Taken for Quality Maintenance

Though there are challenges in higher education in India due to its diversity, large population their needs, financial requirements and a vast area to be covered, it becomes paramount important to maintain the quality of higher education in order to compete with the world; other wise we will be pushed out from competitive world. The higher education institutions should therefore, be more conscious of the quality, component of the education provided.

Quality assurance has to be grounded in the actual practices of systematic quality management which have been created on the basis of the requirements of the community, the nation and the world. It is therefore, suggested that the number of students to be admitted to a college or university department should be determined by the availability of the staff, laboratory, faculty library and other infrastructure facilities.

Considerable care is to be taken while establishing new colleges and universities. These should be started only after making the need assessment of the community, availability of adequate funds for the purpose and due care should be taken to ensure proper standards and quality, maintenance.

National Knowledge Commission (NKC) suggested that there should be frequent revision of universities curricula at least once in three years. As there is change in the content in almost all the subjects due to innovations in science and technology frequent revision becomes essential.

Annual examinations, which test memory rather than understanding, should be supplemented with continuous internal assessments which could begin with a weight of 25 per cent and be raised to 50 per cent over a stipulated period. This will demand systematic and continuous studies on the part of students, instead concentrating only on end examinations.

NKC proposes a transition to a Choice Based Credit Cystem (CBCS) where degrees are granted on the basis of completing a requisite number of credits from different disciplines, according to student's choices.

Retention of Quality Teachers

More teachers are leaving the profession or there is high mobility among the teachers because they are burnt out, disillusioned, or have found better jobs in other places. When many experienced teachers, retire education institutions are hard pressed to find qualified candidates to fill those positions. Teachers are the most important factor in the effectiveness of the quality in education. Hence, there must be a conscious effort to attract and retain talented faculty members by creating better working conditions combined with better incentives for performance.

The elements of infrastructure that support the teaching–learning process, such as libraries, laboratories and connectivity, need to be monitored and upgraded on a regular basis to make the teaching learning environment to be more conducive for both teachers and the students.

There is need to bring in reform in the structures of governance of universities and colleges so that it preserves autonomy and promotes accountability.

There is an urgent need to restructure the system of undergraduate colleges affiliated to universities. To promote autonomy to colleges either as individual colleges or as clusters of colleges, on the basis of criteria that have been stipulated. Autonomy will promote innovations in curriculum, strategies of teaching and evaluation. There is possibility for quality improvement in autonomous colleges as there is freedom in evolving their own programme and make changes as and when it is required.

Some of the affiliated colleges could be remodeled as community colleges, which could provide both vocational education and formal education, by updating knowledge and skill. Today we lack work force as every body wants to enter the white colored jobs without soiling their hands.

The system of higher education must recognise that there should be diversity and pluralism in any system of higher education, and avoid a uniform 'one–size fits–all' approach. Pluralism must recognise, rather than ignore, such diversity and differentiation.

Education is the fundamental rights mechanism for social inclusion through the creation of more opportunities, for all to have access for all the deserving students without any discrimination.

Educational systems around the world today are under increasing pressure to use the new information and communication technologies (ICTs) to teach students the knowledge and skills they need in the 21st century. It is therefore, important to enhance the ICT infrastructure and its use in all the higher education institutions. Teachers and students should be exposed to the use of ICT in the class room and in the community, for both teaching and learning in the world of technology.

Creating of a portal on higher education and research by higher education institutions such as UGC, AICT, NCERT, NCTE etc. would increase interaction and accessibility within higher education system. A knowledge network would connect all universities and colleges for online open resources for quality higher education. Connectivity will also help the teachers and students to have access to latest information from any part of the globe.

There is a paradigm shift that we have started thinking about quality higher education for all which is going to be a great boon to the youths of this county. As the future is in their hands of our youths they will make our nation to be the fore runner in the competitive world. India will definitely lead the globe.

We should therefore, have quality consciousness and move towards providing the quality education. All the stakeholders of higher education as suggested by NAAC. The following seven steps are required to Quality and maintenance in any educational institution.

Quest for excellence

Understanding the concept

Action–orientation

Learner-centric approach

Innovation for change

Training to build competencies

Year–round activity.

3

Education for Holistic Development

"A teacher affects eternity: he can never tell where his influence stops."

Education needs a more holistic approach rather than approaching it in a fragmented way. The challenge confronting our educational systems today is how to transform the curriculum and teaching-learning process to provide students with the skills to function effectively in this dynamic, information-rich, and constantly changing world.

We need a learner centered education system built on the assumptions of connectedness, and wholeness. Therefore, the goals of education should reflect the fundamental needs such as economic prosperity, healthy democracy, personal, community and environmental well-being and its progress. Community well-being requires an inclusive, compassionate and cohesive approach that provides social and emotional support to people. We need active community participation in decision-making and the co-creation of what is required by each community.

People need access to productive and meaningful learning to help them achieve educational, vocational, personal goals and self-determination. The cultural identity and diversity with artistic, sporting and recreational excellence should be promoted through education. It should be a rich experiential journey of discovery, expression and mastery where all students and teachers learn and grow together. But it is felt that current education systems do not satisfy needs of students for meaning, wholeness and fulfillments. Education is to be fully human-recognising the physical, emotional, mental and spiritual dimensions of being human; recognise the importance of opportunities for the creative expression of individuals and communities; transformation and growth by providing opportunity to each person to reach for the highest aspirations of individuals.

Strong foundation and cornerstones are to be laid on this type of education. This will lead to true freedom, democracy, wellbeing and sustainable human development. Only such type of schools will stimulate creativity, intellectual curiosity and honest inquiry among students. No school can survive in isolation. All the stakeholders in education should actively participate to provide meaningful, quality and total education.

The major function of education is therefore; to produce socially fit persons who are conversant with the social traditions and cultural background of their community. Those educational institutions which are equipped to coordinate with community alone can provide quality education and produce quality and efficient people who would work in tune with the social needs and demands reflecting ethos, aims and values of the society.

Education and poverty are linked with total development of an individual and the society. Education develops intellectual capacity and social skills, and children who complete at least ten years of schooling, considered as the minimum requirement for achieving basic literacy and numeracy and they are better equipped to move out of poverty. As households become impoverished, older children are often pulled out of school to supplement family income by joining labour force as child lab our and support their younger siblings resulting in wastage and stagnation leading to increase in dropout rate.

Constraints in Achieving the Goal

One of the greatest impediments to provide meaningful education today is not lack of good programme, or innovation, or good teachers, but a lack of up-to-date perspective plan for future. There is more information than any one person can keep up with-even in very specialised fields. Due to knowledge explosion in the world the sum total of human knowledge is estimated to be growing very fast. National Knowledge Commission (NKC) 'believes that providing universal access to quality school education is a cornerstone of development and a minimum necessary condition for any progress towards making India a knowledge society.'

Drastic changes in the primary education in India should be attempted as it is the foundation period and highly flexible including universatisation of and quality primary education for all without any discrimination. In the last 50 years, the government of India has taken several steps. Commissions have been formed; reports have been submitted but not received attention except gathering dust. The main thrust should therefore be given to the Primary Education. This area has been grossly neglected in the last five decades, and, that is why we find that, even after 64 years of our own rule, more than 50 per cent of our Indian population is still illiterate. Basic facilities in all schools, use of electronic media for promoting education will increase the literacy rate of primary educated students and change the environment at our schools, and ensure quality education.

All the Five year plans in India places high priority on education as a central instrument for achieving rapid and inclusive growth with specific emphasis on expansion, excellence and equity. Implementation of the scheme successfully rests with the teaching community and their commitment to teaching and welfare of children.

Holistic Education

Free, compulsory and quality education to all at least up to Vth Std. should be ensured to remove illiteracy from India. Primary Education provided to children in the rural areas, where real India exists will definitely improve the human resource development required to build a strong and vibrant India. Provide holistic education which is concerned with the growth of every person's intellectual, emotional, social, physical, artistic, creative and spiritual potentials. It actively engages students in the teaching/learning process and encourages personal and collective responsibility. All students are not fully engaged in the current curricula; many students drop out, or absent or don't participate. School education has to be a crucial area of focus if the foundation of a knowledge based society is to be built.

Holistic education recognises that all knowledge is created within a social and cultural context it encourages the transfer of learning across separate academic disciplines. It encourages learners to critically approach the cultural, moral and political contexts of their lives in the specific society. Holistic learning organised around relationships within and between learners and their environment empower learners to live fully in the present and to co-create preferred futures.

Providing education for girls is one of the best strategies for breaking the cycle of poverty and disempowerment on account of greater externalities. Educated girls have greater capacity to apply their learning to their decision making at home and at place of work. Their marriage is postponed due to education and is more likely to space pregnancies. As a result, they tend to have fewer children and are more likely to seek medical attention for themselves and their children. They are better informed about good nutrition and childcare. Women who are educated will enroll their own children in primary school. Educating children, particularly girls, is therefore is an essential strategy of breaking of poverty. It is an assurance of equality of status for girl child as an individual and as a citizen in her own right through promotion of opportunities for her growth and development.

The adolescents should be provided with education and development opportunities so that they can participate in the life and progress of community as productive citizens. They should also be provided with opportunity to develop life skills and self-esteem, decision-making ability and provide education and training opportunities to adolescents to help them prepare for sustainable livelihoods.

Steps to be Taken

Millennium Development Goal emphasises that as per UNESCO, by 2015, children everywhere, boys and girls alike, will be able to complete a full course of primary education without any discrimination with increase in Net enrolment ratio in primary education (UNESCO), Proportion of pupils starting grade 1 who reach grade 5, and the Literacy rate of 15-24 year-olds should go up.

All children in the age groups of 6-14 to have access to primary schools, upper primary schools or their alternatives within a distance of 1 km. and 3 kms. respectively and all schools to have buildings, toilets, drinking water, electricity, playgrounds, blackboards and other basic facilities, with special attention to disadvantaged children. Improve the quality of education through various interventions and stress upon the relevance and quality of girls' education for their empowerment and to facilitate retention of girls in schools.

MDG emphasises that it is to be ensured that every child at the elementary school gets cooked mid day meals and progressively move towards providing cooked mid-day meals to all children in higher classes in Government, local bodies and Government aided schools.

Generate interest in sports and games among school children and also place greater emphasis on the organisation of tournaments and sports and games at various levels.

Involve and enhance the effectiveness of the role of NGOs in educational development programmes.

To reduce the drop-outs motivate community and parents to bring children back to school to complete their education. Provide suitable alternative education systems such as bridge courses, remedial teaching, and back to school camps for school drop-outs, so that they can be mainstreamed into the formal system.

Develop a community based monitoring system to ensure cooperation between community and Panchayat Raj Institutions. This will also ensure the community's commitment.

Encourage opening of new secondary schools, expansion of capacity of the existing schools including two shifts, upgrading of upper primary schools in backward, unserved and underserved areas through expansion and diversification of open schooling and distance education systems.

Ensure inclusion of all children with disabilities in regular schools with special facilities for those with severe disabilities; establish and recognise existing special schools and admission procedure, followed evaluation systems and ensure alternative and flexible testing procedures.

Eliminate all forms of discrimination and exclusion in the curriculum, structure and services of education by providing a common school system.

Emphasize child centered education and appoint qualified and committed teachers at the primary level.

Quality education could be ensured through quality and appropriate curriculum development, textbooks and teaching learning materials, proper infrastructure and teacher training.

Take measures to prohibit and eliminate corporal punishment in all schools and provide learning facilities to help children love coming to school.

Efforts to be taken for mainstreaming 'out of school' children with special interventions and strategies to include girls, SC/ST children, working children, children with special needs, urban deprived children, children from minority groups, children below the poverty line, working children, migratory children and children to join the main stream and continue their education.

Ensure enrolment and make available mobile schools for migrant children and children from transient communities.

Establish residential schools and provide basic education infrastructure and facilities in educationally backward minorities areas and provide liberal financial assistance. Efforts to be made to explore areas of public-private partnership in education by Government, local bodies, and recognised aided schools.

Since teachers play critical role to ensuring the quality of education, it is particularly important to lay down well-defined but flexible norms for the minimum qualifications and other essential qualities required to be efficient and committed of teachers.

Ensure that teachers adopt interesting and appropriate teaching techniques and motivate the learners. Encourage modernisation of Madrasas/Maktabs and other such educational institutions by adoption of mainstream syllabus and teaching methods with specific attention to the education of the girl child.

There is a need for flexibility and innovation by teachers. We must stop our resistance to innovations and negativities and work toward the positive and must remain positive to encourage holistic development among the learners.

A Latin Proverb Says

"By learning you will teach; by teaching you will understand".

Only those teachers who refine their teaching on the basis of the feed back they receive from the stakeholders can move towards excellence in teaching. To refine teaching teachers continue to be the learners must develop the competence needed for effective teaching.

4

Education for a Global World

"Education is not the filling of a pail,

But the lighting of a fire".

—***W. B. Yeats***

Education is the foundation that creates a civil society. Educational institutions are an integral part of the rapidly changing world and they have to contribute appropriately to the growth and development of the world through their three fold functions of, Teaching, Research and Extension. There are about 350 Universities and 16000 Colleges with nearly 947000 students in India.

There are large numbers of Youth between 17-26 years of age who aspire to have higher education in India. Higher education institutions to day have to face many challenges, to meet external pressures and expectations despite inadequate funds. Discoveries and inventions in Science and Technology with extensive use of Information Communication Technology the world are moving at a faster rate than ever before.

Knowledge, qualification, labour, capital and skills are key elements of the future development of the world. Knowledge provided researches and outreach programmes undertaken should be according to the needs and demands of the society of 21st century. Link between Teaching, Research and Extension is to be established in higher education institutions. These should meet the global competition in the knowledge system, research dimension and skill provided. Institutes of higher education should be able to analyse the challenges, commitments and constraints so that the ways and means to face them could be found out and society can move towards the changing global world with confidence. In an increasingly shrinking world, we need a more sophisticated understanding of national and international dynamics at work and work place.

Education in New Millennium—A Paradigm Shift

The new millennium has to develop a creative society that is based on interaction among the individuals, institutions, societies and nations so that a comprehensive and cohesive world could emerge for a peaceful coexistence. Creative knowledge and creative skills will help to develop a creative world. Education, should, therefore aim at promoting a creative society.

Population explosion demands not regional concentration or urbanisation of the available services like health care, educational and employment opportunities. They are to be decentralised in order to prevent immigration and over concentration in one place. People, wherever they are, should be able to enjoy all these facilities for which they are entitled to. Inequality, marginalisation and global divide should not be permitted to continue. Knowledge divide between developed and developing countries will lead to inequality in job market. So efforts are to be taken to bridge the information divide.

Reducing the Gap

Without providing strong base and opportunity to individuals, where ever they are, in which ever circumstances they are born, they should be able to move to higher education. Only then there will be equality of opportunity based on merit and excellence on which the legitimacy of the society depends. Deepening social gaps in the community, work place and place of learning are responsible for spreading "culture of emergency", which creates tension and anxiety among the people. In order to promote a sustainable development to enrich the individuals to face global challenges, institutions of higher education should link the needed knowledge and skills. If this is not created we will lag behind in the race of progress. Expertise for various jobs, especially today being Information Technology turned world education should enlarge the scope for providing such type of education and promote research in such areas.

Towards a Global Welfare State and Information Society

Education should aim at providing free access to information, freedom to think creatively, innovate and perform as per the global requirement. This effort will lead the world towards a Welfare State and Information Society in future. The goal of a welfare state is possible only when there are innovations and researches in education towards this end. In a combination of a welfare state and information society there will be values of caring, confidence, communality, encouragement, freedom, creativity, courage, vision, balance and meaningfulness. All these values in a welfare state and information society will lead to a creative economy, a creative welfare society, humanly meaningful development and a global culture.

In a welfare state and information society the taxation system will promote job/work opportunities that enhance common good, entrepreneurship and creativity. Thus finance is generated for the society. Tax revenue is generated by work and not by tax rate. The philosophy underlying the idea of welfare state is that people have equal opportunities to realise their potential and are protected against the misfortunes of life. This includes equal access and opportunity to education, training, health care, job opportunity etc.

The future of the welfare state depends on the maintenance of the welfare state by improving its productivity through innovations, by combining technological and process-by networking institutions for greater strength and sharing of expertise. The success of this welfare state depends on, eventually an inclusive high quality education and training system. In the information society, learning continues through out life. Education is expected to disseminate not only information, but also build self-confidence, social skills as well as to identify the creative talents and skills of people, identify problems, generate new ideas and solve problems. The success of education is the foundation to achieve these goals. Education, research and training should be of high quality, through out the country through providing equal opportunity.

Access to Research

We must promote open access to research and research articles to all those who are in need (The Hindu. dt. Nov. 2006). It is noted that more than 205 million articles are published every year in the world.

But 24000 research articles are not available to the potential users, especially in the developing world. Easy access could be made through web.

In the global development, we must progress towards joint development that is sustainable on a world scale, with greater open mindedness from the whole world. Developing countries need not wait for the developed countries to mandate self achieving. Infact it is noted that the impact and access of research of others is greater in developing countries as developing countries have more urgent need for these.

Internalisation-Two Way Road

Our education system should attract foreign students and similarly our students and teachers should go on to learn and contribute to other countries. We can begin with attracting students from abroad to study customized courses like religion, culture, sociology, rural development, politics, women's movements and basic sciences. This means internationalisation must be a two way road. It is observed that during 2004-05, 800466 Indian students enrolled in US institutions alone. And more have gone to other countries for higher education. Graduates of accredited foreign institutions play crucial role in shaping Indians to perform better on their return to India. Most of the students, who can afford it, want to obtain the best from other countries so that they can have better chance in the job market. US Universities are interested in attracting the best students from India as they feel that India will be a potential force in the millennium.

We can benefit from global expertise by exchanging teachers and students for education, to participate in conferences, seminars, research and jobs. It would be more profitable and cost effective to provide more funds for research in overseas, participation in international conferences to obtain leading edge on international expertise. Immigration, studies and research periods carried out abroad and international networks must be considered to be mutually complementing strategies that are needed for a globalise collaboration.

Consideration for Globalisation of Education

Higher education when accepts globalisation in the new millennium should consider the following while implementing it:

Globalisation must be reciprocal-two way process of flow. There should be freedom to Indians to go abroad and foreigners to come to India. It should not be only one way channel.

Going abroad either for education or for employment to be considered as "brain circulation" and "mutual gain" not as brain drain, as there is changing dynamics domestically and globally.

Establish net working with domestic institutions and companies first to strengthen ourselves then think of other countries.

Accept free flow of materials and men, from-to any place in the globe.

There should be both specialisation and interdisciplinary studies and research at the higher education to promote an integrated growth and development of the country and meet constitutional rights and responsibilities.

Education at all levels should be according to the global demands/ market. Higher education should display the ethos of India at the same time must be demand driven.

Mass education, education for all and promotion of highly talented individuals should be the aim of education. If we cannot educate all to the highest level, we leave all of them at the lowest.

Education should be flexible and diversified according to the interest, abilities and needs of the individuals in order to stop dropouts, wastage and stagnation in education. Ensuring every individual of quality education is critical to our future.

Keep pace with innovations in research and in teaching and learning technology to use them in the class rooms including virtual learning.

Quality education at all levels should be ensured in order to reduce achievement gap between rural, urban elite and poor. Proper infrastructure facilities should be created for teaching, research and extension so that equal opportunities are made available everywhere and social justice could be brought through higher education.

Institutes of higher education should be places of ideas, rather than idea of authority. There should be no question impossible to ask, no subject that should be beyond the scope of inquiry, no issue should be regarded finally settled and no one who should be above or beyond debate. There should be transparency every where and in every thing for easy movement.

Invest liberally in education to bring people out of poverty and prepare them for global interaction. A liberal funding can boost the caliber of educational institutions and raise their capacity to provide quality education.

Efforts are to be taken to increase student enrolment in higher education institutions. Student enrollment in higher education in India is only 6 per cent as against 88 per cent in Canada, 80.9 per cent in USA and 79.8 per cent in Australia.Evenwhile compared with Asian countries. It will be possible to increase the enrollment only when higher education is diversified, equipped with the knowledge, skills and perspectives that will ensure success in a global age.

Institutions with potentials should be identified for various disciplines and performance based funding be encouraged to promote healthy competitions among the institutions.

All the higher education institutions should volunteer for accreditation by national as well as international organisations, to know their stand in providing quality education.

Summer schools and special coaching camps should be arranged for high achievers every year for fine tuning and focusing their attention.

Faculty improvement programme should be insisted upon at least once in every three years. This exposure will bring new knowledge and fresh thinking in them to teach and guide research projects.

Conclusion

While concluding I would like to say that our main thrust of education in India should be to facilitate human resource development and make it a knowledge reservoir to disseminate and radiate to the whole Universe what is unique to India.

"Think globally and Act locally" should be the slogan of this era by encouraging everyone to have a broad mind at the same time not to forget the ethos of India.

5

Access and Equity in Higher Education Challenges in 12th Plan

"The most important and urgent reform needed in education is to transform it, to endeavor to relate it to the life, needs and aspirations of the people and thereby make it the powerful instrument of social, economic and cultural transformation necessary for the realisation of the national goals. For this purpose, education should be developed so as to increase productivity, achieve social and national integration, accelerate the process of modernisation and cultivate social, moral and spiritual values."

— ***S. Radhakrishnan***

The vision of Radhakrishnan Commission and Kothari Commission has the following five main goals for Higher education—Greater Access, Equal Access or Equality in education, Quality and Excellence, Relevance and Value Based Education.

Active involvement of all stake-holders in education alone can strengthen higher education. It is therefore suggested that Private sectors should come forward to make higher education available to all eligible and deserving people without any deprivation.

As Knowledge Commission says, "by 2020, the population of India will be better educated, healthier and more prosperous". The pace of India's future progress will depend on the type and quality of education available. Hence it is inevitable that higher education is made available to all. But, the major challenges before the Indian higher education system are to bring equity and quality of education across the country.

Several social, economic and political constraints are there to have access and equity in higher education in India. Poverty leads to high drop-out rates at primary, middle and secondary school levels. Lower status of women, lack of easy access, lack of implementation of existing programmes, inadequate utilization of resources, absence of political will and inadequacies in coordinated actions even within institutions are the other reasons. Financial constrains form a significant factor in achieving equity, in education. At this back drop the Planning Commission has designed the vision and mission of 12th Five-Year-Plan as follows:

Vision

To realise India's human resource potential to its fullest in the higher education sector, with equity and inclusion.

Mission

Provide greater opportunities of access to higher education with equity to all the eligible persons and in particular to the vulnerable sections. Expand access by supporting existing institutions, establishing new institutions, supporting State Governments and Non-Government Organisations/civil society to supplement public efforts aimed at removing regional or other imbalances that exist at present; Initiate policies and programmes for strengthening research and innovations and encourage institutions — public or private to engage in stretching the frontiers of knowledge and Promote the quality of higher education by investing in infrastructure and faculty, promoting academic reforms, improving governance and institutional restructuring towards the inclusion of the hitherto deprived communities".

Of course there is many fold increase in the number of institutions and enrolment of students in Universities and Colleges during the last 11 Five-Year-Plans and the 12th plan Approach paper is under preparation. The enrolment rate is still just within 12 per cent to 14 per cent only which is relatively low by international comparison. The number of universities in the country has increased from 20 in 1947 to 378, number of colleges, from 500 has gone up to nearly 19000, after independence, the number of teaching staff has increased from 15, 000 to nearly 5.00 Lakhs; The number of students enrolled in higher education too has gone up to 115 lakhs. This has, in turn; enhanced access to higher education, the enrolment ratio has increased from less than 1 per cent in 1950 to about 14 per cent during 11th plan in spite of regional imbalance and inter-social groups' imbalances in enrolment rate, in term of male female, castes, religions, occupations and poor and rich disparities.

The priority, at this juncture during 12th plan therefore, appears to be enhancing access to higher education, by increasing the intake capacity in higher education institutions. There are also number of challenges to be faced in higher education sector like availability of adequate and qualified teachers, infrastructure for teaching and learning process and discipline in the educational institutions. While concentrating on the enrolment we should also ensure that the higher education is made equitable and inclusive, by minimizing regional and minimising social imbalances.

The 12th Five year Plan identified the task for the next five years, building on the momentum generated in the past 10 years and continuing the focus on expansion equity and excellence steps are to be taken to reform higher education to achiever the quality. Universities should become role model's and contribute to strengthen other institutes of higher learning in their vicinity and reduce the academic in balances.

Equality of Educational Opportunity- Access, Equity and Inclusion

"Equity and Inclusion implies removing barriers in access to higher education by the deprived, marginalised social groups and economically backward." "Equality of Opportunity" is an important feature of the Constitution of India. "Equality of education" may mean here equality of access to education, equality in educational treatment and equality in educational performance and achievement. About 18 per cent of eligible population aged 18-23 years enters the higher education stream in India, where as in developed Countries it is 54.6 per cent, developing Countries 11.3 per cent and World average 23.2. This shows that India is moving fat in increasing the Gross Enrollment of the eligible youth in higher education. 12th Five year plan aims at raising the GER to 25 per cent by 20 per cent which is both desirable and achievable. Students from the lowest income groups are still significantly under-represented in some of the popular professional courses like medicine, law or technical courses in IITs and IAMs. Graduates from these types of courses and institutions earn high remuneration. The deprived, religious minorities and the castes-

SCs, STs, Tribals, female and the low income group suffers social discrimination, economic exploitation and political marginalisation.

Reservation in Higher Education

Quality education is not accessible to all. In most of the tribal, rural and urban areas the quality of education at the elementary and secondary level available to backward community is very poor which leads to poor achievement at the school. This makes the students difficult to get admission in top colleges and Universities. Therefore the students from the deprived category getting admission, is difficult if they are not offered reservation in the top colleges as there is high competition in these institutions, These HEIs are dominated by the candidates mostly from the upper castes who have inclination towards education as well as they are afford to spend. Appropriate actions are needed to reduce the gap between the most affluent and most disadvantaged school-leavers, so that they could get HEI in quality HEIs.

Parameters of Higher Education

Quantity, Quality, and Flexibility, are the major parameters identified in Higher education system.

Quantity

To provide education for growing population we need to have a holistic and balanced expansion to accommodate under represented sections in HEIs. We need to consolidate and improve the capacity and quality of the existing institutions immediately though there is substantial improvement in the number of institutions started during the last 11th Five-Year-Plans still there is imbalance and disparity in providing special requirements of the people from different socio economic status. During the Twelfth Plan period, there is an attempt to enroll additional 10 million-20 per cent in higher education by March 2017. This would significantly increase the GER bringing it broadly in line with the global average.

Dr. Ved Prakash the Chairman UGC said "We are ensuring increased participation rates by girls, students from Scheduled Caste and Scheduled Tribes, minority communities and Physically Handicapped. We have to increase the intake in universities and will have to give additional financial assistance," He also pointed out that where there are no adequate HEIs "The Government of India has proposed to set up 1,543 public institutions by encouraging" "harmonious coexistence" between public and private players. Government also proposes to increase the financial outlay from 1.12 per cent of GDP to 1.5 per cent for higher education. An increase of 0.38 per cent of GDP means an additional allocation of about Rs. 25,000 crore to higher education to raise the gross enrolment ratio in higher education by 5 per cent, "Establishment of new universities and colleges, consolidation and strengthening of existing institutions of higher education is another concern of 12th plan". It is also argued that open and distance education and Community Colleges could be deployed to enhance the GER in the country, in Higher education.

Quality assurance in HEIs remains a challenge in India. The present assessment system is being conceived as cumbersome and failed to cope with all the colleges and universities needing certification. Only in few states in India it is made mandatory that Institutions that are not acceptably accredited cannot get government funding or loan or any funds from any agencies and cannot attract many students. Thus, accreditation is a major necessity to maintain and indicate quality in higher education. Quality and Excellence emphasises identifying the causes of inter-institutional variation in higher education and improving quality and excellence in higher education such as Academic and Administrative reforms, Infrastructure, Admission System, Examination System, Faculty appointment, selection procedures, Performance, Student-evaluation, Curricula and Pedagogy, Governance, appointment of Vice Chancellors, University autonomy, Public accountability, Role of the UGC in higher education development; and the issues of the colleges in affiliating system of higher education;

The effort should be not only increasing the enrolment and starting more number of institutions but to have a paradigm shift to provide quality higher education to all the deserving people. Thrust should therefore, be on consolidating and improving the capacity and quality of the existing institutions, by providing proper and adequate infrastructure facilities and other requirements. Diversity among the HEIs institutions should be encouraged so that institutions could grow along their own uniqueness without being clones of each other.

For maintaining quality multiple independent accreditation agencies are to be created. Periodical assessment and academic audit even by the peer groups will help enhancing quality in HEIs. Autonomy with self regulation also will improve the quality assurance. The regulatory body should be accountable to the Parliament of India and State legislatures. The quality of regulations should be monitored in respect to relevance effectiveness, quality, efficiency of demand and supply, impact and sustainability. Specific commitments should be made; and they should be subjected to some well-defined social and economic obligations to society and other regulations so that there is less uncertainty in the system. In other words, pre and post-establishment norms for the institutions should be defined by the regulatory body without frequent changes. HEIs should go in for evaluation of courses and teachers by all stack holders that will lead to improvement in Teacher Education and enhance the ICT infrastructure. Create Websites and Web based services to have connectivity and a networking, rethinking on salary structure, creating a system of accountability and Accreditation, recognise diversity and evolve appropriate policies for the entry of foreign Institutions.

Performance Based Funding

Both the Central and the State governments should have a friendly partnership in funding HEIs, in achieving the goal of quality and Access to higher education for all. Such resources should be largely used for ensuring equity for providing higher education to poorer section of the society. We need to evolve policy through which private resources are mobilised by encouraging private participation in all sectors of education especially in higher and Technical education. Facilitation and regulation of private investment in higher education is an important component of ensuring relevance of higher education. Fee related issues, funding mechanism, public-private partnership; private investment in higher education and challenges and issues arising out of them are to be analysed while involving them in higher education. Raising fees should be left to the HEIs that will look into the economic positions of the candidates and their earnings after graduation.

The need for private participation in bringing out world class institutions of higher education was strongly felt and accepted, to-day but with caution. Most private investment requires regulatory approval, and its character will be determined by the character of regulatory regime.

State universities and their affiliated colleges that enroll more than 90 per cent of the students; suffer from fund constraints and poor governance leading to poor quality. Current spending on education in India is even less then 4 per cent of GDP. Even with 6 per cent of spending by the Centre there will not be a modest improvement in the status of Higher Education. Allocation of funds in the budget should be based on competitive grants and performance of the institute. Institutions should be encouraged to raise their own funds through various legitimate means. Reasonable tuition fees in higher education need to be supplemented with appropriate public funding. The availability of scholarship schemes and student loans need to be enhanced. The central principle should be that no student who is eligible to be admitted should be deprived of higher education due to financial reasons.

The funding could be quality linked that will boost the performance of institutions and the stakeholders will be encouraged as they are also rewarded for their performance. Attempts should be made to appoint well qualified teachers. The issue of Faculty shortages could be tackled through innovative ways such as technology enabled teaching and learning and use of collaborative Information and Communication Technologies (ICT). Academic Staff Colleges that provide refresher and orientation courses for teachers are to be strengthened and activated.

Research culture in HEIs is to be strengthened to create new knowledge and innovations in teaching and learning process. Higher education Institutes should come out of excessive government control. There is multiplicity of regulatory agencies with confusing and overlapping mandates, rules and regulations from each. An agency which has clear vision about HEI's should be made the regulatory body.

Flexibility

To meet the challenges of changing society there must be flexibility in higher education system. Multiple entry and exit system and lateral entry should be permitted in admission. Choice Based Credit System (CBCS) will enable the students to opt for courses that are more relevant to their career option and interest. This will permit even those employed to continue their studies to upgrade their qualification–academic and skills while earning. Hence it is suggested that UG colleges could be remolded as Community colleges which has high flexibility with local requirements.

The educational institutions could be benefited by establishing link with industry. Industry participation and the feedback from employers will help in designing need based curriculum, teaching learning process and research and development. It will also help HEIs to produce employable graduates who could become entrepreneurship and improve the financial position and resources of the institutions. Experts from industries could be utilised for imparting quality education to the students by providing hands on experiences.

The 12th Five Year Plan

India enrolls about 12 per cent of its university-age population less than enrollment rate of developed countries. Foreign academics and universities cannot help India to find solutions for domestic higher education challenges. It could be done by Indians only who are familiar with the problems and the complexities of Indian society. It is therefore, hoped that the 12th plan will focus on all the issues relating to higher education in India including problem of employment at the global level.

Various committees of 12th Planning Commission which commenced in 2012, have started its tasks. The 12th plan is to target 100 per cent adult literacy, universalise secondary education and increasing a proportion of GDP for higher education. Dr Balaghrusammy member, State Planning Commission said that it will plan to increase the higher education Gross Enrolment Ratio (GER) in Tamil Nadu from 16 per cent as against 12 per cent of the national average to 25 per cent during the 12th Five Year Plan period by making necessary improvements in higher education. He also has stated that during the 12th plan there will be "proper allocations and priorities. Accessibility, equity, employability, expansion and addressing the issue of shortage of teachers in higher education are some of the crucial aspects that will find solutions in the 12th Plan document," By totally revamping the higher education system in Tamil Nadu it is expected to "make our students thinkers and doers rather than be rote learners and mark scorers alone." New ideas and solutions are required to have a plan for handling unemployment, under employment, teachers' shortage, accessibility to rural students, good allocation of funds for higher education and so on," Dr Balagurusamy the member planning commission pointed out.

The philosophy of the 12th Plan policies will follow the vision of the Government of Tamil Nadu and the action plan will be on the basis of the 12-point programme proposed by the government in it vision 2023 to revitalise higher education. At the same time the basic tenets of the national higher education policy of expansion, equity and excellence will be kept in mind.

The government is giving a big boost to science and technology during the 12th Five-Year-Plan. The expenditure on department of science and technology will be doubled to Rs.1,50,000 crore amounting to 0.6 per cent of country's GDP. 'We have decided to give great significance to science and technology–related research studies to enthuse people to pure sciences, applied sciences and research. There has been a significant decline in interest of students in science and technology but we are going to reverse this," Minister of State for Science and Technology Ashwani Kumar said. Along with the partner institutes of higher education, schools and science institutes to make science popular among students. The government is also planning to increase the grants for INSPIRE — scholarship for science students - from Rs. 640 crore to Rs. 3,000 crore in next five years. Private sector growth in higher education including technical should be facilitated and innovative Public Private Partnerships (PPP) is going to be explored and encouraged in the Twelfth Plan. The Ministry of Youth Affairs and Sports take steps to channelize the energy of the youth into constructive work and to inculcate in them noble and patriotic values. These programmes stress promotion and up-gradation of necessary life skills amongst the youth through vocational training besides creating employment opportunities for them.

In the 11th Plan Rs. 7,000 crores was allotted for minorities. For the 12th Plan now under preparation, a massive sum of Rs.15,000 crore is proposed to be allotted for scholarship and other schemes under the Ministry of Minorities Affaires, Maulana Azad Foundation, towards free coaching and allied schemes, equity to the National Minorities Development Fund, research and monitoring, grants in aid to state governments, schemes for leadership development among young women, interest free subsidy on bank loans for studies abroad and for centrally sponsored scholarship schemes. But it is observed that funds are not fully utilised by the minority institutions and students. If it is true, efforts should be taken to popularise the schemes and the minority institutions should make use of the funds to the optimum extend.

There is a paradigm shift in higher education from 'national education' to 'global education'; from 'one time education for a few' to 'life-long education for all' and from 'teacher-centric education' to 'learner centric education'. These changes make new demands and pose fresh challenges to the education systems and practices in the country. Indian higher education system has now a challenge to provide to the nation and the world at large, skilled human power at all levels to reach the social and economic realities. Thus access, equity, accountability and quality should form the four guiding principles, while planning for higher education in India in the twenty-first century by keeping in mind rural, urban and gender disparities in the higher education system.

"Education to provide the skills for learning to know, learning to live together, learning to do and learning to be" (UNESCO).

6

Education at the Door Steps– IGNOU's Initiative

"He indeed must be blind who does not see that mighty are the political changes; far deeper are the fundamental question which will be decided by what happens in the universities"

— S. Radhakrishnan

"Build excellence in the educational system to meet the knowledge challenges of the 21st century and increase India's competitive advantage in fields of knowledge," says Knowledge Commission.

The Constitution of India, Education Policies and Right to Education insist that education is the fundamental right of all. As Dr Kothari has stated in the Secondary Education Commission Report, "the destiny of the Nation is being shaped in her class rooms" This statement is no more a rhetoric. The Governments and the private initiatives have determined to expand the educational opportunities to all to provide quality education to all. Providing access to knowledge is the most fundamental way of increasing the opportunities and reach out to individuals and groups. Education has come to serve the administrative and economic interests of the nation and become an essential aspect of development of national identity. When we think about quality education for all we should begin with addressing the issues related to school education so that we could build a strong foundation for a knowledge society.

Education is considered to be something more than mere acquisition of knowledge and skill. As Swami Vivekananda said, "education is what makes a person." Which means education cultivates values in man. Through education higher value system of the society and a balanced personality of an individual is promoted. Further, it unfolds the potentials embedded in the learners. With all these objectives of true education the teachers' task becomes manifold to achieve these national, social and personal goals. Education should aim at providing free access to information, freedom to think creatively, innovate and perform as per the global requirement. This effort will lead the world towards a Welfare State and Information Society. This enables us to move towards the total development of the nation.

Development does not imply the economic growth measured in terms of Gross National Product (GNP) or Gross Domestic Product only. Development embraces wider concerns of the quality of life, education attainment, nutritional status, access to basic freedom and spiritual welfare by providing infrastructure such as transportation, Communication, energy and other basic amenities and services required for the total development. These will help to have more employment opportunity and the mobility of people in rural areas to other places and at the same time arrest migration. Thus sustainable development is ensured, without affecting the cultural ethos of the rural India. Sustainable development is a positive change towards improvement of environmental and social systems on which the human race depends. This requires a coordinated approach to planning and policy making that involves public participation. An important dimension of India's rapidly growing economy is the development of a skilled and educated workforce.

Technology helps to achieve a paradigm shift from Unskilled to skilled work and there by move large numbers of the rural poor from the primary to the secondary and tertiary sectors of economic activity.

Higher education in India should attempt to increase the gross enrolment ratio from 11 per cent to 20 per cent. This would expect doubling the scale of higher education in the next few years without diluting quality. Student enrollment in higher education in India is only 7 to 11 per cent as against 88 per cent in Canada, 80.9 per cent in USA and 79.8 per cent in Australia. It will be possible to increase the enrollment ratio only when higher education is diversified, equipped with the knowledge, skills and perspectives that will ensure success in a global age.

Thanks to the giant strides of science and technology due to which the world has shrunk in size and has come to be known as a 'Global Village'. Human capital is much more important than financial capital if one wants to make his mark in the world market. To survive and succeed in a world economy, it is imperative that India has an educational system on par with world standard. Politicians and sociologists have been predicting that India will emerge as a super power by 2020 for which Indian Education to be well planned and equipped. Our main thrust of education in India should be to facilitate human resource development and make it a knowledge reservoir to disseminate and radiate to the whole Universe what is unique to India.

As pointed out in Millennium Development Goals in the Human Development Indicators we must enlarge People's choices to lead a Long and Healthy Life, to Acquire Knowledge (Education), to have Access to Resources needed for a decent standard of living, preserving Energy and Environment for future generations, protecting Personal security and achieving Equality for all women and men; rich and poor; rural and urban.

The curriculum should be driven by aims and goals by giving importance to "substantial weight to personal, social and emotional education," and value system which falls outside boundaries of traditional subjects.

As Mrs Indira Gandhi has stated "Education is a liberating force and in our age it is also a democratizing force cutting across the barrier of caste and class smoothing out inequality imposed by birth and other circumstances". Her vision and dream have become realty through IGNOU which stretches out far and wide in the country and abroad as well. Education is made available according to their convenience at any time and anywhere with high flexibility to the poor and rich men and women; urban and rural and old and young with a large number of options.

All those who receive their Degrees and Diplomas today from the portal of Indira Gandhi National Open University which provides education to the people in remote places which are unreachable, are the fortunate few. We should be grateful to IGNOU for their effort which also aims at a national character. Knowledge and skill acquired by you the graduates, is to be shared with others. As C. Davis-Mary says:

"We do not own our knowledge; it is not ours to keep. We must share our gift of knowledge with those seek knowledge. Learning is a blessing, teaching is a gift and knowledge is power. Let us empower others."

The great visionary poet Rabindranath Tagore says we must make our nation move forward a world:

"Where the mind is without fear and the head is held high;

Where knowledge is free;

Where the world has not been broken up into fragments by narrow domestic walls;

Where words come out from the depth of truth;

Where tireless striving stretches its arms towards perfection;

Where the clear stream of reason has not lost its way into the dreary desert sand of dead habit;

Where the mind is led forward by thee into ever-widening thought and action…

Into that heaven of freedom, my Father, let my country awake".

I would like to quote Mahatma Gandhi who cautioned us long back by saying.

"I do not want my house to be walled on all sides and my windows to be stuffed. I want the culture of all the lands to be blown about my house as freely as possible. But I refuse to be blown off my feet by any."

7

Globalising Higher Education–An Analysis

A balanced intellect presupposes a harmonious growth of body mind and soul

— Mahatma Gandhi

Globalisation for Balanced Intellect

In the current world where globalisation is a by-word in every field 'a balanced intellect' is possible only through globalisation of higher education. Thanks to the giant strides of science and technology, the world has shrunk in size and has come to be known as a 'Global Village'. This term of appellation is not a fantasy but a fact. Gone are the times when one thought of the other countries as 'far' and 'remote'. The boundaries of the countries are steadily being marginalised and nominalised. Rapid developments in information technology have brought about drastic changes in our spatial perception. The advancement in the field of digital network, internet and satellite communication systems have promoted communication at a mind-boggling speed. The traditional concept of distance has gracefully bowed its way out to facilitate globalisation.

Economics and Education – Kindred Linkage

Marketisation, liberalisation, privatisation and globalisation have been the key words so far in economic reforms. Till recently education has not had not been realised that it has place in economic reforms. But now people have started seriously thinking of education in global context.

Economists like Amartya Sen have repeatedly emphasised the kindred connection between education and economic development as education has both inherent and instrumental value in the context of development. The core of any economic reform is promotion of competitive market:

- Abstract of the paper to be presented at the International Conference on 'Globalisation: What issues are at Stake for Universities' organised by International Association of Universities, in Canada from 18-21 September 2002.
- Vice-Chancellor, Gandhigram Rural Institute (Deemed University) Gandhigram 624302 Tamil Nadu economy. Human capital is much more important than financial capital if one wants to make his mark in the world market. To survive and succeed in a world economy, it is imperative that India has an educational system on par with world standard. Politicians and sociologist have been predicting that India will emerge as a super power in the 21st Century. This will turn out to be an idle boasting unless and until we think of globalising our educational system.

Main Objectives of Globalisation of Education

Globalisation of higher education has four major aims/goals. They are as follows:

1. creating favourable conditions for outwardly mobile students and teachers, who are willing to do a part of their studies or teaching in another country,
2. creating conditions that make it easier for foreign students to gain access to or participation in local study programmes,
3. adding an international dimension to the course contents and teaching practice of all programmes of education; and
4. Cooperating with foreign partners in developing future curricula and educational methods.

Process and Approaches

India has already started the process of globalising education in certain areas like management, technology and a few areas of science. The process is still in its infancy and universities have to think in terms of rapid strides. A university is essentially a social system. It has to accept the new role of economic catalyst in the context of globalisation as it plays a lead role in dissemination of information and in charge of creative ideas. It will be a centre of policy formulation gearing up total economic activity and employment.

Sitting in an ivory tower anyone can speak of any kind of reform in any field. But when we come to the implementation of the programme we have to think of the practical issues that are involved. Internationalization of higher education sounds an ideal solution to market Indian education in the world market and vice versa. But how to do it? What is the role and approaches of Indian Universities in this process of internationalisation of education?

Implication

What will be the implications of internationalisation of education in the different spectrum of life of an individual and the nation? We have to consider the following aspects when go for globalising higher education:

1. The political, social and cultural aspects of a nation should in no way be compromised while partnership in education is promoted. As two/three countries work in collaboration with each other they get a chance to exchange knowledge of the other country's systems. Knowledge should be enriched without in any way jeopardizing the national, religious, cultural security of the individual and the nation.

2. We have to seriously take into account the economic considerations. When we treat education as an industry where the product is enriched knowledge, we have to work out a method of supply/demand network for successful marketing of education. The quality of education attains paramount importance to ensure dependable markets. The teachers have to have exemplary ability to provide quality education to face the competitive world.

3. While designing the curricula one has to keep in mind quality control and quality assurance systems. The courses offered should be meticulously framed and a tool to evaluate the quality of education should be systematically prepared. The examination system to be followed should be carefully analysed and what is evolved after deliberation should be acceptable to the countries

in partnership. Similarly suitable methodologies to teach the courses should be carefully deliberated upon and the teachers to be suitably trained. This means innovation in syllabus, methods and evaluation and teachers education.

Any reform–social, political, economic, educational–is challenging and not immediately acceptable as it involves changes in patterns of life. But life becomes meaningless if there is no challenge, sequential mobility and consequential development. Once the idea globalisation of education becomes acceptable and the implication cease to appear insurmountable one can think of the academic and administrative strategies. Once the activities and assignments to be carried out are decided, the approaches are determined the actual programme becomes less tantalising and more of reality.

Relevance and Importance

Education has come to serve the administrative and economic interests of the nation and becomes an essential aspect of development of national identity. Internationalisation of learning is founded on cooperation and exchange. For example, Mahatma Gandhi is taken to American Universities by our teachers and Martin Luther King is brought to our university by their teachers. Senator Fulbright speaks of educational exchange as 'from the standpoint of future world peace and order, probably the most important and potentially rewarding of our foreign policy activities'. The exchange programmes will produce thousands of young men and women "who may go back to their countries with a deeper emotional attachment to their own nation and often with a deeper nationalism than the one with which they came' as remarked by Scientist *Karl Wolfgang Deutch*. Besides, educational exchange establishes bonds of friendship that transcend national boundaries and lays the foundation for shared and common understanding.

Looking before Leaping

So many queries are to be answered before the final launching of this venture. Will internationalisation stabilise itself as an integral part of higher education? Will it be a solution to the problem of multicultural society? Will it bring the local and global into perfect harmony or is it a means to merge multiculturalism? Will it pave the way for world peace and mutual understanding? Is it really the process of integrating an international/ intercultural dimension into the teaching, research and service function of the institution as defined by Institutional Management of Higher Education (IMHE)? Is it cost effective? Is it economically, socially, culturally viable.

Answers to these are to be found only through experiments. We have to take some definite steps. As President Bush has remarked 'International exchanges are not a great tide to sweep away all difference. But they will slowly wear away obstacles to peace us surely as water weans away a hard stone'. We have to take some definite step for 'promoting vigorously the internationalisation of our institutions and the global competence and literacy of our students as being essential to the long term pursuit of a more peaceful world where international understanding and cooperation in solving problems will be increasingly critical for the quality of life and sustained economics, social and cultural development.'

Small Steps before a Giant Leap

Once we decide to accept the challenges of globalisation of higher education we have to start optimistically planning the actual process. Academic planning and administrative support are the two sides of educational system. From the academic side we have to think of globalising education in two phases–one is offering a partial programme where one or two interchangeable papers will be offered in a course by the two countries. The other option is a full course which takes care of the entire programme. The next step will be to design a suitable syllabus followed by evolving suitable methodology of teaching and subsequent evaluation strategies. The administrative side will concentrate on providing proper infrastructure, recruitment of staff, deciding the fee structure, providing accommodation and boarding facilities, publicity preparing brochure etc. The list is long and daunting. Nevertheless break ups always facilitate long term/short term planning meticulously.

Globalisation

The purpose of globalisation of Indian education according to the Ministry of Human Resource Development is threefold. Globalisation of education helps the government learn foreign exchange, quality of education is improved and it gives India an opportunity to spread its culture and values. Indian universities have a major role to play. To quote Dr S. Radhakrishnan:

"He indeed must be blind who does not see that mighty are the political changes; far deeper are the fundamental question which will be decided by what happens in the universities".

India is a vast country with diverse culture. It may not be possible to propagate a universal model to meet all the challenges. Each university may have to develop depending upon the expertise it has and the local conditions, its own innovative strategy to meet the challenges.

8

Challenges in Education

"Education is the most potent tool which needs improvement and modification to suit the present and future needs" as only through education we can shape and create the future of the world.

India is a vast country with a population crossing one thousand million. Besides poverty one of the greatest problems of the country is illiteracy with a total number of illiterates being 296 million as per the 2001 census. Though there has been an increase in the literacy rate from 51.63 per cent in 1991 to 65.38 per cent in 2001 with 75.96 per cent male literates and 54.28 per cent female literacy rate this increase is meager. Though this is the grim picture on one side, India is definitely a technologically advanced country and its contribution in the field of Information technology is matchless.

Technological changes provide new opportunities as well as challenges in higher education sector in the 21st century. Technological advances are fundamentally altering and redefining our information and its modes of dissemination. Education has come to serve the administrative and economic interest of the nation-states and has become an essential aspect of the development of national identity. In the present fast-changing technological world with quiet crisis in higher education how a nation can well educate its citizens without constantly updating its educational strategies to suit the present and future needs? Planning, management and evaluation of educational institutions vis-a-vis social needs and priorities are major areas of concern.

Challenges in Higher Education

Higher education in India has evolved in distinct and divergent streams with each stream monitored by an apex body, indirectly controlled by the Ministry of Human Resource Development and funded by both central and the state governments. Education serves a critical role for society by cultivating future generations who will be able to express their individuality and creativity, thus improving society as a whole. An analysis of existing system of Higher Education indicates a need for major changes in our perception, policy, and the practice of our educational objectives.

The major challenges before the higher education in the country are listed as follow:

Internationalisation of Higher Education,

Accreditation and Quality Assurance,

Curriculum and Pedagogical Issues,

Accountability,

Funding,

Technology enhanced higher education,

High competion in higher education.

Internationalisation

There is an emerging need for internalisation of education especially at the tertiary level. This calls for international cooperation, relevance, quality, management, and financing of higher education. "Internationalisation of higher education is the process of integrating an international/intercultural dimension into the teaching research and service functions of the Institution." Higher education should be characterised by its international dimension of colleges of higher education, interactive networking, mobility of teachers and students and international research projects also taking into account of the international culture, value and circumstances. More emphasis on professional education, continuing education, on new areas such as environmental studies, information science, etc. requires a comparative and international dimension from both the teachers and the students. The emphasis is no longer on specialised knowledge, within a few disciplines, but on promoting the ability to interact and understand other people and nations and thus to operate with wisdom in the global networks that shape us all.

Internationalisation of education gives its attention on the following aspects which are reciprocal in nature.

1. Mobility of Students and faculty members;
2. Strengthening international research collaboration.
3. International dimension in curriculum;
4. International development projects;
5. Joint academic programmes,
6. Development of twinning programs;
7. Establishment of branch campuses; and
8. Commercial export/import of education programmes.

Accreditation and Quality Assurance

The quality of a country's higher education sector and its assessment and monitoring is not only important to its social and economical well-being; it is also a determining factor affecting the status of that higher education system at the international level. The establishment of quality assurance systems has become a necessity, not only for monitoring quality in higher education delivered within the country, but also for delivery of higher education internationally. There should be more transparent information on procedures and systems of quality assurance, accreditation and the recognition of qualifications, at the global level so that the acceptability of mobility of our students and faculty members are made possible.

Teaching Strategies

Teachers play a crucial role in providing and maintaining quality education. Great teachers may differ in personality and individual teaching styles, but they share a common devotion to excellent teaching. They also derive a common enjoyment of their work and an understanding that, by helping to shape the minds of today's students they are making their imprint on tomorrow's world. Perhaps most importantly, they share their faith in the capabilities of their students and an absolute commitment to enhance the lives of the young people they teach. To achieve this ambition it is essential that they update both the content and their teaching strategies to suit the individual differences. As NKC says teaching and research should go hand in hand as research creates new knowledge. Research should enrich teaching and teaching should lead to research. Care should be taken to allot fund for the purpose.

On the subject of work and the mission of one's life, DuBois wrote:

"The return from your work must be the satisfaction which that works brings you and the world's need for that work. With this, life is heaven, or as near as heaven as you can get. Without this…, life is hell."

Curriculum

The curriculum should be driven by aims, and give "substantial weight to personal, social and emotional education," and value knowledge which falls outside the subject areas also. Focus should be on revising as often as possible so that new inventions and discoveries can be incorporated and updated. The stakeholders should have the freedom in curriculum revision. It should be need based for easy mobility. Transparency in curriculum construction with inclusion of new concepts helps the teachers and the students have easy access to move around the globe. Students should most readily see and accept the reality and the benefit of "Research-linked" curriculum and teaching. The expansion of education activities are conducted keeping in mind the institutional, national and International ethical codes of good practice and strategy to sustain quality control. One broad strategy is to audit the teaching strategies and practices that are already in vogue and/or develop current implicit strategies at institutional and at departmental levels. Globalisation also provides opportunities to the graduates access to international employment market, provided they have relevant needed skills, knowledge and self-awareness. They should also have adaptability and sensitivity to the impacts of globalisation in the course of their personal and professional lives. These dimensions are to be taken into consideration in curriculum formulation.

Accountability

Accountability within the system as well as to the society, its stakeholder is another major requirement of any educational system. When any institution utilises the public money it should be the responsibility of the institution to serve the society with commitment and devotion by providing quality education. NKC points out that "an expansion in education which provides students with choices and creates competition between institutions is going to be vital in enhancing accountability."

Funding

Another challenge is to determine who will pay the cost of higher education. There is much written about the cost of education but any answer must account for: (1) Significant societal changes including the advent of the knowledge based global economy, and (2) The growing population approaching college age. With the students and their families to bear the cost of the education when the total cost of education becomes the responsibility of parents then the deserving students will not get opportunities. But it is the responsibility of the state to ensure that all deserving students get access to higher education. No one should be denied the opportunity for higher education due to financial constraints. Scholarships and fellowships should be assured to the deserving and needy students. Expansion and quality improvement in higher education will not be possible without finance. From where can we get adequate funds? Essentially it should be both from public and private sectors and individual HEI should also come forward to generate income by themselves. The principal challenge for higher education is to respond to more competition, more scrutiny from inside and outside the academy, an uncertain economy and hence diminished public appropriations, more demands for increased health benefits, better financial aid, updated technology, and increased security.

For nearly 30 years, most states have tried to solve short-term budget problems by reducing their rates of investment in higher education and allowing institutions to augment their revenues by increasing tuition and other fees. The result is that universities and colleges have become market enterprises increasingly dependent on their own ability to compete for student enrollments, research grants, and service contracts to fulfill their own agendas. The Governments should give importance to higher education and allocate funds in their budget. In a survey conducted in America top priority was given to education and 76 per cent of the respondents asserted that the federal government should increase spending more for education, thus ranking education as the most important issue among 14 issues listed. The Government of India and the State Government should allocate more funds for higher education in India.

New generations of highly educated self-reliant men and women are ready to face challenges, adventures, relationships and meaning at every stage of their life. People now live in cycles, are ready go back to school in their 30's or 50's, change careers often, "unretire" in their life.

Technology Enhanced Higher Education

Information and Communication Technology (ICT) is believed to be a revolution with profound influence on economic development. The rapid advancements in ICT are making it economically feasible to collect, store, process and transmit information at breathtaking speed, reduced cost, raised productivity and increased economic welfare and the life style of people. ICT has expanded opportunities for learning in the workplace. In fact, learning through distance mode in the workplace is the fastest expanding area of learning, education and training today. A large company makes available an array of education and training programmes to its employees in the work place itself so that they could update their knowledge and skills, produce more and earn more.

As Gita says "Work hard, work as a team, maintain good human relations, bring happiness and welfare to the society at the same time bring peace and joy for yourself. Be strong, manly and fearless because you are really the eternal Atman."

We have to face the problems and challenges boldly and be the master of the environment and not the creature of the environment.

Fearlessness, purity of heart, steadfastness in the yoga of knowledge, alms giving control of the senses, sacrifice, study of the Sastras, straight forwardness and austerity are the essential virtues which every one should keep in mind. This has been emphasised by Rabindranath Tagore in his Gitanjali by saying that our country must become a free nation where people live in peace and harmony.

Swami Vivekananda said, "We want that education by which character is formed, strength of mind is increased, the intellect expanded by which one can stand on one's own feet".

The end of all education, all training is to make the man grow in a balanced way. It should help in controlling the vices and bring in new and desirable virtues. We have to imbibe the values by precepts, inspiring examples from your role models and by experience make them your own. This will build the character to serve oneself and to serve society and become worthier human being.

I would like to quote again Swami Vivekananda who said "Be and Make," be our motto. Be good men and women to make others good men and women.

High Competition in Higher Education

It is regretted to make that no Indian University could compete with the universities of the world. The dearth of talent for important academic activities teaching, research and extension or dissemination or research findings are common today in the institutes of higher learning. Those are the major challenges we have to face in the higher education. Another daunting task is the regulatory system and quality of governance. Therefore, the focus now should be on policy formulation that will promote autonomy and good governance with high promote autonomy and good governance with high competition to provide quality higher education, for which the talented teachers are to be attracted to stay on in the country with conductive service conditions and incentives. Hidden these steps will improve the enrolment ratio and the talents and energy of the youth will be attracted and utilized for nation building activities. At the same time our concentration should also be or quality improvement. Expansion without quality improvement serves very little purpose. It is developing to note that Indian University finds it difficult to complete with the universities in the world our higher education institutions are not upto the mark. There is unnecessary rigidity both for the faculty and students. These should be flexibility in the higher education system and odhast good, efficient faculty members, raise the standard of teaching, encouraging cutting edge research and nurture their talents. Today there are new challenges and also new opportunities. Our collective task ahead entails putting in place an educational system that would help India into a modern, prosperous and progressive economy and society in the 21st century.

9

Right to Education or Right Education

"Education is a human right with immense power to transform. On its foundation rest the cornerstones of freedom, democracy and sustainable human development."

— ***Kofi Annan***

Constitution of Post-independence India stated in Article 45 that the State shall endeavor to provide within a period of 10 years from the commencement of the Constitution-1950 free and compulsory education to all children until they complete the age of 14 years. Millennium Declaration, of United Nations in the Millennium Development Goals (MDGs) also ensures that all children around the world are in primary school by the year 2015.

Of the estimated 200 million children who enroll annually in India's 900,000 primary schools, 53 per cent drop out before they reach secondary education (class VIII). Of the remaining only 10 million enter institutions of tertiary education, of whom some 3 million only graduate every year. In 2009, India guaranteed its citizens the right to education. But critics say the policy is marred by a dangerous move toward privatisation. The majority of the population started getting into private schools that has increased inequality further.

The government schools today, especially the primary schools, have mostly illiterate/semi literate parents. Ten/20 years ago, there was a better social mix it used to be a heterogeneous group in government schools as there were very few private schools. Unless the school system encourages a mix of students from several social strata learning together, we will not be able to raise the standard of life and equality among the people. It does not possess a mobile phone or a TV and other modern gadgets in our house things are going to change.

Right to Education (RTE)

The Right of Children to Free and Compulsory Education Act or Right to Education Act (RTE), which was passed by the Indian Parliament on 4 August 2009, describes the modalities of the importance of free and compulsory education for children between 6 and 14 in India under Article 21a of the amended Indian Constitution. Sixty-three years after independence, India enforced a historic Right to Education (RTE) on Thursday, the 1st April 2010, act that promises freedom from illiteracy for this vast and diverse country.

The Right of children to Free and Compulsory Education has been a part of the directive principles of the State Policy under Article 45 of the Constitution, which is part of Chapter 4 of the Constitution, came into force from April 1, 2010. This was a historic day for the people of India as from this day the right to education will be accorded the same legal status as the right to life as provided by Article 21A of the Indian Constitution. Every child in the age group of 6-14 years will be provided 8 years of compulsory and quality elementary education in an age appropriate classroom in the vicinity of his/her neighbourhood.

Any cost incurred for a child to access to school will be borne by the State which shall have the responsibility of enrolling the child as well as ensuring attendance, retention and completion of 8 years of schooling. No child shall be denied admission for want of documents; no child shall be turned away if the admission cycle in the school is over and no child shall be asked to take an admission test. Children with disabilities will also be educated in the mainstream schools-and provided inclusive and integrated education.

All private schools shall enroll 25 per cent of their enrolment from weaker sections and disadvantaged communities. No seats in this quota can be left vacant. These children will be treated on par with all the other children in the school and the cost will be subsidised by the State at the rate of average per learner costs in the government schools.

The National Commission for Protection of Child Rights (NCPCR) has been mandated to monitor the implementation of this historic event. A special toll free helpline to register any complaints will be set up by NCPCR for this purpose. NCPCR will involve all civil society groups, students, teachers, administrators, artists, media, writers, government personnel, legislators, members of the judiciary and all other stakeholders to join hands and work together to build a movement to ensure that every child of this country is in school and enabled to get at least eight years of quality education without dropping out.

We are committed to ensuring that all children, irrespective of gender and social category, have access to education–an education that enables them to acquire the skills, knowledge, values and attitudes necessary to become responsible and active citizens of India. We must have institutions which have inspiring learning ambience, caring and competent teachers who can satisfy the stakeholders of the society.

Highlights of RTE Act

Following are the key points of the legislation that expects to empower the nation through education. The RTE includes the following minimum benchmarks that all educational institutions are required to adhere to make India a literate nation:

1. Free and Compulsory Education to all Children in India of six to 14 Years of Age Group;
2. No Child shall be Held Back, Expelled, or required to pass a Board Examination Until He/She of Completes Elementary Education (up to Class Eight);
3. A Child who Completes Elementary Education shall be Awarded a Certificate;
4. There Should be a Fixed Student-Teacher Ratio;
5. Will Apply to all of India Except Jammu and Kashmir;
6. Provision for 25 per cent Reservation for Economically Disadvantaged Communities in all Private and Minority Schools. The expenditure will be reimbursed by the State as Part of the Public-Private Partnership Plan. The Reservation to Start with Class one beginning 2011;

7. Improvement in Quality of Education;
8. School Teachers will need adequate Professional Qualification within five years or else will Lose Job; Teachers in all Schools will have to Subscribe to these norms within 5 Years.
9. School infrastructure to be Improved in three years, else Recognition will be Cancelled;
10. Financial Burdens will be Shared between State and Central Government on the Basis of Sarva Shiksha Abhiyan (Education for all).
11. Private Schools will have to Pay Penalty for Violating RTE.
12. It also prohibits all unrecognised Schools;
13. There is no Provision for Donation or Capitation Fees;
14. No Interview of the Child or Parent be Conducted for Admission;
15. There is Provision for Special Training of School Drop-Outs to Bring them up on Par with Students of the Same Age.
16. RTE Requires that surveys be conducted periodically to measure the School-Age population of every neighbourhood and make sure every child has a School to Attend.

School Management Committee–(SMC)

Per the section 21 (1) and 21(2) of Right of children to free and compulsory education Act, all government and government-aided schools shall constitute School Management Committee (SMC) in their schools that will consist of the elected representatives of the local authority, parents and guardians of children admitted in those schools and teachers. As per the act the SMCs should perform the following functions and ensure that the school functions effectively and regularly monitor the working of the school. (SMC) should prepare and recommend school development plan every year. It is expected that it monitor the utilisation of the grants received from the appropriate government or local authority or any other source and Perform such functions as may be prescribed time to time by the competent authority or body. Though the SMC have such laudable functions by and large they do not have proper guidelines regarding its functions and duties and are either inefficient or are found to be working for vested interests.

Some of the parent representatives who are in the committee are not aware about why this committee has even been setup and what they are expected to do.

Constraints

About 20 per cent of government primary schools are multigrade teaching institutions with 2 teachers; another one-fifth don't have a proper building; 58 per cent can't provide safe drinking water, and 70 per cent lack toilet and sanitation facilities. Considering the increase in quantity/number of students in the classroom and schools there is a lack of corresponding increase in number of teachers and infrastructure facilities in most schools.

Inadequate funding and allocation in the budget both by state and centre for education is a major constraint in achieving the objective of quality education for all. The combined annual outlay of central and state governments for education in India has never crossed the 4 per cent of GDP. Compared it to the global average spending of 5 per cent of GDP per annum and 6-7 per cent in the developed nations of the western world ours is very low that needs to be increased. Kothari Commission recommended in 1966 itself that 6 per cent of GNP for education would be necessary to attain the goal of education for all. Even after 47 years India is not allotting at least 5 per cent of GDP.

Right Education –The Quality of Education

The state of primary education in India has always been a point of concern. With the RTE Act being implemented, it was expected that this would enhance the access, scope and quality of education to all young children across the country. But while the RTE's potential to provide significant uplift to primary education is undeniable, some questions still remain on the quality of education provided at all levels from pre primary to tertiary level. An analysis of RTE's impact could provide a broader understanding of why an increase in quantity does not always equal an increase in quality.

Studies undertaken by few agencies highlight some of the major issues in primary education. Top of the list are the issues pertaining to reading and writing levels of children in India. A study under taken by an NGO in 2010 reveals that nationally 46. 3 per cent of all children in std V could not read a std II level text. This proportion increased to 53.2 per cent in 2012. Reading and writing abilities of school children are dipping to alarming levels. Some blame the deterioration in standards on the new educational policies that now allow children to move from one class to another with no fear of detention for academic non performance. Others argue that if students are detained and made to repeat classes, will only increase dropout rates and rob disadvantaged children off even the most basic schooling rights.

Continuous and Comprehensive Evaluation (CCE) that has been initiated for students from class 6 to 10 is a good measure but it has practical shortcomings. It is important that teachers are properly trained in carrying out Continuous and Comprehensive Evaluation, to reduce teachers' burden with administrative duties and focus more on CCE since it need continuous monitoring the performance of the students on a regular basis. Overworked teachers are unable to implement these mechanisms with the energy and time that is required for this task. In addition, there has been very little emphasis on skill development especially in subjects such as Mathematics and English which has led to very poor performance of students not only at that level but also in higher classes.

The definition of literacy and education has of course progressed from a standard of barely being able to read and write; a more inclusive definition now calls for any literate person to have the 'ability to read for knowledge, write coherently, and think critically about the written word', which essentially means the ability to process information. This shouldn't surprise, because one of the major issues in primary education has been the quality of teacher training and the pupil teacher ratio in the system. It is said that, poor monetary benefits provided to teachers have led to a reduction in quality of people who are entering the teaching profession. It is no more a truth. Teachers are well paid compared to even corporate sectors. Still we don't get teachers with competence. Besides this the problems lie with quality of training provided to teachers that have been amply highlighted in the recently conducted Central Teacher Eligibility Test (CTET) in which 99 per cent of the teachers failed to clear the examination.

The overall quality of education has deteriorated. It is said that the quality of education provided by majority of government schools remains a big question. While it remains the largest provider of elementary education in the country forming 80 per cent of all recognised schools, it suffers from shortages of teachers, infrastructural facilities. There are also frequent allegations of government schools that there is absenteeism, mismanagement and appointment of teachers are based on political convenience and other criteria. Despite providing free lunch-food, uniform and other requirement in the government and aided schools, many parents send their children to private schools where teachers are paid considerably lower than that in government and aided schools but they are made to work very hard.

Children attending the private schools are seemed to be at an advantage position, thus discriminating against the weakest sections that are forced to go to government schools. Furthermore, the system has been criticised as catering to the urban and rural elites who are afford to pay school fees in a country where large number of families live in poverty. The act has been criticised as discriminatory for not addressing these issues.

It is observed by many educationists and social activists that RTE is slow in moving towards achieving its goals and objectives. In fact, it only made the present multi-layered, inferior quality school education system where discrimination continues to prevail. 54 per cent of urban children attend private schools, and this rate is growing at 3 per cent per year. "Even the poor children are abandoning the government schools. They are leaving because the teachers are not showing up. However, other researchers have countered the argument by citing that the evidence for higher standards of quality in private schools often due to other factors such as family income, parental literacy—all correlated to the parental ability to pay. Increase in number of schools led to more number of children who are enrolled, but learning little'. Increased access to education has led to reduced efficiency, which detracts from the noble objective of 'quality education for all'.

In order to address these quality issues, the Act has provisions for compensating private schools for admission of children under the 25 per cent quota.

Section 12 of the Right of Children to Free and Compulsory Education Act 2009 (the Act) has made it compulsory for every private unaided school to admit at least 25 per cent of its entry level class from children belonging to weaker and disadvantaged groups. For this category of students the state government shall reimburse schools an amount equal to either the fees charged by the school or the per child expenditure in state schools, whichever is lower. This minor social engineering has produced some ridiculous protests from the elite. Yet, equally ridiculous is the claim that this will significantly help the poor. Of India's hundreds of millions of school children, only a few thousand poor will enter the elite havens. The others will remain at the mercy of government schools that provide no worthwhile education."

"If it's hard to look beyond the socio-economic differences, schools must be urged to develop a class-neutral atmosphere. Like discouraging bringing lunch from home-and having a common canteen for all the students, a common stationery shop where everyone buys their supplies. The other drawbacks such as inadequate number of playgrounds, toilets and drinking water facilities are to be taken care of at least with the participation of community along with the government. In addition to these there is adequate availability of teachers. The pupil teacher ratio should be regulated.

The small schools with two teachers or less would find it hard to provide quality education for a number of reasons. For one it requires very dedicated teachers who can function without much supervision. Teachers have to simultaneously cater to different classes which make it difficult for teacher to pay attention to individual students or for students who seek individual attention from teachers. Teaching students of different ages at the same time is not an easy task. Teachers shortages is a major problem which is difficult to tackle as the possibilities for sharing workload are very limited. These small schools are also usually deprived of appropriate facilities and basic services like libraries or properly trained teacher. Students suffer when teachers spend time on administrative work or go for collection of salaries or for other official meetings often with higher authorities. And the problems are further amplified by the time the teachers are forced to spend on non teaching activities like ensuring mid day meals or for conducting census or election duty as frequently called upon by the government. However, the special nature of these small schools is not recognised by the policy makers.

Conclusion

The RTE, enacted in 2009, is highly laudable, but today faces a number of implementation roadblocks, including inadequate funding, shortage of trained faculty, inadequate infrastructure and a controversy on the applicability to private schools. The government is contemplating on extending RTE to pre-schools and classes 9-10. Proper analysis of the functioning of the scheme is essential before its expansion. A coherent, realistic and effective roadmap for implementation of RTE is desired before they are extended to other segments of school education in India. To sum up increasing access, affordability and quality of education in India is the need of the hour. Quality of education, especially school and primary education, has been a major cause of concern for some years now. But those long-term goals of the RTE Act themselves need to be met with an equal emphasis on quality and not just quantity alone.

Dear teachers of the emerging digital world and who are going to be major stakeholder in successful implementation of RTE must understand the scheme better and contribute your best. Your creativity, resourcefulness, commitment and competence will pave the road to the success of making RTE a community friendly scheme benefiting millions of children of India. The teachers who have already graduated and those who will be leaving the portal of this college of education in few days should take a vow that you are going to be the torch bearers and will light thousands of lights that will continue to illuminate in the world. I wish all the graduate teachers a bright future.

10

Internal Quality Assurance Systems and Curriculum Transaction

"Quality is an ever-extending goal-the better you are, the better you need to be."

Quality assurance refers to measures with which both customers as well as other stakeholders are convinced of the fact that the requirements pertaining to products are met i.e. external confidence of the customers is achieved and that the institutions have reasonable facilities and capabilities for providing quality education. In general terms, quality assurance, or a quality management system, is a method of ensuring a consistent standard of deliverables. A quality assurance process is at the heart of producing a professional and consistent product or service. Unlike in industries and military activities where there are definite and measurable input and out put, it is difficult to decide and measure the parameters/standards/ benchmarks in education. Bench marking helps to decide the best practices to be adopted to improve the quality of educational practices education at all levels. Steven M. Bragg defines a Best Practice as any improvement over existing systems. SACUBO (Southern Association of College and University Business Officers) defines it as creating better, more efficient and customer friendly business practice But in the recent past there is greater awareness in fixing the Benchmarks and how to measure the quality of education, as is said, "Quality products and quality service begin with quality thinking." A well defined and need based curriculum, accountability in teaching, learning and evaluation process, socially relevant researches, extension and consultancy services to the society, functional and effective student support services along with adequate infrastructure facilities decide the quality of education provided.

Since the inception of the National Assessment and Accreditation Council in India, in 1994, there is a great wave on providing quality education which created awareness and quality culture among the stakeholders, especially at the higher education institutions. NAAC has been responsible for triggering the colleges and Universities to be quality conscious and is moving towards providing quality education. The MHRD announced the year 2002 as the year of Quality in Higher Education. We could observe that there is high competition among higher education.

India has been a centre of excellence Since ancient times, in the field of higher education. Nalanda, Vikramashila and Takshashila were few of the oldest universities in the world and were the most renowned seats of higher education during their time. Students' from far off countries came to study in these universities. Today India has one of the largest higher education systems in the world and also there are some world-class institutions for higher education which provide quality education. With population explosion, the educational expansion, universalisation of elementary education, vocationalisation of secondary education, higher and professional education and overall quality of education are major challenges before the country.

Education is the most important public attributes of social, economic, political and human development in service sectors. Education is a human right with immense power to transform an individual, as an individual as well as a responsible citizen in the society. The major function of education therefore, is to produce fit persons who are conversant with the societal needs, traditions and cultural background of the society. Educational institutions which assume these as their goals and are to be equipped to coordinate with community, alone can provide quality education. And only this type of institutions especially at the higher education level, students on completion of their studies enter the world of work, would produce quality people who would work in tune with the social needs and demands reflecting ethos, aims and values of the society. To imbibe these qualities a suitable ambience is to be created at the institutional level.

Curriculum Transaction

Quality of education largely depends on quality of curricula and its transaction. Where as the affiliated colleges have very little role to play in curriculum construction. It is decided by the authorities of the concern Universities, though there are representations in the Board of Studies, from affiliated colleges. Therefore, the challenge confronting our educational systems, especially in affiliated colleges, today is how to transform the curriculum and teaching-learning process to provide students with the skills to function effectively in this dynamic, information—rich, and continuously changing environment. If we carefully analyse, in our curriculum transaction there is fragmentation, isolation and purposelessness which create feelings of alienation and powerlessness that are believed to contribute to depression among students, leading to substance of abuse and suicide of youth. Quality education could be ensured through quality curriculum development, innovative strategies, using ICT, quality textbooks and Teaching Learning Materials, researches, consultancy and outreach programme of the colleges, proper infrastructure and teacher quality. Education should enrich the mind, the heart and awaken the spirit of each student. It should provide opportunities for students to be creative, contemplative, and imaginative through innovative curriculum transaction.

High quality curriculum outlines what students are expected to learn and be able to do, in all subjects and grades and is designed to help students achieve their individual potential and create a positive future for themselves, their family and their community. However, teachers have flexibility to decide how to teach and the methodology to be followed. Curriculum must provide students with the knowledge and skills needed for the present and future. If it is determined through the regular review process and feedback sessions from the stakeholders, that there is a need to make minor or major revisions to the curriculum that could be done periodically. It is therefore mandatory that Education institutions conduct consultations as often as possible and take initiative to modify the curriculum. The draft may be shared with a wide variety of education stakeholders through advisory committees, online feedback forms, conferences, authorities of the Universities such as Academic council, Board of Studies and presentations to specialist teacher councils. Teachers play a vital role in this process. They use their practical knowledge and experience about a subject and about students' needs at specific age levels to provide input and feedback during the process. The implementation of new curricula is to be supported by providing resource support and professional development opportunities along with the best possible instructional materials for the implementation of approved programmes of study.

Expectations of the Future

Education system in 21st century must meet the needs of the whole-person and be built on the assumptions that there should be connectedness, linkages and wholeness. It needs a more holistic approach rather than approaching in a fragmented way. The challenge confronting our educational systems is how to transform the curriculum and teaching-learning process to provide students with the skills to function effectively. Curriculum for 21st century should value and give importance to physical, mental and spiritual knowledge and skills needed to face the world confidently. It should present knowledge within cultural and temporal contexts, rather than as facts to be memorised or dogma to be followed. It should be integrated into all disciplines emphasising inter-relationship and inter-connectedness. It should challenge students to find their own place in space and time, and to reach for the highest aspirations of the human spirit.

Holistic curriculum that recognizes all knowledge is created within a cultural context and that the content is related to expectations of people. This will include the sciences and the humanities, including music and art. It encourages the transfer of learning across academic disciplines. A holistic curriculum encourages learners to critically approach the cultural, moral and political contexts of their lives. This type of Holistic learning organised around relationships within and between learners and their immediate environment empower learners to live fully in the present and to participate in co-creation of preferred futures. Holistic Curriculum is inquiry driven, interdisciplinary and integrated, and is based on explicit assumptions of interconnectedness, wholeness and multi-dimensional. Current education systems do not satisfy student needs for meaning, wholeness and fulfillment.

The XI Plan places high priority on education as a central instrument for achieving rapid and inclusive growth with specific emphasis on expansion, excellence and equity. Adopting internationally proven but flexible curriculum frameworks with different social, ethnic and cultural environments will help the students and faculty to study at other campuses. Students will be able to specialise in the fields of knowledge most required for the development of their own and their neighbouring societies, within the context of a broad and meaningful education. Corresponding to this global reach, the curriculum will include mastery of more than one language so that, while English will be the medium of instruction, the students will be encouraged to be bilingual, and perhaps multilingual. They will also excel in the use of modern information technologies to enable them to access the world's most sophisticated knowledge bases.

There are unacceptable differences in the outcomes of education for people from different social and cultural groups. We need an inclusive education system that provides learner centered education for everyone regardless of disadvantage. The education system needs to work collaboratively with the whole community to support the diverse needs of all students. High quality and well transacted curriculum ensures that students have a comprehensive education. And they are well-prepared for the future, including for post graduation and professional education, world of work and life out side the protected portals of education institutions.

Internal Quality Assurance

The higher education Institutions like Colleges and Universities, in large number volunteered to go in for Assessment and Accreditation by the NAAC since NAAC began to assess and accredit higher education institutions in our country. This process in turn helped the institutions to realise their strength and weaknesses in seven criterion identified by NAAC. This assessment system is both internal and external by a peer team. Self-assessment/evaluation is of immense help to the stakeholders as they themselves are able to locate their strength and weakness and take initiative to rectify short comings, weakness and errors if any and introduce innovations, even before the peer team visits the institutions. Thus, quality culture and quality consciousness is created once they think of going in for accreditation. After the Peer, Team visit and their assessment and accreditation on the basis of direct observation and interactions with various stakeholders their remarks and suggestions become eye openers to the institutions as to how they should function during the coming 5 years. Here comes the role of Internal Quality Assurance Cell in higher education institutions. NAAC thought that as post accreditation measure, an internal system could play vital role in quality up gradation and sustenance of quality of the institution and insisted on establishment of IQAC in all the accredited institutions. To day we observe that even in non accredited institutions there is greater awareness on the importance of IQAC and they started establishing IQAC.

Functions of IQAC

IQAC in higher education institutes have got definite and greater role to play in up grading the quality of education in the institution by improving the ambience of the teaching and learning atmosphere. I have just listed a few functions of IQAC here.

Bring in internalisation and institutionalisation of quality enhancement.

Make quality enhancement as a continuous process.

Help the institutions realise the goals of quality enhancement and sustenance.

To develop a system for conscious, consistent and catalytic improvement in quality development of the institution.

To disseminate information on quality aspects of education among the stakeholders of the institution.

Organise discussions, workshops, seminars to promote quality culture.

Recording and monitoring measures of the institution and periodically communicating the progress of the institution to NAAC.

Acting as the nodal agency of the institution of the quality related activities.

Make all the stakeholders of the institution responsible for quality maintenance.

IQAC's in higher education institutions thus have a vital role to play as an internal body, which has immediate access to all the activities in the institution and to guide towards excellence in all the seven criteria. At the same time be of link between the stakeholders and the institution in bringing about change in curriculum up gradation and the curriculum transaction.

11

Stakeholders are the Best Assessers of the Quality of Institutions

"It is not the strongest of the species that survive, or the most intelligent, but the one most responsive to change".

— ***Charles Darwin***

Customer satisfaction is the major goal of any service sector and business sector by providing quality products. They want to be assured of the quality in what they use. Quality assurance refers to measures with which both a customer as well as other interested parties—the stakeholders is convinced of the fact that the requirements pertaining to products are met and that the organisation has reasonable abilities for the purpose. There are direct users and indirect users-Stakeholders in education such as students, parents, alumni, teachers, principals, employers and the public and they are the best judges, is gaining momentum in higher education system. Customers of both direct and indirect who come to us are the important persons. They are integral part of our system and programme. We depends on their satisfaction. But for them we could neither sell our products nor exist.

The customers or the stakeholders are the important persons whose needs are to be satisfied first as they are the investment in our effort to provide quality education. The biggest contributing factor to quality is building the capabilities and satisfaction of our stakeholders. In order to achieve stakeholder-driven excellence, we have to know who they are what their expectations are and their capabilities. Quality assurance once established is not an end by itself; it is an ever-extending and ever growing process. You need to go on trying to be better and better. The management of the quality process is infinite and marked only by milestones as we see some thing new and better is emerging in the world of education.

It is a planned and systematic means for assuring management that the defined standards, practices, procedures, and methods of the process and goals are applied. A planned and systematic pattern of all actions are necessary to provide adequate confidence to the stakeholders that an item or product of the institution conforms to their requirements and satisfaction. Assurance of quality in higher education is a process of establishing stakeholders' confidence that there is provision for quality input, process and outcomes that fulfils their expectations and requirements Quality assurance is an all–embracing term covering all the policies, processes, and actions through which the quality of higher education is maintained and developed. (Campbell & Rozsnyai, 2002).

The UNESCO definition enlarges on that and says: Quality Assurance an all-embracing term referring to an ongoing, continuous process of evaluating-assessing, monitoring, guaranteeing, maintaining, and improving the quality of a higher education system, institutions, or programmes.

Quality Assurance

Planned and systematic review process of an institution or programme to determine that acceptable standards of education, scholarship, and infrastructure are being maintained and enhanced periodically and systematically. It includes expectations that mechanisms of quality control are in place and effective and confirms that the conditions are in place for students to achieve the standards set by the institution or other awarding body.

Duff *et al.*, (2000, p. xv) define quality assurance as a process of demonstrating excellence, accountability and value for money: Quality assurance is a process through which a higher education institution guarantees to itself and its stakeholders that its teaching, learning and other services consistently reach a standard of excellence. Such assurance is a necessary goal for the institution itself. Increasingly, it is also necessary for publicly funded institutions to be accountable, and provide assurances, to society and the state that they are delivering the services for which they are funded, thus ensuring that they are providing value for money.

Centrex (2004) Frames it Simply as an Institutional Confirmation of Achieved Standards

Quality Assurance is the means by which an organisation confirms that conditions are in place for students to achieve the standards set by the training organisation. Internal QA is crucial to sustainable quality improvement and quality culture. Hence the Partnership must start at the grass root through Student involvement Accreditation is based on optimum standards, professional accountability and encourages organisation to pursue continual excellence.

Role of Stakeholders in Quality Sustenance

Students

Quality assurance and sustenance systems should involve all stakeholders in higher education and enable them to formulate their demands and duties/responsibilities to sustain the quality of the institution. Stakeholders should have equal Partnership to Developing a sustainable partnership and promote Partnership culture.

Students as the direct first stakeholders—consumers they are the experts to assess on the institution and other conditions of the institution. This is the group which has legitimate interests in the QA and QS. They are the responsible co-actors, full and equal partners in maintaining quality.

Higher Education Institutions

Valuable feedback and reflected decisions of the stakeholders enhances the Accountability towards the external world be able to get more support for their work in appreciation of the quality maintenance. This will also be able to promote developing a sustainable partnership with stakeholders. Institutions also develop ability to make well-reflected decisions on the basis of the feedback from its stakeholders.

For the Labour Market/ the Consumers/Social Partners

They express their expectations for their service and business and expect the higher education institutions to supply employable graduates who will have potentiality and suitability for the job, sincerity, punctuality, leadership quality and other soft skills needed for an efficient professional/worker.

Use of Feedback in Quality Assurance and Sustenance

Systematic and periodical feedback and regress analysis of the responses of the stakeholders will help the institutions to identify stakeholders' quality expectations and refine educational practices and implement effective quality management and follow the best practices in all the seven criterion-Curricular Aspects, Teaching-Learning and Evaluation, Research, Consultancy and Extension, Infrastructure and Learning Resources, Student Support and Progression, Governance and Leadership and Innovative Practices as identified by NAAC of India. The HEIs will start apply proven techniques, practices and standard templates to create Total Quality Management (TQM) on the basis of Stakeholders' quality expectations and requirements by initiating the following steps:

- Generate a quality assurance tasks list that incorporates best practices for sustainability.
- Transform quality assurance recommendations into corrective and improvement actions so that the best is sustained.
- Raising change requests as appropriate to the institution and the programme and set the tasks systematically by assessing the weakness and the strength.
- Identifying improvement opportunities in various aspects-criterion and ensure that best practices are maintained.
- Updating the organisational processes so that best organisational climate and culture is established in the institution for continuous quality improvement.
- A set of activities designed to evaluate the process by which products are developed or manufactured.
- Promote 'Quality Culture' as a prerequisite for efficient functioning of HEIs and lasting quality.
- Make quality visible to all the stakeholders as it has become the watchword in the community. Today all the stakeholders are conscious of the standards of the institution even before admitting their wards in the higher education institutions. Even the students are interested in knowing the quality of the HEIs before joining any institution of HEIs.

Conclusion

Developing the quality culture in higher education, at all service levels such as teaching, research, administration and student support services is vital to the higher education system. Quality management, quality enhancement, quality control, quality sustenance and quality assessment are means through which quality assurance is ensured. Duff *et al.*, (2000, p. xv) define quality assurance as a process of demonstrating excellence, accountability and value for money. Quality assurance is a process through which a higher education institution guarantees to itself and its stakeholders that its teaching, learning and other services are consistently modified, sustained and march towards excellence. Such assurance and sustenance are necessary goal for the institution itself.

I would like to conclude by quoting Leonardo Da Vinci who Quotes for Teachers "Iron rusts from disuse, stagnant water loses its purity, and in cold weather becomes frozen, even so does inaction sap the vigour of the mind." So let us continue to refresh ourselves and our education system so that we could provide quality education to the youth who are the hope of the future.

12

Net Working Teacher Education Institutions for a New Era

"United We Stand, Divided We Fall."

— ***Proverb***

Teacher education has to play a crucial role in evolving and delivering quality education at all levels-Pre-Primary to Professional. This indicates that teacher education programme in any country in the globe should aim at quality delivery of the system. After independence there is tremendous growth in education. Number of schools, colleges and universities has grown manifold. Especially during the last two decades. Existing teacher education institutions are scattered with their own standard and quality. The diverse teacher education institutions preparing the teachers for Pre-Primary, Secondary and Tertiary education in the formal system of education and personnel for adult education, technical education and vocational education in the non-formal system seem to be diverse and face challenges.

Though there are different issues relating to teacher-education of both pre-service and in-service. We have not yet tackled them effectively or brought any innovation in teacher education system. Even when in some corner of the country, there are sporadic experiments and innovations they are not brought to the limelight and experimented for their suitability and sustainability in preparing the teachers. The teacher education institutions are isolated and stand aloof.

Thanks to the National Council for Teacher Education (NCTE) which played unifying role by prescribing a common curriculum framework and having a control and monitoring teacher education in India. NCTE has made it mandatory that all the existing teacher education institutions should be accredited and should obtain permission for starting any new teacher education institutes. It has formulated bench marks for assessing the quality of teacher education institutions along with National Assessment and Accreditation Council (NAAC). In few countries even the individual teachers are assessed and their license for teaching is renewed periodically. It is also insisted that the accredited institutions should prepare quality teachers who would permanently stay in teaching. Such teachers are also given incentives so that well qualified and committed teachers stay on. Whether is would be possible to maintain the same standard in providing quality teacher education; and bring equality and social-justice to all those who undergo teachers training. We find this diversity throughout the country especially with regard to the status of the teachers serving in the schools and the teacher educators serving in teacher education institutes.

It is observed that there are diversities in teacher-training programmes provided in (DIETs) District institutes of Education and training. Secondary teacher education/college of education institutes of advanced studies in Education (IASW), then state councils of educational research and training (SCERT), National council for Education research and training (NCERT), and university departments of education. Which impart teacher-education on a regular basis as well as through distance mode? After the establishment of NCTE all these systems of teacher education are compelled to follow its norms. In this context of diversity and the NCTE playing a vital role in providing quality teacher education; it is high time we think of coming together to provide the quality teacher education in India, through networking teacher education institutions. Only when the teacher education institutions come together and jointly aim at promoting the effective and sustainable application of standard teacher education at all level we cannot think of promoting quality of education in schools, colleges and universities, as well as teachers to work in the informal sectors. We must unite around for the cause of quality teacher education in India and compete with the rest of the world. A collective effort alone will ensure this.

Networking of Teacher Education Institutions

Networking of teacher education institutions will be a medium for bringing together well experienced teacher educators and will facilitate sharing of both positive and negative experiences in curriculum frame work, teaching learning strategies, evaluation, research and development of new knowledge and skills. It is applicable to both the pre-service teacher education programme as well as for serving teachers who have to continually update their knowledge and skill in teaching in the from of in-service trainings.

Through networking teacher education we come to know some one who knew some one which creates a great source of knowledge, skills, understanding, sharing and know-how to strengthen teacher education and thus whole gamut of education system in the country to face the global requirement.

The differentiated forms of teacher education, though try to enhance the potential of teachers and teacher educators it is done in segregation or in isolation. Is it possible for us to unite by net-working all the teacher-educators who are isolated, to form a great force to improve the quality of teacher education, as well as education in general? From a loose group of teacher education institutions to a united group, to know more about each other, pool their expertise, for the benefit of education system we must come together. It is essential that net-working of these institutions is initiated to evolve, a model and sustainable teacher education system. The teacher education network will provide a platform for teacher education institutions to share training facilities and expertise available in each institute. This will enable us to develop competence and effectiveness to evolve a curriculum to suit the changing scenario and follow innovative techniques of teaching by using technology.

Objectives of Net-Working of Teacher Education Institutions

The following should be the goals/objectives of networking teacher education institutions:

- To unite teacher–education institutions with key institutions of teacher education in India and at the global level.
- To design curricula in primary and secondary education institutions for deeper learning and instructions.
- To improve teaching efficiency of teacher educators by using variety of techniques including electronic media.

- To identify the local needs and tailor the programme to suit the community, by reflecting the campus, local, regional to make it culturally appropriate and locally relevant.
- To share the infrastructure and expertise to strengthen each other.
- To work with ministries of education, departments of education, and other educational agencies to create professional development programmes related to teacher-education.
- To tap and use community resources to tackle local sustainability issues.
- To identify common issues and try to solve jointly. United action will be of great strength.
- To find out new models for professional development in teacher education by drawing together the needed skills, curricular approaches and activity based learning models.
- To re-orient teacher education as a viable avenue for research and development in educational institutions.
- To facilitate and promote easy and quick ways of interactions.
- To make the administrators and policy makers aware of the need for reorienting the teacher education programme.
- To identify local and global issues for sustainability of the inter-disciplinary courses to be offered.
- Demonstrate pedagogical techniques that would foster higher order thinking skills, support decision making, involve participatory learning, and stimulate skill of questioning.
- To identify new sources of finance by establishing contacts for undertaking sponsored researches.
- To collaborate with NGOs, environmental and social foundations.
- To identify the ways to overcome difficulties and barriers at institutional departmental and government levels.
- To establish strong base for research and developmental work.

- To document, publish and disseminate new knowledge to improve teaching-learning process.
- To provide opportunities to the teacher educators to improve their professional career to use Information Communication Technology (ICT) for teaching.
- To create collaboration and exchange teachers in the teacher-education institutions.
- To establish an electronic, paper and talking library by networking the teacher education institutions.
- To make available the profiles of teacher-education institutions.
- To develop common in-service training programmes.
- To develop and implement continuing professional developmental programmes for teachers and teacher-educators.
- To integrate teacher education with school education directly and exchange teachers for better understanding of school curriculum.
- To create partnership with schools to evolve appropriate curriculum and teaching technology.
- To move towards virtual class rooms.

Strategies of Networking

Like minded institutions with social commitment should join together and discuss the need for networking their educational institutions. They should come forward to share the infra structure facilities and the expertise available in their institutions. A good contact should be established with national organisations like University Grants Commission (UGC), NCTE, NCERT, NEPA (National Educational Planning and Administration) to obtain financial assistance and other guidance. The UGC has come out with a scheme of connecting all the higher education institutions in the country through 'inflibnet' to reduce the expenditure on college and university libraries and provide an easy access to latest information to students and the teachers across the country. It is estimated that this scheme would cater to the needs of approximately (11) eleven million students and four million faculty members of nearly 1600 educational institutions in the country. ISRO (Indian Space Resource Organisation) has been helping for developing the 'inflibnet' and connecting clusters of educational institutions through networking. It is a boon to the students and the research scholars. Inflibnet also would bring a drastic change in the structure of academic libraries, which would be equipped with computer and printers, in future.

NCTE integrated the teacher education, the technical teacher training institutes and the special education programmes for preparing teachers for disabled children vocational education and some special education units recently started in some universities and informal sectors. It is involved in non-formal education and adult education also in its networking, and has provided the visibility and stability to these institutions. The NCTE has made use of EDUSAT (Educational Satellite) for reaching out to different levels of teaching and learning. This is also made possible for us to link with global communication network. ICT has raised the quality of school education as; ICT made use of multimedia and made learner centred education. Using ICT also creates a novel learning atmosphere. The NCTE has two schemes to network nearly 3000 teacher education institutions, 25,000 teacher educators and about thirteen lakhs teachers in service, 1. Through internet and 2 though. EDU-SAT. This will break the isolation and barriers among various institutions. A set of CD ROMS developed by NCTE, and distributed to all the recognised teacher training institution would also provide new resources for teaching and learning.

There are also professional organizations through out the globe that provide online services to teachers and teacher educators through which the teacher educators could share and disseminate their views on different issues relating to teacher education, school education, curriculum, teaching learning process, evaluation and research. At the international level UNESCO CHAIRS and UNIT WIN networks E-MAP-E-NET work on planning and management.

Conclusion

If teacher-education institutions come closer to these national and international organisations after common understanding at the local level, we may begin networking institutions at least within the university area first, then at the state level, national and international level. This will boost the image of teacher education institutions and faculties. Networking will bring the teacher education programme on a smooth platform and enhance the quality of education at all levels, in the new era by disseminating information, knowledge and skills through researches, websites, electronic publications such as *e*-journals, organising workshops and conferences and exchanging the infrastructure and expertise. This united action will bridge the digital divide and bring us all together.

While concluding I would request all the teacher education institutions and the teacher educators commit to change. Unless we commit to change we will not accomplish anything.

UNITY WILL BE OUR STRENGTH. Let us all come together for the cause of education and provide challenging and quality inputs to our future citizens to shoulder higher responsibilities and face new challenges with vigour and knowledge in the new millennium. As a teacher educator nearly for four decades, I strongly believe that networking of teacher education institutions will be a timely and worthwhile attempt to improve the quality of education in India. I congratulate Sri Sarada College of Education for taking initiative to think about this crucial issue. I wish the deliberations during two days will be fruitful and result in action.

13

Role of Teachers in Building Human Resources

"By education I mean an all-round drawing out of the best in the Child and man-body mind and spirit".

— Gandhiji

"Teaching is leaving a vestige of one self in the development of another. And surely the student is a bank where you can deposit your most precious treasures."

— Eugene P. Bertin

A balanced intellect presupposes a harmonious growth of body, mind and soul. Education should promote in every child the ability to discriminate what is good and what is bad. Swami Vivekananda said, "Education is what makes a person." Which means education cultivates values and peace in man. Through education higher value system of the society along with peace in the globe and a balanced personality of an individual is to be promoted. Teaching is the profession that teaches all the other professions. Teachers unfold and bring out the potentials embedded in the learners by using the methods of problem solving, decision-making, and creativity. When the students enter the class-room, they bring with them great enthusiasm and energy. That energy and enthusiasm should be then pumped into the teachers and it begins a positive cycle between the teachers, the students and the environment to play a pro active role.

According to Horace Mann, "A teacher who is attempting to teach without inspiring the pupil with a desire to learn is hammering on cold iron". As William Arthur War expresses "The mediocre teacher tells. The good teacher explains. The superior teacher demonstrates. The great teacher inspires." This should be the maxim of teaching.

Education is for Holistic Development

Children should not be taught the skill of reading, writing and arithmetic-the 3 Rs. only. They should be prepared to face the challenges in the globe with confidence by learning life skill experiences creativity and critical thinking. Literacy is not the end of education nor even the beginning. Our vision for 2020, should therefore be quality education for all with greater emphasis on nurturing broad human development. Education is the stepping stone for social, emotional, physical, intellectual and creative development and wellbeing of children. Education should therefore be designed in such a way that it promotes the quality of life by providing inputs for facing the challenges in the fast challenges in the fast changing world. New knowledge is to be created and students should be exposed to new knowledge and make the knowledge an action plan to make India excel in the world. Education should therefore promote the total development of the human being by teaching them the values of life, peace, providing opportunity for character formation, self-confidence to face any problems in life; promoting the mind which is highly receptive and creative in a healthy body. It is believed that consciousness-based education, developed by Maharishi Mahesh Yogi, does promote holistic brain functioning and expansion of mental capabilities through the Transcendental Meditation technique. They are found to be more committed academically, more alert, healthier and balanced, more self-actualised, more satisfied with their education, more harmonious in their relationships, and more mature in moral judgement, compared to students at other educational institutions.

Towards a Knowledge Society

The Knowledge Commission constituted by the Prime Minister of India under the Chairmanship Sam Pitroda aimed at preparing a blue print to tap into the enormous reservoir of our knowledge base so that our people can confidently face challenges of the 21st century. The commission aimed at building excellence in the educational system by creating and applying new knowledge in the fields of Science and Technology and Agriculture and Industry to face the challenges of the 21st century. In turn, it is believed that it will encourage the use of knowledge capabilities in making government an effective, transparent and accountable service provider to the public.

To achieve the above said target the NKC identified the following five aspects of knowledge paradigm: Access to Knowledge, Knowledge Concepts, Creation of Knowledge, Knowledge Applications and Delivery of Services. The Report categorically states that Knowledge concepts could be organised, distributed and transmitted through the education system. It also firmly believes that it is only through education that an individual can make better informed decisions, keep abreast of important issues and trends around him or her and most importantly, question the socio-economic arrangements in a manner that can lead to change and development. Our education system should therefore, move towards that direction which enables an individual not only to question but prepares him to build a new world. To create such type of education atmosphere we should start upgrading the knowledge from school level itself as it is the foundation and highly flexible period to construct new knowledge and skills and expand it to higher education.

Education is Investment

Providing Education to the children means investment for future. A Chinese proverb says "If you are planning for a year, sow rice; if you are planning for a decade, plant trees; if you are planning for a lifetime, educate people." Every child has the right to education. A child's right to development and quality life includes the right to education. As *John F. Kennedy the former President of United States of America expresses* "Let us think of education as the means of developing our greatest abilities, because in each of us there is a private hope and dream which, fulfilled, can be translated into benefit for everyone and greater strength of the nation." What is really needed today to make democracy function is not knowledge of facts, but right education with social commitment. Achievement of an individual in life will show the real education he/she received. "Education is not the filling of a pail but the lighting of a fire." —*William Butler Yeats*

It is a superstition to think that the fullest development of man is impossible without knowledge of art of reading and writing. "While that knowledge undoubtedly adds grace to life, it is in no way indispensable for man's moral, physical or material growth." Children can no more be taught only the skill of reading, writing and arithmetic they should be prepared to face the challenges in the globe with confidence by learning life skill experiences, critical thinking. Our vision for 2020, should be quality education for all with greater emphasis on nurturing broad human development. India is to promote human resource development by creating a legacy of hunger free nation with no malnourished child. The healthy children of today will ensure the healthy generation of tomorrow. Education is the stepping stone for social, emotional, physical, intellectual and creative development and wellbeing of children. Education should therefore be designed in such a way that it promotes the quality of life by providing needed inputs for facing the challenges in the next millennium.

Right to Education

Constitution of India emphasizes in Articles 24, 39 and 45 about protection of children from being employed in hazardous employment, protection against moral and material abandonment, and provision of free and compulsory education for all children up to 14 years of age. Constitution of India also ensures that the State shall take measures to ensure that every child up to the age of 18 years has the Fundamental Right to free, quality and compulsory education in neighbourhood schools with common school system till completion of Higher Secondary Education (12th Standard) or equivalent.

The State shall ensure physical education, games, sports, Human Rights education, Life Skills and other types of recreational as well as cultural and scientific activities in educational institutions so that well balanced human resources could emerge. Education not only unearths and exposes the learners to new knowledge and moulds the present generation, it reflects a society's goals and the tasks to be performed to achieve them.

Getting students excited about learning is absolutely the best way to teach.

Right to Education Act passed in 2009 (RTE) provides a right platform to reach the unreached the poor, villagers, tribals other disadvantaged groups such as child laborers, migrant children, differently abled, girls or those who are deprived of education owing to social, cultural economical geographical, linguistic, gender and other reasons. India wants to make Schooling compulsory for all children below the age 14 and the Government pledged to double spending on education, to 6 per cent of GDP. There is an increase in primary school enrolment overall by 13.7 per cent and by 19.8 per cent for girls, reaching close to universal enrolment in Grade 1. It is not enough that we enroll them we should ensure that all boys and girls enrolled in primary school complete a full course of primary schooling to achieve universal primary education.

Poverty and Education

The children are the primary victims of poverty in the world over Due to poverty they are forced to take up jobs for a very low wage or start begging at an early stage when they are expected to enjoy life, learn and build their capacity to face the future with confidence. As per the National Labour Institute 92 million children in India are neither enrolled in school nor in labour force but are 'nowhere' children. Nearly one lakh children live in street without parental care. Efforts are to be taken to regulate the age of admission to employment, the hours of work, the type of employment, remuneration and holidays. If, there is need for employment of children care should also be taken to see that children below 15 years of age are protected from entering bonded labour, physical and moral dangers. India's economy is rapidly growing and we therefore require more skilled and educated workforce, Sudip Mozumder writes "India needs to equip the 12 million young people who join its labor force every year with higher levels of education and skills to be able to access better-paying jobs, and to benefit from the demographic dividend," says a new World Bank report. To improve Secondary education in India we have to increase investments in additional infrastructure and highly qualified and dedicated teachers, improved curriculum and textbook; more effective teacher education; use of new educational technologies and strategies of teaching, accountability systems; and examination reforms that will improve access, quality and equity of secondary education.

Teacher as Emancipator

Right to education also focuses on the quality of teaching and learning, which emphasises on the third parent- the teacher and their commitment and the ability to teach well. As Khalil Gibran says "The teacher who is indeed wise does not bid you to enter the house of his wisdom but rather leads you to the threshold of your mind." "We should not teach children the sciences but give them a taste for them," Says *Jean Jacques Rousseau.* The basic idea behind teaching is to teach people what they need to know. They should teach from their heart, not from the book.

A good teacher is a good student first. He/She should continue to be a learner and update the knowledge. Only when a lamp continues to be burning can light another lamp. Creative and sustained initiatives are crucial to train more than one million new and untrained teachers and to reinforce the skills of existing teachers to ensure child-friendly education.

Education to Empower Women

Empowering women is an important end in itself, not only as a human right but as having the potential to enhance human well-being. Empowering women and improving their status are essential ingredients of realising the full potential of economic, political and social development and ensuring sustainable development as they constitute fifty percent of our population. Efforts are to be taken to promote gender equality and empower women. Eliminate gender disparity in primary and secondary education preferably by 2005, and by all levels by 2015. Equal rights of men and women are explicitly mentioned in the Preamble to the Charter of the United Nations. All the major international human rights instruments include sex as one of the grounds upon which States may not discriminate. Develop a comprehensive human rights education programme to raise awareness among women of their human rights and raise awareness among others of the human rights of women. Girls are strong, smart, and bold, but need encouragement to overcome society's messages and pressures that make them doubt their potentials. Girls gain confidence when they are encouraged to set achievable goals, explore their worlds, and dream beyond their realities as parents, caregivers, and the teachers we have to play an essential role in shaping their futures.

The following poem reveals the influence of teachers and their long lasting effect on learners.

"It was with the blessings of the preceptor that I was freed from illusion.

It was with the blessings of the perceptor that I was freed from forgetulness.

It was with the blessings of the perceptance that I was freed from worldly bondages.

It was with the blessings of the perciptor that I was fred from the bondage of sins."

— ***Channabasavanna***

14

Quality Teacher Education and ICT

"I never Teach pupils, I only Create Conditions in which They can Learn Themselves."

— Albert Einstein

We live in a digital world. Information and Communication Technologies (ICTs) have a major role to play in every walk of life of the mass. Educational systems around the world are expected to use the new information and communication technologies (ICTs) to teach students the knowledge and skills they need in the 21st century. Use of technology provides opportunity to both teachers and students to experiment with teaching and learning. The emphasis on *e*-learning and *e*-teaching is in increase. Improving the quality of education through the diversification of contents and methods and promoting experimentation, innovation, the diffusion and sharing of information and best practices as well as policy dialogue are UNESCO's strategic objectives in education.

While talking about the teachers it is said that "Of all the factors which determine the quality of education and its contribution to national development, the teacher is undoubtedly the most important factor. The success of all educational endeavours ultimately depend on his/her personal qualities and character, educational qualifications and professional educational qualifications".

Let us now analyse what is ICT and its role in teaching. ICT has been described in the Conference Proceedings of First Annual Conference of SETRAD as "Educational Technology is the development, application and evaluation of systems, techniques and aids to improve the process of human learning". As Des Wallemoor) says, "You can lead a computer to the Superhighway but you can't make it think." It is only the human being who can think. Use of ICT can facilitate and motivate learning but can not replace teacher. It is only a tool and an aid to make teaching more interesting by creating a novel atmosphere in the class room that will motivate learners.

Educational systems around the world today are under increasing pressure to use the new information and communication technologies (ICTs) to teach students the knowledge and skills they need in the 21st century.

Conditions Required for Effective use of ICI

To effectively harness the power of the new information and communication technologies to improve learning, first of all a mindset is essential for which the following conditions must be fulfilled:

Students and teachers must have sufficient access to digital technologies and the Internet facilities in their classrooms, schools, and teacher education institutions.

High quality, meaningful, and culturally relevant digital content must be available for teachers and learners.

Teacher education institutions face the challenge of preparing a new generation of teachers to effectively use the new learning tools in their teaching practices. If students to achieve high academic standards Teachers must have the knowledge and skills to use the new digital tools and resources and this task requires the acquisition of new resources, expertise and careful planning.

Using ICTs effectively, support communication between learners, society and beyond classrooms. Here the teacher's role is to be of a facilitator of establishing collaboration and networking with local and global communities.

Teacher education Institutions must have sufficient number of ICT equipment to create the atmosphere and motivate the teachers and students use them as often as possible.

Teacher Education and ICT

Approaches to the professional development of teachers should dependent on the demand driven-need based, local specific, context and culture of the society. Experience has shown that a number of essential conditions must be met to successfully integrate ICTs into teacher education programmes. Technology should be infused into the entire teacher education programme at different levels. Throughout their teacher education experience, trainees should learn how to incorporate ICTs in their teaching. Restricting technology experiences to a single course or to a single area of teacher education, such as methods of teaching, will not prepare students to be effective users of technology. Pre-service teacher education students should learn about a wide range of educational technologies across their professional preparation, from introductory and foundations courses to student teaching and their professional development

Students should experience innovative technology—supported learning environments in their teacher education programme. Technology can be used to support traditional forms of learning as well as to transform learning. A Power Point presentation, for example, can enhance a conventional lecture, but it does not necessarily transform the learning experience. On the other hand, using multimedia to teach topics that have previously been addressed through lectures is an example of a learning experience transformed by technology. Students should experience both types of uses of technology in their programme; however, the brightest promise of technology in education is as a support for new, innovative, and creative forms of teaching and learning

Professional development to Incorporating ICTs into teaching and learning is an integral part of teacher education and should not be thought of as one 'injection' of training. Teachers need to update their knowledge and skills as the school curriculum and technologies are constantly change. Owing to the emerging new technologies, the teaching profession is evolving from an emphasis on teacher-centered, lecture-based instruction to student centered, interactive learning modes. Designing and implementing successful ICT-enabled teacher education programmes is the key to fundamental, wide-ranging educational reforms. If the Teacher education institutions do not assume a leadership role in the transformation of education they will be left behind in the swirl of rapid technological change. For education to reap the full benefits of ICTs in teaching and learning, it is essential those pre- and in-service teacher education programmes are able to effectively use these new tools for teaching and learning as their technique.

Steps to Incorporate ICT in Teacher Education

Integrate ICT as an innovative approach to teaching and learning in teacher education programme to make the teachers and trainees draw inspiration from the innovations made in science and technology.

Arrange special lectures cum demonstrations by experts on ICTs in professional development of teachers.

Help the trainees develop skills in preparing lessons using appropriate technology to teach a particular lesson, first in a small class room situation, few concepts and for a shorter period, then to a whole lesson to a whole class.

Make teacher educators and teacher trainees understand, appreciate and use ICTs in the class rooms more effectively in varied situations.

Learn to prepare soft ware for teaching different subjects.

Organise training progamme to prepare and use Web based teaching learning materials.

Teach teacher trainees how to prepare *e*-content and how to use it to a large group of people in the community.

Learn to use the internet for teaching and learning.

We will make use of the ICTs only when we understand and appreciate the impact of technology on global society and the implications for education, the extensive knowledge that has been generated about how people learn and what this means for creating more effective and engaging student-centered learning environments. The stages of teacher development and the levels of adoption of ICTs by teachers, dependence on the critical importance of context, culture, leadership and vision of the teacher education programme. Life-long learning, and the change process in planning for the integration of technology into teacher education, the ICTs competencies required for teachers relating to content, pedagogy, technical issues, social issues, collaboration, and networking, the importance of developing standards to guide implementation of ICTs in teacher education, the essential conditions for successful integration of ICTs into teacher education and the institutional readiness to accept it by understanding the benchmarks and the standard required for the use if ICTs in teacher education, easy access to tools required are the important strategies to be considered in planning for the infusion of ICTs in teacher education and managing the change process.

Information and communication technologies (ICTs) play major role in shaping the new global economy and producing rapid changes in society. Education is at the confluence/link of powerful and rapidly shifting educational, technological and political forces that will shape the society and the structure of educational systems across the globe. To accomplish this goal requires a change in the traditional view of the learning process and an understanding of how the new digital technologies can create new learning environments in which students are engaged in learning process as participatory learners, able to take greater responsibility for their own learning and constructing their own knowledge. In contrast to the traditional teaching-learning paradigm, a new paradigm shift in the teaching-learning process is emerging, based on three decades of research in human learning.

A Shift from Teaching to Learning

As technology has created change in all aspects of society, it is also changing our expectations of what students must learn in order to function in the new changing world economy. Students, now have to learn to navigate through large amounts of information, to analyse and make decisions, and to master new knowledge domains in an increasingly technological society. They have to be life-long learners, collaborating with others in accomplishing complex tasks, and effectively using different systems for representing and communicating knowledge to others.

A shift from teacher-centered instruction to learner-centered instruction is needed to enable students to acquire for the 21st century knowledge and skills. Shifting the emphasis from teaching to learning can create a more interactive and engaging learning environment for teachers and learners. This new environment also involves a change in the roles of both teachers and students. The role of the teacher will change from knowledge transmitter to that of learning facilitator, knowledge guide, knowledge navigator and co-learner with the students. The new role does not diminish the importance of the teacher but requires new knowledge and skills.

Students will have greater responsibility for their own learning as they become participant in learning process. In this new environment they seek out, find, synthesise, and share their knowledge with others. ICTs provide powerful tools to shift to student-centered learning and the new roles of teachers and students. New learning environment can be created without the use of technology also. But in teaching and learning process ICTs provide powerful tools to help learners access vast knowledge resources, collaborate with others, consult experts, share knowledge, and solve complex problems.

Constructivism in Learning

ICTs in learning promote a new style of learning called Constructivism, where the learners are active participants. The learners engage themselves in their own knowledge construction by integrating new information into their own schema or mental structures. The learning process is seen as a process of "meaning-making" in socially, culturally, economically, historically, and politically relevant contexts. In a constructivism learning environment, students construct their knowledge by testing ideas and approaches based on their prior knowledge and experience, by applying and integrating new knowledge and experiences gained with pre-existing intellectual constructs.

A constructivist environment involves developing and promoting learning communities comprised of students, teachers and experts who construct new knowledge. A constructivist learning environment also provides opportunities for learners to experience multiple ways of teaching and testing. Through discussion and debate, learners are able to analyse issues and problems from different points of view, to negotiate meaning, and develop shared understandings with others. The constructivist learning environment also emphasizes on assessment of learning using different techniques. Contrutivistic learning also promote creativity and originality in gaining knowledge.

Global Context

As noted in the UNESCO World Education Report, "*Teachers and Teaching in a Changing World*" (UNESCO, 1998), "the young generation is entering a world that is changing in all spheres: scientific and technological, political, economic, social, and cultural. The emergence of the 'knowledge-based' society is changing the global economy and the status of education. Information and communication technologies (ICTs) are a major factor in shaping the new global economy and producing rapid changes in society. Within the past decade, the new ICT tools have fundamentally changed the way people communicate and do business."

There is growing awareness among policy-makers, business leaders and educators that an educational system designed to prepare the learners for an agrarian or industrially-based economy will not provide students with the knowledge and skills they need to thrive in the 21st century's knowledge-based economy and society. The new knowledge-based global society is one in which there is realisation that there is knowledge explosion every day through research and inventions in the field of science and technology and these findings are published. This has made the present day learners to realize that they learn much more than their parents and grand parents when they were of their age.

The teacher provides the repertoire-the learning atmosphere to his/her students that will help them learn according to their choice, capability and speed with which they can learn. Teachers at every level have to decide how to balance the past and the future so that learners have no confusion in achieving new learning. Teachers should have the necessary threshold of knowledge and skills to charter a course in ICT based programme as well as what is required by the community.

To reach this goal teachers should be innovative, flexible and committed to change and development that occur in every learner. And they are also expected to counteract/mitigate and solve problems created by any new challenges that emerge due to changes. Teacher educators have many real and hard pressing challenges while using ICTs in new challenging atmosphere of preparing the teachers for next generation. But there is no option other than to face the challenges as education is powerful and rapidly shifting in various fields such as educational, technological and political forces that will shape the structure of educational systems across the globe.

Technology co-ordinators view the problems of insufficient hardware, software, and training as major obstacles. Teachers consider the lack of time to develop technology-based lesson a concern. Administrators identify teachers' lack of experience using technology in instruction as yet another challenge. Simply providing the technology for learners and teachers is not enough. Interest and commitment on the part of both teachers and learners should be ensured. Availability of the type of ICT equipment and level of access is also important. ICTs will improve learning very little if teachers and students have only rare and occasional access to the ICT tools for learning. For the acquisition of competence with hardware and software, especially for teachers there should be reasonable access to both teachers and learners. For example, provision of portable computers-laptops/notebook is a boon for ICTs teacher education, so that they use them for both teaching in school and for other professional activities elsewhere.

Web based and Electronic Model

The Web based model encourages teachers to create new activities for their students. This in turn will encourage students develop their own Web based activities to support what they are learning and share it with others by designing and using Multimedia objects such as text, graphics, video, animation, and sound to represent and convey information. Many teachers find that students are motivated to learn if they can use technology appropriate to convey what they want at the apt places/situations. Some examples of multimedia presentations include: creating a web page or site; using a multimedia slide show to make a presentation more interesting and shooting, editing video shows to create a computer-generated movie, photos, scanned images, movies, and text.

Telecommuting, Internet-enriched learning activities often actively involve students in learning process. They may share with others what they have learnt and what they know. Telecommuting tools include email, electronic mailing lists, and electronic bulletin boards, discussion groups, web browsing, chatting, and audio- and video-conferencing. Online resources include web sites, interactive environments, and remotely operated robotic devices.

Conclusion

Thanks to the innovations in the field of teaching strategies and use of technology in teaching and learning. Today it is emphasised that we should start using ICTs at the planning of Curriculum, administration and in Evaluation also. It is one of the recommendations of the National Knowledge Commission that to interconnect all knowledge institutions throughout the country, through an electronic digital broadband network with gigabit capabilities, to encourage sharing of resources and collaborative research. NKC has proposed creating national web based portals on important components of education so that it will have a wider publicity, sharing and use from where knowledge society could emerge.

It is true that technology can not replace a teacher. At the same time we should also remember that if we do not use them judiciously a teacher who uses them effectively, will replace us. Use of ICTs will enable us to reach the mass without much difficulty in conveying the concepts and their learning with ease. Let us therefore, imbibe the culture of technology where ever it is essential, for effective teaching and communication and lead the prospective teachers to changing scenario of Indian education system. Aiming at global connectivity will bring the people and their culture closer and bring peace and harmony in the world and make Education an instrument for social change.

As Henry Ford Says

"Any one who stops learning is old. Any one who keeps learning stays young.

The greatest thing in life is to keep your mind young."

So, let us continue to be the learners and keep ourselves young and be burning as bright torches to light another torch.

15

Teacher Education in the Changing Scenario of Globalisation

"We do not own our knowledge; it is not ours to keep. We must share our gift of knowledge with those seek knowledge. Learning is a blessing, teaching is a gift and knowledge is power. Let us empower others."

— C. Davis-Mary

Introduction

The global challenges of the Millennium encumber various fields-economic, political, social, environmental, physical, and technological and education. The advancement in the field of digital network, internet and satellite communication systems have promoted communication at a mind-boggling speed. The traditional concept of distance has gone. The world has shrunk in size and has come to be known as a 'Global Village', making Vinobaji's dream of "Vasudeva Kudumbakam" a reality. The traditional concept of distance has gracefully bowed its way out to facilitate everything to go global Globalisation is changing our aspirations and achievements which have changed our life style. Global economic systems shape our job opportunity. Though privatisation, marketisation, liberalisation, globalisation have been the key words so far in economic reforms, today it has political, social and educational implications as well. Till recently education had not been realised that it has a place in economic reforms. But now people have started seriously thinking of education in global context which has less controversy. Human capital is much more important than financial capital if one wants to make his mark in the world market. To survive and succeed in a world economy, it is imperative that India has an educational system on par with world standard.

Globalisation has multidimensional impact on the educational system at all levels. Education as a service industry, is part of Globalisation process under the umbrella of General Agreement on Trade in Service (GATS). It may therefore demand a different type of education system which some time cause inequality in our country. As for as Teacher Education is concerned, which prepares the key persons to carry on the responsibility of producing the teachers for excellence in education should have its indicators of such qualities.

Objectives of Globalisation of Teacher Education

Teachers are the catalytic agents of any change in the society through their students. They are to be provided with proper and quality education and its transaction to inspire and attract others to enjoy and use education received. Teaching is not merely imparting the knowledge from teachers to students; teaching is inspiring the young minds to achieve higher values in life, to lead next generation.

The National council for Teacher Education (NCTE) document (1998) stresses that teachers are to be the torchbearers in creating a new society, with social cohesion and national integration by revealing and elaborating the secrets of attaining higher values in life. Only enlightened and emancipated teachers could lead the communities and nations in the right direction, march towards better and higher quality of life.

In the changing scenario, of education system, due to Globalisation Teacher education has to rethink and reformulate its aims/goals in order to compete with the structure and quality of teacher educators in the rest of the world. The purpose of globalisation of Indian education according to the Ministry of Human Resource Development is threefold. Globalisation of education helps the government earn foreign exchange, quality of education is improved and it gives India an opportunity to spread its culture and values. Indian universities have a major role to play, in this regard."

Only those who have resources, competency and the knowledge could become mobile and participate in global market for education and employment, they become human capitalists and others have to be confined to purely local and may lose the opportunities. Globalisation has a positive influence on the quality as well as quantity of knowledge through interaction among the countries. The explosion of knowledge in the fast developing world has opened up the door for life long learning. Learning is a continuum without confining to a specific period of life and barrier restricting the process.

In this back drop teacher educators and teachers should be equipped with the cognitive structure and the skill to be teachers and teacher educators at the local and when there is demand at global. Our students are also to be mobile, they go out to other countries and the foreign students come to India for their higher education and employment. Hence teacher educators and the teachers should have the competency, be ready to compete with their counterparts in any part of the globe. Can we say that the present Teacher education in India is really meeting this requirement? Keeping this in view the following objectives of Teacher Education could be formulated:

1. To create favourable conditions in the Teacher education Institutions for outwardly mobile students and teachers, who are willing to do a part of their studies or teaching in another country.
2. Creating infrastructure facilities and other conditions that make it easier for foreign students to gain access for participation in Indian Institutions of Teacher education.
3. To add an international dimension to the course contents with higher quality and teaching practice to make it global with stress on strengthening the competency in foreign languages that produce higher quality manpower who will be ready to face challenges any where in the globe.
4. To cooperate with foreign partners in developing future curricula and educational methods to make our teacher education curriculum global.
5. To motivate teacher educators and teachers to travel abroad to understand various systems of education followed and excel in their competency to disseminate our system as well.
6. To think of recertification process in teacher education on the basis of their achievement in teaching, research and extension.
7. Help to stimulate a new humanism which contains ethical component that would preserve our ethos and culture.

Initiatives to be Taken

Internationalisation of teacher education sounds an ideal way to market Indian education in the world market and vice versa. What are the role and approaches of Indian Universities and other bodies like NCTE which have the control over teacher education in India in this process of internationalisation of teacher education?

When we treat education as an industry where the product is enriched knowledge, we have to work out a method of supply/demand network for successful marketing of education. The quality of education attains paramount importance to ensure dependable markets. The teacher educators and teachers have to have exemplary ability to provide quality education to face the competitive world. Hence while designing the curricula one has to keep in mind quality control and quality assurance systems. Similarly suitable methodologies to teach the courses should be carefully deliberated upon and the teachers to be suitably trained. This means there should be innovation in curriculum, methods and evaluation in teachers' education. When the idea globalisation of education becomes acceptable and the implication cease to appear insurmountable, one can think of the academic and administrative strategies. Once the activities and assignments to be carried out are properly worked out it gives clarity as to how we should proceed with internationalising teacher education in India.

We speak of educational exchange as 'from the standpoint of future world peace and order, probably the most important and potentially rewarding of our foreign policy activities'. The exchange programmes will produce thousands of young men and women "who may go back to their countries with a deeper emotional attachment to their own nation and often with a deeper nationalism than the one with which they came' as remarked by Scientist Karl Wolfgang Deutch. Educational exchange establishes bonds of friendship that transcend national boundaries and lays the foundation for shared and common understanding. When education stresses on value education, it will help in co-operation, rather then competition, sharing of experience, rather than personal gains and leaning to live together rather than hostile behaviour.

A combination of essential conditions is required for teachers to create learning environments conducive to powerful uses of technology. The most effective learning environments would we to facilitate learning of relevant content while addressing individual needs. For these new learning environments we have to insist on, certain prerequisite factors/essential conditions that must be present in every phase of an aspiring teacher education institution. During first-year teachers cannot be expected to put into practice what they have learned about how to use technology without the presence of these essential conditions in their new job environment. Policy decisions supporting technology use, greatly affect a new teacher's ability to use technology effectively.

As it was envisaged in the National Policy of Education (1986) efforts are to be taken to integrate pre service and in service components of teacher education. This will provide feed back from the field which will enrich the teacher educators with the latest information, need based and the skills needed to equip the teacher educators as well as the future teachers.

Cautions to be Taken

So many queries are to be answered before the final launching of this globalisation of teacher education. Will internationalisation stabilise itself as an integral part of higher education? Will it be a solution to the problem of multicultural society? Will it bring the local and global into perfect harmony or is it a means to merge multiculturalism? Will it pave the way for world peace and mutual understanding? Is it really the process of integrating an international/intercultural dimension into the teaching, research and service function of the institution as defined by Institutional Management of Higher Education (IMHE)? Is it cost effective? Is it economically, socially, culturally viable? Are we cautious about unregulated entry of foreign institutes of higher education? Do we accredit all the higher education institutions which enter India? Do we insist on reciprocity of our institutions of higher education to be established in their countries?

We have to take some definite step for 'promoting vigorously the internationalization of our institutions and the global competence and literacy of our students as being essential to the long term pursuit of a more peaceful world where international understanding and cooperation in solving problems will be increasingly critical for the quality of life and sustained economics, social and cultural development.' Once we decide to accept the challenges of globalisation of higher education and teacher education we have to start optimistically planning the actual process. Academic planning and administrative support are the two sides of any educational system. There should be proactive leadership and administrative support from the entire system. The administrative side will concentrate on providing proper infrastructure, recruitment of well qualified and competent staff, deciding the fee structure, providing accommodation and boarding facilities.

The next step will be to design a suitable curriculum followed by evolving suitable methodology of teaching and appropriate evaluation strategies. In Teacher Education the matters of evaluation and assessment should be linked to what happens and what is expected and intended with curricula in schools. As it is stated in the Curriculum Framework for Teacher Education, curriculum to be linked to the pedagogical and professional concerns of the child and the teacher, so that both teacher and the learner could be empowered. Interfacing of school curriculum with teacher education curriculum will enrich teacher education and the learning atmosphere and the capability of the learner.

In the new millennium we observe that there is knowledge explosion. New knowledge is emerging everyday. Only those who are able to have efficient use of the innovations made and are able to create new knowledge will be able to be successful in their life and career, others will be thrown out. This means teaching, research and outreach programme should go hand in hand. Educators are expected to be knowledgeable in their subject matter and teaching methodologies in their discipline. They should also encourage innovations among the teachers under training besides they being the creators of new knowledge, as the new knowledge is the key indicators of the growth of any nation.

Teacher education faculty should develop skill in using technology systems and software appropriate to their subject area specialty and model effective use as part of the coursework. Technology keeps improving faster and is becoming more powerful. Keeping abreast of the latest changes can be a challenging task even for the most informed educators. Educators should have access to current technologies, software, and telecommunications networks and are to be skilled in the use of technology for learning and teaching. Teacher educators are to be provided with technical assistance for maintaining and using the technology. Technical assistance for teacher education faculty and students should be readily available so that they could easily use technology resources for teaching and learning.

Technology-based curriculum resources that address subject matter content, standards and support teaching, learning, and productivity should be made available to teacher candidates that will motivate them to be knowledge creators and effective communicators of the knowledge.

Teacher educators must be familiar with various techniques of measurement and evaluation that will satisfy the requirement of all. Teacher education faculty and professional teaching staff will integrate teaching and assessment to measure the effectiveness of technology-supported teaching strategies.

Teacher preparation programmes should also provide teacher candidates with opportunities to participate in field experiences at partner schools and other stakeholders.

They should be exposed to and familiar with Policies associated with accreditation, standards, budget allocations, and personnel decisions in teacher education programs and field experience.

Conclusion

"The destiny of India is shaped in her class room", by Dr. Kothai, as the opening remark of the report of the Education Commission (1964-1966) is a classical example to stress the importance of education. This will become a reality only when the teachers are properly equipped with the aptitude, positive attitude for teaching profession, commitment, knowledge, and the competency. In the present context of globalisation it becomes still more relevant as the teacher educators and the teachers face the challenges from the learners and the world around.

The true teacher is one who learns from teaching rather than one who has finished learning. A teacher should continue to be a learner. This has been aptly expressed by Rabinadranath Tagore as:

"A teacher cannot teach unless he is teaching himself.

A lamp cannot light another lamp unless it continues itself to burn."

I would like to quote Mahatma Gandhi who cautioned us long back.

"I do not want my house to be walled on all sides and my windows to be stuffed. I want the culture of all the lands to be blown about my house as freely as possible. But I refuse to be blown off my feet by any."

16

Rural Institutes Towards Quality Rural Higher Education

Education from the dawn of history has been a process of handing over knowledge and awareness, culminating in the growth of every aspect for human kind. Education is a process of transformation that enables mankind to become more civilised.

During ancient times teachers of exceptional knowledge and wisdom were revered as the upholders of civilisation. Ancient Indian Tradition of Gurukula System laid emphasis on a deep personal relationship where teachers and pupils freely interacted and the teachers were the friends, philosophers and guides in the true sense.

In India, both Braminical and Buddhist education systems took shape into systematic learning centers. Takshasila, Nalanda, Valabhi, Kasi, Kashmir etc. were samples of those great traditions.

During the pre-independent era, the British found it difficult to administer the vast country all by themselves. The British government utilized the immense intellectual potential and manpower in India to administer the vast country through imparting western education to the Indians. The education thus imparted focussed on creating bureaucrats to satisfy the British needs.

The demand for English education was growing strong and the government declaration in 1844 that English knowing Indians would be given preference in public employment made English education more popular. The advent of western civilisation on the Indian ethos and in particular, Macaulay's concept of education had a great impact on the education system and went to the extent of shaping the out look of Indians. Though Mahatma Gandhi called for an innovation in Education to suit the life of individuals and the soil by introducing a system of education which he named "Nai Talim" new education, it was not accepted widely. Nai Talim or Basic Education from Pre Basic - Nursery, Basic to Post Basic-Secondary level, then to Social or Adult Education and Higher Education aimed at providing education through life, for life and of life.

Gandhian principles of rural development, a self-sustaining village community and the concept of gram swaraj were the main concerns of this system of education. The Indian Government, after independence realised the need for unique kind of institutions to cater to the educational needs of millions of rural populace living across the country.

Conventional university education system, which encouraged academic advancement, detached itself from the rural realities. To counter this Rural Institutes were conceived as the culmination of the experiment in Gandhian Basic education at the higher education level. The emergence of the concept of Rural Institute though belated created consciousness among the educationists of the academic needs of our rural population.

It was felt that in order to mould the rural intellectuals and to develop personnel who could understand the rural realities Rural Institutes would be an alternative system of education at the higher education level where all the three components of education–teaching, research and extension could be successfully carried out.

Genesis of Rural Institutes

In 1949, immediately after independence the University Commission constituted under the chairmanship of Dr S. Radhakrishnan strongly emphasized the need for starting Rural Institutes/Rural Colleges to improve the Higher Education System in rural areas.

Subsequently in 1954, a Committee on Higher Education for Rural Areas: Rural Institute was appointed Chaired by Dr. K. L. Shrimali. The Committee recommended that "Rural Institutes should help in breaking down economic and geographic barriers between rural and urban population. They will also help to bridge the gulf between culture and work, between humanities and technology and between practical and the ideal".

The committee suggested certificate courses in Agriculture, Sanitation, Rural Health, Overseers, Teaching etc. and a three year Diploma course in Rural Services equivalent to first degree. These courses were open to the candidates who completed the Post Basic or Higher Secondary courses.

To administer the Rural Institutes (RIs) the committee recommended to form a National Council for Rural Higher Education as an Advisory Body to the Central Ministry of Education and at the State level a State Council for Rural Higher Education for Rural Areas in the Department of Education.

On the basis of the recommendations of Shrimali Committee the following Institutes which were pioneers in the field of education in rural areas were recognized as Rural Institutes in 1956:

1. Shri Shivaji Lok Vidyapeeth Rural Institute, Amaravathi - Bombay
2. Balwant Vidyapeeth Rural Institute, Bichpuri (Agra)
3. The Gandhigram Rural Institute of Higher Education, Madras
4. Sarvodaya Mahavidyalaya, Sundar Nagar, Bihar
5. Shri Mouni Vidyapeeth, Gargoti, Kothalpur - Bombay
6. Lok Bharati Rural Institute, Sanosara - Bombay
7. Sri Ramakrishna Mission Rural Institute, Coimbatore - Madras
8. Sriniketan Rural Institute, Shantiniketan
9. Vidya Bhawan Rural Institute, Udiapur, Rajasthan
10. Jamia Millia Islamia, Jamia Nagar, New Delhi.

The following Institutes were added from 1959 to 1963:

1. Kasthurba Rural Institute, Rajpura (Punjab) - 1959
2. Rural Institute, Wardha (Maharashtra) - 1961
3. Rural Institute, Hanumanamati (Mysore) - 1961
4. Kasturibagram Rural Institute, Indore, (Madhya Pradesh) - 1963
5. Rural Institute, Thavanur (Kerala) - 1963.

The above 14 Rural Institutes were administered by National Council for Rural Higher Education with 75 per cent financial assistance from Centre and the balance from the Stage Governments. A Committee under the Chairmanship of Mahonjani appointed by the University Grants Commission in 1964 considered the scope and standard of education in Rural Institutes and suggested that Rural Institute should not function in isolation from the general stream of higher education, and instead they should be affiliated to the existing universities in the respective vicinity.. It also suggested that deemed university status could be considered to Rural Institutes. In 1967 a Committee on Rural Higher Education, headed by Shri G. Ramachandran went into the satisfactory functioning of the Rural Institutes for Higher Education and suggested measures to improve working conditions of these institutes. Followed by the UGC's committee's recommendations and the recommendations of Committee on Rural Higher Education, National Council for Rural Higher Education recommended that Rural Institutes may seek affiliation to the neighbouring Universities. Almost all except Gandhigram Rural Institute got affiliated to the neighbouring universities.

Basic Principles of Rural Institutes

The basic principles of Rural Institutes are as follows:

- Rural Institutes should identify themselves with the people and strive to raise the living standards in the rural areas,
- should serve the rural community and be an instrument for social change,
- should develop courses that are need based and locate specific,
- should develop the social consciousness among the youth and motivate them to focus their energy to ameliorate the conditions of the rural life,
- Yet another principle that foregrounds the Rural Institutes is that the Rural Institutes do not impose their ideas and ideals on the villages but encourage the villages to evolve their own strategies for development and growth,

*Rural Institute in Shantiniketan was merged with Visva Bharati University in 1963.

- should strike a balance between pure and applied research. Scientific research in the Rural Institutes is to focus on the sustainable development, ecological and environmental preservation coupled with increased prosperity in the rural areas,
- should provide excellent rural oriented education based on rural conditions and needs to the youths and motivate them to go back to the villages to serve and uplift the villages,
- Ultimately, the Rural Institutes will act as a vital link between education and a holistic development of an individual and rural reconstruction programme.

These roles could be summarised into:

1. education/teaching for rural services,
2. research on problems relating to rural life and
3. extension in these areas to achieve the goals.

There are two Rural Institutes functioning now in India — one at Gandhigram Deemed University and another one started at Pochampolly in Andrapradesh inaugurated by Shri P. V. Narasimha Rao in 1995.

The Gandhigram Rural Institute

Veteran Gandhians, freedom fighters, social reformers and educationist of this era, Dr. T. S. Soundram and her husband Dr. G. Ramachandran started Gandhigram in 1947 with the blessings of Mahatma Gandhi. Mahatma Gandhiji's message to the inauguration was: "Success attends where Truth reigns".

Gandhigram, extending over an area of 350 acres, is placed ideally in an enclave of the beautiful Sirumalai hills on the east and south and Kodai hills on the west.

Gandhigram was started in a similar way to that of Phoenix farm of Gandhiji by a few dedicated workers. As the founder Dr. T. S. Soundram was a medical doctor, she dedicated her services to the remote rural people. Thus emerged the Kasturiba Hospital. In order to improve the social status of women and orphans, Kasturiba Sevikashram for destitutes and windows and Children's Home for orphans and destitute children were started along with medical services. Similarly, in order to ensure economic upliftment of the rural poor varied activities in accordance with the principles of Gandhiji were started to provide employment to masses through Kadhi and Village Industries.

Shri G. Ramachandran, the first Director of Gandhigram Rural Institute aimed at synthesizing Rabindranath Tagore's Vishwabarathi and Sevagram of Mahatma Gandhi in his experiment in education at Gandhigram.

To provide quality education to all, especially in rural areas, Pre-Basic, Basic, Post-Basic and Basic Teachers' Training schools were established along with Adult Education Centres in villages around Gandhigram. The idea of establishing Rural University at Gandhigram was first mooted in 1954 when the first batch of pupils from Post-Basic school were to complete their schooling in 1958. This idea and subsequent consultations with Shrimali Committee on Rural Higher Education led to the establishment of Institute that was formally inaugurated on 17th August, 1956, by Rashtrapathi, Dr Rajendra Prasad.

The Institute was started with 91 students. The curriculum approved by the National Council for Rural Higher Education was followed in the courses of study offered by the Institute : (i) three-year Diploma in Rural Services; (ii) two-year Agriculture course and (iii) one-year Preparatory course.

The Diploma courses offered five elective groups namely, Public Administration, Cooperation, Village Industries, Fine Arts (Music) and Home Science. Optionals offered were (i) Elements of Civics and Economics, (ii) Elements of Sociology and Psychology and (iii) Home Science.

Emphasis was also laid on training in the Village Industries course that was considered as training-cum-production unit and it consisted of five industries, namely, (i) Hand-pounding of Rice, (ii) Ghani-oil Pressing, (iii) Hand-made paper, (iv) Soap making, and (v) Allied Carpentry. Minor Industries of Poultry and Apiary were also offered. Theoretical teaching and practical work were carefully balanced in the courses offered.

Extension services were undertaken in right earnest under the guidance of the staff. Community living had been the core principle of Gandhigram. All the institutions of Gandhigram were built on the twin principles of self-reliance and self-government.

Community life bound all students and teachers together and it comprised common discipline, various items of community work from sanitation to cultural programme. Discipline was evolved from within, and it banished casteism, communalism or linguism.

A tutorial system known as "The Gurukula System" in the spirit of the old Gurukula was evolved in the Institute. A teacher or Guru was given charge of ten students and he acted as a guide and friend and helped in every aspect of his living in order to mould his character and promote the wholesome personality of the students. Indeed it is not a surprise that the students of Gandhigram Rural Institute (GRI) shine as Pole Stars in different walks of life.

Gri Attains the Status of Deemed University

The Gandhigram Rural Institute attained the status of Deemed University in the year 1976 for its exceptional service in the rural extension work. Dr P. Gajendragadkar, former Chief Justice of India and Educationist who prepared the classical document on the Governance of Universities, became the first Chancellor of Gandhigram Rural Institute — Deemed University functioning with the following objectives:

- To provide instruction and learning and to promote a classless and casteless society,
- To provide for research and advancement and dissemination of knowledge, and
- To function as a Centre for extension work leading to integrated rural development.

GRI restricted its courses of study, research and approaches to extension to achieve the above said objectives. The focus on rural development, international peace, research input in rural development, appropriate technology, transfer of technology to the rural areas, etc., have been taken in earnest. In the long run of 25 years since it became a Deemed University, it has acquired many plumes.

At present GRI has the following seven faculties: Faculty of Tamil, Indian Languages and Rural Arts, Faculty of English and Foreign Languages, Faculty of Agriculture and Animal Husbandry; Faculty of Rural Health and Sanitation with single department.

The Faculty of Rural Social Sciences has Department of Co-operation, Economics, Political Science and Development Administration,

Gandhian Thought and Peace Science, Sociology and Rural Industries and Management.

The Faculty of Rural Oriented Sciences consists of Mathematics, Centre for Future Studies, Physics, Chemistry, Home Science, Biology, Computer Science and Applications and Rural Technology Centre.

The Faculty of Rural Development has departments of Rural Development, Applied Research, and Adult Continuing Education and Extension.

The dedication of the Institute to rural development had enabled the Institute to attract and work on projects and special cells. The projects and cells are dovetailed to the idea of sustainable rural development.

The Shanti Sena, Cell for Culture and Arts, Rural Technology Centre, University Science Instrumentation Centre, Rural Extension and Evaluation Cell, Employment Bureau, Information Development and Resource Agency (IDARA), Krishi Vigyan Kendra (KVK), Rural Energy Centre, Participatory Rural Appraisal Unit, Population Education and Resource Agency, Rajiv Gandhi Chair for Panchayati Raj, Centre for Entrepreneurship Development, Museum on Gandhiji's Constructive Programme, Village Industry-training Units, and Publication Division are some of the unique features of Gandhigram Rural Institute.

Village Placement Programme, Shramdhan, Gurukula system and Rural Extension Programme are the integral part of education in GRI, which shape the personality of the students and promote aptitude for services to the humanity.

The university is awarded many projects funded by various Ministries of Government of India, Government of Tamil Nadu, organisations like CAPART, NABARD, UGC, ICAR, HUDCO and Research and Development institutions like M.S. Swaminathan Foundation, Centre for Development Studies (Trivandrum), and Rajiv Gandhi Foundation. Programmes are also being sponsored by World Bank, Ford Foundation and DANIDA.

Besides regular programmes, GRI imparts short-term programmes in various fields, from rural people to government officials on awareness creation, skill development and capacity building. Visits of rural masses to the University for various programmes is a very common phenomenon. Thus it fulfils its objectives of education for rural poor at their doorstep and tries to eradicate illiteracy in rural areas by admitting nearly 85 per cent of students from villages and exploring employment opportunities for them.

Swamy Ramananda Tirtha Rural Institute

Swamy Ramananda Tirtha Rural Institute functioning at Pochampally village in Andhra Pradesh since 1995, is funded by the Government of India and Andra Pradesh. This Institute which aims at rural empowerment was started to fulfil Mahatma Gandhiji's dream of making rural India the focal point of holistic development. As it was emphasized in 1986, Policy of Education the Government of India initiated this movement of Starting Rural Institutes and a National Council for Rural Institutes (NCRI) was set up under the Chairmanship of Dr M. Aram, former Vice-Chancellor of Gandhigram Rural University, who had contributed to the shaping of Gandhigram Rural Institute at Gandhigram. After, Dr M. Aram, Shri L.C. Jain was the Chairman of the Council and now lot of initiatives have been taken by the present Chairman, Professor Briz. Kishore to coordinate and strengthen the existing Rural Institutes and to start more Rural Institutes. The NCRI has its headquarters in Hyderabad.

The main objectives of the Institute are :

- To play a pro-active role in the cause of rural development, with primary emphasis on the principles of equity and social justice.
- To work for the holistic rural development through training, education, extension and consultancy.
- To develop, adopt, assimilate and test technologies, including indigenous and smaller technologies, so as to ensure their relevance to the rural requirements.
- To evolve and implement a package of education, training and gainful employment through encouraging flexible entry conditions into its training and educational programmes.
- To develop and maintain a Research and Documentation centre with a view to act as a Resource Centre for studies on rural development, and to conduct research in issues involved in rural education and development.
- To establish and maintain Information Technology network, so as to enable easier access to information and to create an interface between the rural producers and users.

In order to enable the rural mass to attain economic independence this Institute offers various training programmes.

The Continuing Education Programme is another unique feature which helps the rural people to hone their skills and update their knowledge.

Through Rural Info-net Swamy Ramananda Tirtha Rural Institute (SRTRI) reaches the unreached and assists them in every possible means.

By providing a comprehensive package of Training and Education, Technology Development and Transfer, Extension Consultancy and Research and Documentation, the SRTRI has partially achieved a synthesis of sophisticated technology and simple rural ethos and has envisaged many more future programmes for skill-based academic inputs and training technologies.

This facility offered by the SRTRI is open to all, any one who would like to use these facilities in SRTRI are encouraged to use and be benefitted. Their experiment on providing four tired Pyramidal approach of education, viz. (1) Skilled Worker, (2) Technician, (3) Engineer and (4) Specialist help students to choose from any one offered according to their capability and needs.

Under the first Tier — Skilled worker, the main emphasis is either on skill acquisition or upgradation. The courses are offered to students for this purpose. In the second Tier-Technician is based on the grade points fixed by the Institute. The Third Tier-Engineer-entry is grade based. High level technical education is the aim. A full fledged engineer in his chosen speciality is being aimed at. He should be able to enrich rural technologies and productivity. He should go back to rural area to improve rural economy.

In the Fourth Tier students are exposed to advanced training and research to become specialists in chosen field. The entry point is highly flexible. No time scale or duration of the course is fixed; candidates can upgrade their knowledge through distance education.

There are 12 schools in SRTRI in the main campus which are responsible for providing the four tier programme. Schools of (1) Materials Production and Audio Visual Research Centre, (2) Rural Engineering, (3) Agricultural Engineering, (4) Societal studies, (5) Rural Marketing and Management, (6) Training and Extension services, (7) Rural Non-conventional Energy, (8) Primary Health Care, Nutrition, Sanitation and Indian Medicines, (9) Bio-Medical Engineering, (10) Women's Studies, (11) Continuing Education and Human and Legal Rights.

All the above programmes are conceived as per the programme of Action of National Policy of Education 1986, with a complex of schools which try to integrate all aspects of education, training with productive and creative activities, combining science, technology, humanities and Social Sciences according to the local needs.

National Council of Rural Institutes (NCRI)

In 1995, NCRI was set up in Hyderabad as its Headquarters as a nodal organisation to promote Rural Higher Education on the line of Gandhiji's concept of Nai Talim — Basic Education with the following objectives as stated in the booklet — 'A New Dawn on Rural Higher Education' published by NCRI. (P. 2).

All efforts are taken by NCRI to provide quality Higher Education to Rural Youths who will be taught to be self-employed, or be employed by acquiring skills required for employment. The goal of the programme in Rural Institutes is to produce employable youths. NCRI's emphasis on Health, Rural Water Supply, Energy, Communications and Seed and Post Harvest Technology of Agriculture will help to bring about total and integrated development of villages by combining conventional and modern knowledge and technology.

Conclusion

It is stated in Kothari Commission Report (1964-66) "The destiny of India is now being shaped in her class rooms". It is here that the future of the globe is being decided by the education given to the people. This cannot be suggested from human lines and transplanted. It must be rooted in the soil, at the same time be alert to the changes taking place around the world. Gandhiji's system of Basic Education at the Higher Education also is an answer as he emphasised vocational education/skills along with the sublimation of mental, physical and spiritual faculties of the learners. Quality Rural Higher Education should be made available to the people in Rural areas to promote and improve the life style of the people in villages through Rural Institutes in every state.

17

Teachers for the Digital Age

"We need to develop strong and appropriate human capital to stay in the forefront of competition, and this will be affected by the quality of education delivered by its schools and teachers. One of the best ways to achieve this is to enhance Teacher Education programmes so as to train high quality teachers."

— Ignacio Estrada

There aren't just three Rs anymore-as reading, writing and 'rithmetic-there's a fourth one, the Internet. What once we thought as fundamental aspects of education need to be challenged, and started rethinking what our children's education needs to look like in the 21st century and to enhance teacher education for 21st-century. To be successful now and in the future, students need new skills — 21st century skills. An international effort to transform education for students in the information age is needed. It is therefore necessary to address the complex nature of what skills and knowledge our children will need for the future world.

'Teacher educators are to be charged with preparing teachers, children and young people of the 21st century, to be successful citizens and members of a society that is increasingly being transformed by application of technology in every dimension of life. . . Although most programs for teacher education provide some computer education for pre service educators, many do not have latest equipment or faculty with technology expertise in the teacher education institutions. It is therefore, important, that colleges of education widen their offerings to prepare pre service teachers to use technology effectively, and begin modeling proper applications of technology and teaching strategies in the teaching and learning process So there is need to do a much better job of teaching and measuring advanced, 21st century skills that are the indispensable guarantee for participation, achievement and competitiveness in the global economy.

The critical thinking, problem solving skills and Cognitive skills are more important, for everyone, Thinking critically and making judgments, having multidisciplinary approach, communicating and collaborating effectively, making innovative use of knowledge, information and skills in every day life situations are the essential characteristics of an educated individual of the 21st century. As per Tony Wagner, (The Global Achievement Gap) to help students achieve proficiency in 21st century skills, teachers and administrators should provide education support systems that strengthen their instructional, leadership and management competencies. Both students and educators need learning environments that are conducive to achieve this goal.

Educational system around the world are under increasing pressure to use the new information and communication technologies (ICTs) to teach students the knowledge and skills they need in the next millennium. With the emerging new technologies, the teaching profession is evolving from an emphasis on teacher-centred, lecture-based instruction to student centred, interactive learning environments. The future ahead is going to be digital and the future workforce for 21st century is to be prepared for a global, technology-based society and try to address the following questions: Preparing *e*-content, E-enabled smart class room teaching-enabled evaluation, handling digital equipment and digital library, using *e*-journal and books; networking with alumni, other agencies and institutions through online.

Curriculum for 21st Century Teacher Education

Every aspect of our education system from Pre-Primary to, Post Secondary, Higher Education and Teacher preparation programs must aim at preparing citizens with the skills they need to compete in 21st century as today's students will be the future citizens who will be the teachers, technocrats, scientists, business people and artists who will shape the world of 21st century. Advanced economies, innovative industries, firms, and all high-growth professions require more educated workers with the ability to respond flexibly to complex problems, communicate effectively, manage information system, be a responsible leader to guide and work in teams and produce new knowledge.

In future technology, media and telecommunications, may dominate in emerging industries, such as advanced manufacturing, biotechnology, digital media, geospatial technology, nanotechnology, photonics and renewable energy. Promoting creativity, innovation and adaptability will become the hallmarks of competitive digital world. High-growth and emerging industries require a highly skilled and creative workforce.

The technology has embraced fields like medicine, teaching, transportation, manufacturing, and entertainment. In order to stay current and update in these fields teachers must be exposed to the use of appropriate technology so that their teaching will be towards the next millennium.

Students need to have a, holistic development with global awareness and proficiency in, economic, business and entrepreneurial literacy, civic literacy, communication and collaboration skills, information literacy, media literacy, ICT (Information and Communications Technology) literacy; social and cross-cultural skills, life coping and career skills need flexibility, adaptability, initiative and self-direction, productivity and accountability, leadership and responsibility. These alone will help the people to thrive successfully in the competitive world with challenges of the next decade with integration of technology and infrastructure, modernizing professional learning programmes and models, expand use of public media as a cost-effective asset for teachers and create association of Digital Teachers to share and improve their knowledge and skiil.

Essential and new knowledge creation and skills have created a paradigm shift in the way we educate our children today. These educational goals could become a reality, only when the teachers receive the appropriate teacher training needed to teach the children of the next century at the same time the needs of their childhood. The professionals can become model and guide the teacher candidates to acquire the knowledge and skills that an effective classroom teachers should possess to: Educate all children by providing for individual differences keeping in mind that if a child can't learn the way we teach, we should teach the way they learn; create an atmosphere to promote reading and writing skills of the students for effective communication; produce independent thinkers and problem solvers by giving students the necessary knowledge and skills to enable them to become independent learners and be successful citizens of the digital world in the 21st century.

Teacher Educators and Strategies of Training

As Socrates says "I cannot teach anybody anything; I can only make them think." An efficient and committed teacher educator could make the teachers under training an architect of the future. Teacher educators should have the following qualities to prepare the teachers of 21st century who will promote the needed proficiencies among the students besides being a role model.

"The art of teaching is the art of assisting discovery." — Says Mark Van Doren.

A Teacher educator should possess high quality mentoring relationship between student teachers and the teacher educator-the master teacher, should have a strong mastery over the subject content as well as educational and pedagogical techniques. They should have the ability to establish collaboration with, all the stakeholders in education. Promoting hands-on teaching experience at the micro and macro levels and learning in realistic classroom setting prior to placement is another requisite quality of a teacher educator.

Teachers under training should be given regular feedback at every step to correct the errors if any, preparation and use of ICT and improve further their skill of teaching.

The quality of teachers is, to a large extent, determined by their interest, aptitude and attitude for teaching profession and how they are trained to take up the profession.

The community expects teachers to be sufficiently knowledgeable in the subjects they teach and proficient in pedagogy. Over-emphasis on examinations, rote learning and deteriorating language proficiency of students, pressure from parents, communities and governments, the teaching profession itself has strongly promoted reforms in many areas including continuous professional development for teachers, research-based teaching, reflective practice and attention to issues, arising from the changing demands on teachers in increasingly complex classrooms and community. Changes in political, social and economic forces also challenge teachers and teacher educators. These include the growth of an interconnected, complex global economy, unprecedented developments in communication technologies and school and classroom environments. In many countries, education reform is driven by a community's perception of falling educational standards reflected in reduced student learning outcomes.

We have to be aware of these traditional paradigm differences, and is committed to developing a research and research training environment at the teacher education Institutes that will shape pedagogic approaches and lead to innovation in curriculum design, curriculum transaction, evaluation, research, innovation and outreach programme performance—linked promotion for teachers as well as the need for professional structures that could establish comparable benchmarks for the profession of teaching' comparable to the professional bodies associated with other professional areas.

"We know that old habits are hard to break and that some people are comfortable with technology while others are not," Johnson acknowledged. "Through the professional development, we're breaking down those barriers and making some progress". It appears that key recommendations of the recent reforms, such as curriculum reform, both at the school and tertiary levels, and continuing professional education for teachers, as well as strategies to attract good students into the profession, need immediate attention of implementation.

21st Century Students need 21st Century Teachers. Students are moving forward, in terms of technology, and they are finding limitless opportunities to explore and create on-line. Are we sure that we teach them how to do this wisely? Are we building on these innate interests and talents? Are we harnessing the power of technology to optimise their educational experience? In today's society and generation of students, it is imperative that teachers of today are also for digital age of the 21st century. We need to recognise the importance of technology in the classroom and the benefits they provide to students today. I think it is time for more and more teachers to rise up to the occasion and meet the needs of their students through technology enabled teaching and learning. The most effective pathway to improve student learning outcomes is the quality of teaching, especially teachers' ability to motivate and facilitate such learning. Teacher quality is significantly and positively correlated with pupil attainment–the performance of students not only in class rooms but also the conviction with which they grow to face the world of the future.

Challenges and Opportunities

The teachers as well as teacher educators have to face certain challenges and issues inside the class rooms-dealing with the changing classrooms comprising of multi-cultural and multi-lingual students. The second issue adding to the challenges for teachers relates to the explosion in information and communication technology and the development of education software. This is a significant topic in Teacher Education reform agendas around the world where there is a general call for these technologies to be harnessed for the improvement of teaching and learning. The question of what knowledge, attitudes, behaviours and skills teachers should possess so that the teachers could satisfy the expectations of the stakeholders and be the facilitators of learners' acquisition of the key knowledge, attitudes and behaviours that they will need to be active in society and the economy.

In distance education as teachers learn to teach technologically by integrating technology disciplinary content knowledge and technical content knowledge merge. This connectivity for integration creates the possibility of transforming and extending teaching in ways that reach students across distance. At the institutional level many institutes, mainly private as of now have entered into online distance education by using satellite technology Many teachers who used familiar teaching techniques and skills now quickly discovered that they had to re look at their familiar ways as the landmarks and touchstones of teaching now changed. Change is a painful process for a few but the need of the hour is effective change in their approach to curriculum construction, teaching process, evaluation and class room management which are gradually getting digital and ICT based.

The International Society for Technology Education insists an Educational Technology Standards for Teachers. These standards include 21st century skills such as finding and managing resources, publishing on the web, and connecting with colleagues, students, parents, local and global communities. Teachers must be proficient in these skills in order to promote good practices for their students and to help students include these skills for learning.

I would like to conclude by saying that now it is time for all the teacher education institutions to re look, revisit and redefine the present Teacher Education system as today's teacher trainees are going to teach the Learners of Digital Age. There emerges the need to change the traditional paradigm of teacher education and to create a new model that will be the choice to prepare the education work force of the 21st century.

"Teachers teach more by what they are than by what they say."

18

Teacher is a Learner

The Professional teacher is one who learns from teaching rather than one who has finished learning how to teach. Teaching and learning go hand in hand. It is an inseparable process, like two sides of a coin.

— ***As Rabindranath Tagore***

"A teacher cannot teach unless he is teaching himself.

A lamp cannot burn another lamp unless it. Continues itself to burn."

There is technological change everywhere along with knowledge explosion in this era of science and technology. Technology keeps improving faster and is becoming more powerful. Keeping abreast of the latest changes can be a challenging task even for the most informed educator. Whether one likes it or not has to move along the current, to be accepted Researches reveal that good teachers are always active learners themselves. If any teacher wants to be effective and inspiring teacher in the classroom he/she should look out for new resources, and strategies to be effective and inspiring teachers in the classroom. Those who update their knowledge and technology of teaching are successful teachers and enhance student learning by integrating them in their classroom teaching. An effective teacher is one who starves, starves to excel others in wiring the confidence of his/her students. Teachers should be ready and willing to learn from other teachers as well as from their students how, when and where to incorporate technology, as well the new knowledge gained from various sources. This continuous learning helps the teachers be connected to the changing knowledge system, its application and demands of the society. I quote "The main objective of teaching is not to explain the meaning but to knock at the door of the mind" — *Tagore.*

Teachers are the catalytic agents of any change in the society through their students. They are to be provided with proper and quality education and its transaction to inspire and attract others to enjoy and use education received. Teaching is not merely imparting the knowledge from teaches to students, it is inspiring the young minds to achieve higher values in life, to lead next generation.

The National council for Teacher Education (NCTE) document (1998) stresses that teachers are the torchbearers in creating a new society, with social cohesion and national integration by revealing and elaborating the secrets of attaining higher values in life. Only enlightened and emancipated teachers lead the communities and nations in the right direction, in their march towards better and higher quality of life.

Education is considered to be something more than mere acquisition of knowledge and skill. As Swami Vivekananda said, "education is what makes a person." Which means education cultivates values in man. Through education higher value system of the society and a balanced personality of an individual is promoted. Further, it unfolds the potentials embedded in the learners. With all these objectives of true education the teachers' task becomes manifold to achieve these national and social goals. Hence, quality of education depends of the quality of teacher education. The training for the profession should make individual to think all time what she/he can learn or what she/he can teach; what has she/he got to give to others around and what is he/she able to take from them. Education is not knowledge that is stuffed into one's mind. It is something that enables an individual develops and grows for the rest of life. Education is not more collection of past knowledge and ends there. Future is always new and needs preparation to face the challenges of the future. In facing the challenges the past experience and knowledge will help. Education that we receive and give should be such that it kindles in each a sense of his/her responsibility in nation building and a desire to serve society.

Discussion so far on education would have given an insight into the responsibilities of a preceptor, the educator, the teacher. To discharge these responsibilities teachers are to be prepared and equipped with skills. This capacity building of teacher is a continuous process, before entering the profession (Pre-service training) and while in the profession (In-service training). It is said by some that the teachers are born and some argue that they are to be trained. However, any profession needs certain specific skills to be more proficient in the job. Teachers play crucial role in the nation building activities, as they are the correct interpreters of any policy and scheme of the nation to be implemented successfully.

Pre-Service–Training

When we accept teaching is a profession, teacher education is an education before entering the profession of teaching. They are expected to be concerned with the community the nation, understand the students to whom they have to teach thorough knowledge of the subjects taught, techniques of curriculum transaction, evaluation and interpretation of test scores along with dedication and integrity to the profession. During pre-service training they are expected to be updated with all the above said qualities and their capacity is built but, it is not possible to give all there during the training period. They are initiated and exposed to these concepts which are to be further learnt while teaching. Actual training and learning starts only when they begin to teach.

Components of Teacher Education-Pre-Service Training

There are three major components, theory, and related practical and teaching practice. To promote the competence in teaching, there should be more emphasis and exposure to the skill oriented programme-practicals and teaching practice, so that they develop the following skills of teaching motivation, skill of presentation, and communication, questioning which is an art by itself, skill of teaching small groups and individual instruction, developing students thinking, evaluative skills and classroom management and discipline. Before teachers face a large class or audience they are given the opportunity to face a small group, teach a simple concept, for a few minutes at the micro level. This procedure is called microteaching. This gives confidence and competence to face a large class without fear and hesitation.

It is not that the teachers receive at one time all these skills when they are under training. This initiation should continue during teaching depending on the situations that are demanded in the classrooms and the society. Changing scenario in the world may demand something different from what they learnt during the training period. The foundation laid should encourage and help them to face the new challenges in the area of content and methodology. Emerging inventions and discoveries should be faced with conviction by being a teacher by himself/herself so that they could become effective teachers.

In-service Education

Even if the teachers are fully qualified both in academic and professional, they should not be satisfied and remain with pre-service education only. They should rise to the occasion. As Gabriella Marcell of Argenitina says, I quote — "We must act now-we cannot wait for everything to be right-for bandwidth to increase in schools. Many things in life can wait. But the child cannot. Now is the time when his bones are being formed, his blood is being made and his mind is being shaped. His name is not tomorrow. It is today." Harris (1980) emphases the need for in-service programme and says, "In-service education is to the school operation to tell the child what good eating habits are and a balanced diet to human growth and vitality. So, in-service education could form part of, teachers" professional enrichment.

Both, pre service and in-service education for teachers are essential to enrich the teaching and professional development and they can readapt to the changing world. Especially the induction training to the teachers who join the profession is a transaction from initial teacher education to a real situation where they have to put into practice, what was learnt and identify the challenges, problems and difficulties that are to be over come. Teachers have to make use of various opportunities available to constantly refresh their skills and knowledge, to kelp up with the latest development in education, both pedagogies and technologies. It will also aid to closely examine the vision, dimensions and strategies of the society for introducing anything new. Feed back to the training institutes will promote the training strategies of teachers, which will become more need based. This will be one of the effective strategies of teachers becoming successful teachers who are going to shape the future of the world to be more sound and peaceful.

19

Strategies and Challenges in Educational Research

"Be an opener of doors for such as come after thee".

— Ralph Waldo Emerson

Education research is a field of inquiry aimed at advancing knowledge of education and learning processes and development of the tools and methods necessary to support this endeavour. Educations researchers aim to describe, understand, and explain how learning takes place throughout the life cycle and how formal and informal processes of education affect learning, attainment, and the capacity to lead productive lives. Scholarship in this arena is undertaken at the individual, situational, institutional, and social structural levels of analysis. The unifying purpose for education research is to build cumulative and sound knowledge about human and social process of fundamental significance to individuals, to groups, and to the larger society. Educational research refers to a variety of methods, in which individuals evaluate different aspects of education such as philosophy and sociology of education, student learning, teaching strategies and technology, evaluation and measurement, administration and organisation, teacher training, and classroom dynamics. Researches in these improve education and serve the public good and promote understanding and responding to global change, including the cumulative effects of human activities and natural processes on the environment.

Research is an investigation of finding solutions to scientific and social problems through objective and systematic analysis. It is a search for knowledge, that is, a discovery of hidden truths in a logical and systematic search for new and useful information about matters. The information might be collected from different sources like, human experience, books, journals, nature, etc. A research can lead to new contributions to the existing knowledge. Only through research is it possible to make progress in a field.

Objectives of Research

The prime objectives of research are (1) to discover new facts (2) to verify and test important facts (3) to analyse an event or process or phenomenon to identify the cause and effect relationship (4) to develop new scientific tools, concepts and theories to solve and understand scientific and non-scientific problems (5) to find solutions to scientific, non-scientific and social problems and (6) to overcome or solve the problems occurring in every day life situations, (7) to solve the unsolved and challenging problems (8) to get joy of doing some creative work (9) to acquire respectability in the society (10) to get recognition (11) satisfy curiosity to find out the unknown facts of an event (12) curiosity to find new things (13) to serve the society by solving social problems and issues, (14) Expand the knowledge base. (15) Improve education and training of future scientists, engineers, and citizens. (16) Stimulate knowledge transfer among academia and the public and private sectors. (17) Bring the perspective of many disciplines to bear on complex problems important to the Nation. (18) Enhance components of the infrastructure supporting research and education, including access to the expanded knowledge base (19) to foster the natural connections among the different strategic areas, as these interconnections are critical to success and (20) research also further aims at understanding and responding to global change, including the cumulative effects of human activities and natural processes on the environment.

Characteristics

- Research gathers new data from primary or first-hand sources or using existing data for a new purpose.
- It is based upon observable experience or empirical evidence.

- Research needs accurate observation and description.
- Research employs carefully designed procedures and rigorous analysis.
- There is emphasise on the development of generalisations, principles or theories that will help in understanding, prediction and/or control.
- Research requires expertise—familiarity and understanding of the field; competence in methodology; technical skill in collecting and analysing the data.
- Research attempts to find an objective, unbiased solution to the problem and takes pains to validate the procedures employed.
- Research is a deliberate and unhurried activity which is directional but often refines the problem or questions as the research progresses.
- Educational research attempts to solve a problem.
- Research is carefully recorded and reported to other persons interested in the problem.

Research Areas

The following are being identified as strategic priority areas in educational research Reforming education at all levels-elementary, secondary, undergraduate and teacher education; sustaining quality in education; promoting public understanding of the need for science and lifelong learning enhancing ICT in education; ensuring human resource development; developing an adequate science and technology workforce; and value based education, (8) Organisational and Systemic Reform in educational institutions, (9) Faculty enhancement through both research opportunities and those that combine scientific and pedagogical components, (10) Human Resource Development, (11) Instrumentation and laboratory improvement, (12) Informal Science Education and its application in every day life, (13) Developing psycho-educational instruments, evaluating the quality of measures from those instruments, conducting research relating to testing practices, and developing measurement models, (14) Aternative system of education, (15) Online distance education, (16) Education of differently abled, (17) *E*-learning learning and preparation of *e*-content.

Research Methodology

Research Methodology includes both quantitative and qualitative methods. First, it is a thorough and a systematic way to solve a problem. It is a science of studying how research is to be carried out. Essentially, the procedures by which researchers go about their work of describing, explaining and predicting phenomena are called research methodology. It is also defined as the study of methods by which knowledge is gained. Its aim is to give the work plan of research. Research methods are conventionally divided into quantitative, qualitative and participatory each with differing underlying approaches, tools and techniques.

Research is broadly classified into two main classes: 1. Fundamental or basic research 2. Applied research.

Basic Research

Basic research is an investigation on basic principles and reasons for occurrence of a particular event or process or phenomenon. It is also called theoretical research. Basic or academic research focuses on the search for truth or the development of educational theory.

The pursuit of information that can be directly applied to practice is aptly known as applied or contractual research. Researchers in this field are trying to find solutions to existing educational problems. Study or investigation of some natural phenomenon or relating to pure science are termed as phenomenological research.

Phenomenological Research

The purpose of the phenomenological approach is to illuminate the specific, to identify phenomena through how they are perceived by the actors in a situation gathering 'deep' information and perceptions through inductive, qualitative methods such as interviews, discussions and participant observation, and representing it from the perspective of the research participant(s). Phenomenology is concerned with the study of experience from the perspective of the individual, Pure phenomenological research seeks essentially to describe rather than explain, and to start from a perspective free from hypotheses orpre conceptions (Husserl 1970). Phenomenological methods are particularly effective at bringing to the fore the experiences and perceptions of individuals from their own perspectives, and therefore at challenging structural or normative assumptions. A variety of methods can be used in phenomenological-based research, including interviews, conversations, participant observation, action research, focus meetings and analysis of personal texts.

Scientific Method

The basis for educational research is the scientific method. The scientific method uses directed questions and manipulation of variables to systematically find information about the teaching and learning process. The analysis of data that is collected specifically for the purpose of answering these questions. Hypotheses are written and subsequently proved or disproved by data which leads to the creation of new hypotheses.

Qualitative research uses data which is descriptive in nature. Tools that educational researchers use in collecting qualitative data include: observations, conducting interviews, conducting document analysis, and analyzing participant products such as journals, diaries, images or blogs:

- Case study
- Ethnography
- Phenomenological Research
- Narrative Research and
- Historical Research

Quantitative research uses data that is numerical and is based on the assumption that the numbers will describe a single reality. Statistics are often applied to find relationships between variables Quantitative social survey methods are powerful data collection devices, and the researchers may not know how to use the data collected.

Types of Quantitative Research

- Descriptive Survey Research
- Experimental Research
- Single - Subject Research
- Causal - Comparative Research

- Correlation Research
- Meta-analysis

Action Research

Action research aims to contribute both to the practical concerns of people in an immediate problematic situation and to the goals of social science by joint collaboration within a mutually acceptable ethical framework.'

Information work is carried out in the context of organisations. Either the work is done for people who work within organisations, or the work is done by an organisation for the benefit of the community at large the findings must be perceived by managers as relevant to the organisation or the individuals in the society, changing some aspect of organisational structure, technology, tasks or staff.

It is important for the re-searcher to know not only the research methods necessary for the research under taken but also the methodology. For example, a researcher not only needs to know how to calculate mean, variance and distribution function for asset of data, how to find a solution of a physical system described by mathematical.

Challenges in Research

The growing pressure to transform an entire system of community creates a huge challenge for us and naturally also a lot of angst with its participants. It's not just for individuals within the system to learn new, we need the whole system to shift and learn. We face some additional challenges to conducting our research. Here are some suggestions for overcoming those hurdles, gathered from our peers.

Funding International Travel

Availability of financial assistance to travel abroad and even at the local to collect data, it is very difficult to get assistance from funding agencies. I'm skeptical if changing a single thing can help change a system. It's the nature of system change that nearly everything belonging to the system is changing at the same time.

Recruiting Graduate Students

Recruiting specific individuals to participate in daily data collection after experiencing a construction zone or the like through using Twitter or other programs delivering real-time information on their Smart Phones has been increasingly used.

This can be Challenging for any New Faculty Member, Successful Strategies Include

Network with colleagues who teach undergraduate courses in your specialty.

Go to professional conferences and keep an eye out for promising undergraduate students with interests similar to yours. Serve on the graduate admissions committee for your department.

If there is a required course for incoming graduate students, volunteer to teach it, and use examples from your research in class.

Cultural diversity versus cultural globalisation (local-global), accessibility to education in relation to equal opportunities in education and not only as a technical feature, virtual organising and management of education in order to provide affordable and quality education that is contextual and meaningful for learners. The idea of "localisation" does not connect education to global cultural issues only. In multicultural societies, the diversity of different languages and cultures has been present in education for centuries.

Inadequate Literature

Non availability of relevant literature on the area of study is a big issue. Dissemination of results of the studies conducted in the subjects is limited to certain areas. Researchers don't come out to publish their research findings.

It is obvious that cultural issues have a huge impact on education as a system but also on learning at an individual level as well. Based on the analysis of the research domains and conceptual metaphors, these issues have not really broken through yet in the research on ICT integration in education.

Much of the current research related to the "platform" paradigm and *e*-learning are based on learning theories emphasising contextual collaboration. This means that each interaction should be understood in the cultural context.

Research Applications

Mass media-information seeking and application behaviour

This is not to suggest that some affective or cognitive need will *immediately* 'trigger' the response of information-seeking. Personal needs are at the root of motivation towards information-seeking behaviour. Consumer behaviour, and the disciplines of Psychology, Neuroscience, Sociology, Behavioural Economics, and Cultural Anthropology, all provide advanced understanding and insights on consumer behaviour. Behavioural sciences continue to advance human understanding of the fundamental drivers of consumer behaviour, the future of marketing will be found in those insights.

Today, there are a totally new set of dynamics at play in the mass media landscape. We have conducted research in partnership with the world's largest traditional research agencies focused on providing insights into these vexing mass media challenges. This experience defines how we approach problems and provide strategic new media insights in the mass media space.

Financial Services

No other industry can benefit more from the application of new media strategy than financial services.

More and more users of market research are using research not only as a defense to public or target audience questions, but to develop an offense to help answer questions about or to the audience in advance.

20

Inter Disciplinary Research in Social Sciences

Inter disciplinary research in Social science refers to research conducted by Social Scientists in sociology, psychology, history but also within other disciplines such as Social Policy, Geography, Political Science, Education, Economics, Environment etc. Interdisciplinary research now receives a great attention because of the rich, creative and contributions it generates and their usefulness to the society. But a host of factors-institutional, interpersonal and intellectual-also make a daunting challenge of conducting research outside one's usual domain. Broad range of areas including: Anthropology, Applied Sciences, Behavioural Sciences, Cognitive Science, Communications, Economics, Education, Environmental Sciences, Health Sciences, Humanities, Interdisciplinary Studies, Law, Management, Media, Natural Sciences, Physical Sciences, Politics, Public Policy, Psychology, Social Welfare and Technology.

Interdisciplinary Research is a substantive and practical guide to the most effective avenues for collaborative and integrative research in the social, behavioural, and bio-medical sciences. It provides answers to questions such as what is the best way to conduct interdisciplinary research on topics related to human health, behaviours. This will enable the science and technology students aware of the various issues concerning man and society and sensitise students to the broader social, cultural, economic, ethical and humane issues involved in social change and social interactions.

The Interdisciplinary Social Science Program combines two or more social sciences for students who wish to study a particular area of interest that transcends the traditional academic disciplines. It encourages students to think in multidimensional and dynamic ways, to see how life today is shaped by the varied elements of modern society. This multi-disciplinary approach will help the social scientists explore the new developments and changes of the idea of pluralism and their implications for social and political processes in contemporary societies. Interdisciplinary research promotes complex national and international social issues and critical social needs.

Broad Areas of Interdisciplinary Research

It is attempted to list under each subject some broad areas which could be integrated with other subjects to make the researches more meaningful and socially relevant. Our approach is to establish, facilitate and maintain collaboration between academics whose expertise can contribute to Bridge the Global Digital Divide. Interdisciplinary Research Programme will promote initiatives to dissolve academic department boundaries within academic institutions and increase co-operation between institutions, train scientists to cultivate interdisciplinary efforts. The interdisciplinary social sciences offer a programme of integrated study that exposes students to diverse methodologies, philosophies and controversies that define the social sciences

Political Science

- Type and system
- Local Government and its Evolution
- Government Polices
- Party and Party Politics
- Party less Democracy
- Leadership
- War and Peace

Sociology

- Social system and structure
- Social institutions,

- Social Organisation their diversity and functions
- Family, Society, Culture
- Social cohesion, conflicts and ethnic groups
- Social Movements
- Social Change
- Borderless world
- Religion and Communal harmony
- Caste system and war against Racism
- Industrialisation and Urbanisation

History

- Anti-colonial struggle and freedom
- New social history,
- Interface of memory and history,
- History of art and architecture,
- Landscape archaeology
- Emergent sub-field of historical fieldwork
- Indian Constitution
- Human Rights and Duties

Economics

- Development of Economics theory and practice.
- Income and expenditure
- Per capita income
- Agriculture and food security
- Impact of Technology on production and consumption
- Globalisation

- Employment–Types-Un-employment and under employment-causes
- Poverty–causes and poverty reduction measures, Mal/Under Nutrition
- Industrialisation by ignoring traditional SIs.
- Property Rights
- Intellectual Property Rights–IPR

Psychology

- Growth and Development.
- Psychology of human behaviour
- Cognitive, Affective and Psychomotor behaviour
- Mental Measurement and interpretation
- Learning and Conditions of Learning
- Study of individual and Group
- Personality and Measurement and interpretation
- Mental Health
- Individual conflict and resolution
- Cultural psychology and psychohistory

Education

- Education-system, evolution and issues.
- Historical perspective
- Type and Relevance
- Globalisation and Education
- Evolving objectives
- Curriculum development
- Strategies of curriculum transaction and evaluation

- Preparation of textbooks and revision
- Providing resource support to governmental and non-governmental initiatives education

Gender Equality, Equity, and the Empowerment of Women

- Conditions and Status of women
- Education for empowerment
- Participation in the labour market
- Women in decision-making
- Female-headed households
- Search for identity
- Female infanticide
- Programme of Action relating to gender equality, equity and empowerment of women
- Feminisation of poverty
- Violence against women

Health

- Child Health
- Maternal Health
- Major Interventions of the Programmes
- Needs and Deficiencies in Contraceptive Services
- Schemes of the department of health
- Schemes of department of family welfare National Family Welfare
- Medical Termination of Pregnancy Act
- Pre-natal Diagnostic Techniques Act,

- Infrastructure Facilities
- Women's Health Policy

Environment

- Exploitation of Mother Earth
- Environmental Degradation
- Environmental Pollution
- Environmental Hazards
- Environmental Management
- Population Growth
- Industrialisation and Urbanisation
- Change in the Climate

Advantages

Based on the idea that "the world is interdisciplinary" our research programme should provide opportunity to take up interdisciplinary researches, especially in social sciences which have direct bearing on the society. Advantages of interdisciplinary research in social sciences are listed below:

Provide students with historical and theoretical perspectives from the social science disciplines.

Enable students to identify and analyse different disciplinary approaches.

Conceptualise the linkages among the social science disciplines.

It encourages researchers to think in multidimensional and dynamic ways to solve problems.

Preparation for careers in government, business, law, teaching or pre-professional training in any social sciences.

Sharpen students' ability to think critically, to practice sound methodological skills, and to communicate effectively.

Able to see how life today is shaped by the varied elements of modern society.

Prepare for the holistic problem solving required in the public and private sector.

Contribute to an integrative perspective to improve Nation's development.

Provides flexibility to pursue a course of study or do research from a range of disciplines rather than simply looking at the world through the lens of one discipline.

Understand the linkages between social science disciplines and natural sciences.

Develop the ability to creatively synthesize the tools of traditional disciplines to examine and analyze social issues in new ways.

Conclusion

Interdisciplinary researches and integration of social and/or behavioral sciences with other disciplines encourages that integration of various levels of analysis from the genomic to the global level will lead to a dynamic result. This will also lead to pluralism as an approach for conducting innovative, collaborative research and study. Epistemological pluralism recognises that, in any given research context, there may be several valuable ways of knowing, and that accommodating this plurality can lead to more successful integrated study.

21

Value Creation for Holistic Life

Values are not just words; values are what we live by. Our goal is to aid in personal, team and organisational transformation through a better understanding of values and culture. Values are described as 'deeply held beliefs about what is important or desirable. They are expressed in the ways that people think and act.

The values must be of the people, for the people, and by the people. They must embrace common moral values such as altruism, integrity, freedom, justice, honesty, truthfulness, responsibility, compassion, and must reflect the normative standards human beings discover and develop through living together. Value development must draw upon reason, science, the arts, and must express concern for justice and fairness and concern for the physical and mental well – being of every human being in an effort to maximize individual freedom without limiting the freedom of others.

Sathya Sai Baba while talking about human values he says that, "If we want the coming generation to preserve the validity of human beings, it becomes our utmost responsibility to see that our children do not get into this mad, material race, chasing after nothings. All the so-called valuables such as gold, diamond, currency etc. are given value by us (humans) and apart from that; they do not have any independent value of their own. Thus, if we want to revalue the human values, we have to devalue these "precious" commodities by giving less importance to these commodities. It is also reiterated that values can never be got from outside i.e. from books, shops, etc. but are something inherent in us that is our Conscience. We must follow what our consciousness says are the values. This Conscience is something which all of us possess, is the most precious gift from God.

Education and Values

There are two aspects to education: imparting knowledge and instilling character value creation in learners. There is saying that "if wealth is lost nothing is lost, if health is lost, something is lost, if character is lost, everything is lost". We firmly believe that Education transmits civilisation; it is an instrument for social change. Schools are one of the first places where kid's behaviour and future educational success is being shaped. In the present scenario the philosophy of education itself needs to be modified without just insisting on producing great engineers and doctors, there is need to produce, basically a good human being who has heart, and not machines that work only for themselves. Unless we take immediate action against this trend, the world will surely be ruled by robots. But today, education has become synonymous with gaining more and more knowledge neglecting inculcation of values in younger generation. In the case of knowledge even if the teacher does not teach students have other sources like books, internet etc. For creating character, it is the parents and teachers who could perform this task of inculcation of values. A parent/teacher with good character can produce students of great character, even against the so-called peer pressure.

Value Creation

The accepted value system be embraced, taught, encouraged, and supported internationally, nationally, locally, and personally. The ethical value system that will create a world of peace and harmony for co existence of a human diversity should be respected, tolerated and nourished. The values must be of the people, for the people, and by the people. They must embrace common moral decencies such as altruism, integrity, freedom, justice, honesty, truthfulness, responsibility, compassion, and must reflect the standards of human beings and develop through living together. Value development must be based upon reason, science, the arts, concern for justice and fairness, the physical and mental well-being of every human being by endorsing the individual freedom without limiting the freedom of others.

Human Values

Humanistic values espouse cooperation and peaceful living in the society and reject the use of violence to settle problems/issues whether international, national, local, or familial. They recognise cultural and religious diversity and individual creativity while rejecting the religious, spiritual superiority or political autonomy over others. Values are pluralistic; to accept this spirit of tolerance is expected to be developed. Tolerance does not mean ignoring the behaviour that violates or the rights and freedoms of others. Tolerance marks the recognition of the wide variety of human expressions and patterns of living; without ignoring injustice, cruelty, or inhuman actions of anybody. Education programme at all levels from Pre primary to tertiary should insist on the following values:

- The right to personal security and protection.
- The right to personal liberty.
- Right to privacy which demands for respect for the rights of others as well.
- The right to intellectual and cultural freedom which requires a spirit of toleration and understanding.
- The right to adequate health care.
- Freedom from want which means that society must guarantee.
- Economic freedom.
- Moral equality, which entails equal opportunity and equal access.
- Equal protection under the law which is vital to a free, democratic society.
- The right to democratic participation in government which include.
- The right to hold religious beliefs or not hold religious beliefs.
- The rights of marriage and the family.

The school curriculum should therefore include the following programme that will promote the value system such as excellence, innovation, enquiry and curiosity, diversity, equity, community and participation for the common good, ecological sustainability including care for the environment, integrity and respect for themselves, others and human rights. These will help the students to express their own values and explore the values of different kinds like moral, social, cultural, aesthetic and economic values and critically analyse these values and act up on them.

Role of Teachers in Inculcation of Values

"A good teacher not just imparts training but also inspires the student to learn" says Leonardo Da Vinci. The role of a teacher in society is both significant and valuable. It has far–reaching influence on the society he/she lives in and no other personality can have an influence more profound than that of a teacher. Students are deeply affected by the teacher's love and affection, his/her character, competence, and his/her moral commitment. A popular teacher becomes a model for his/her students. The students try to follow their teachers, their manners, costumes, etiquette, style of conversation and their get up. They become their role model in life.

They adhere to a set of ethics and code of conducts of their profession. A Code of Ethics enables them to; Set out the ideals and responsibilities of the profession, Exert a defacto regulatory effect protecting both clients and professionals; Improve the profile of the profession; Motivate and inspire practitioners, attempt to define their roles and functions; Provide guidance on acceptable conduct; Raise awareness and consciousness of issues and improve quality and consistency of the tasks to be performed.

Therefore, good teachers with great vision can play a pivotal role in making the future of their students while as a bad and corrupt teacher will harm his/her students much more than a corrupt, bad and perverted judiciary, army, police, bureaucracy, politicians or technocrats. Bad and incompetent teachers create a corrupt and incompetent generation. The importance of a teacher as an architect of our future generation demands that only the best and the most intelligent and competent members of our intelligentsia should be allowed to take up this noble profession. When we speak of a good teacher it means that a teacher must be a model of faith and piety and should have a fairly good knowledge. A good teacher should be proud of his/her culture, national dress and his/her national language. He/She should be a missionary, a mentor, a reformer, a philosopher, a guide and a friend to the students.

While highlighting the role of a teacher in the society, it is imperative to involve the role of parents, too, in the process of character building of the students. In the past, parents and teachers both used to provide a congenial atmosphere to their children to develop higher virtues and morals. But the present social scenario due to urbanisation competition for financial gains demanding both the parents to be the wage earners and heavy preoccupation in every day life have taken away the parents from their parental role. Children are left in the hands of care takers and children learn the culture of the care takers than family. All these have led to erosion in the value system of the present society.

Strategies of Value Creation

"Iron rusts from disuse, stagnant water loses its purity, and in cold weather becomes frozen, and even so does inaction sap the vigor of the mind."

Students will be made to feel, as Kevin Carter wrote:

"I promise I will never waste my food no matter how bad it can taste and how full I may be. I pray that he will protect this little boy, guide and deliver him away from his misery. I pray that we will be more sensitive towards the world around us and not be blinded by our own selfish nature and interests."

Out standing teachers may have very different personalities and approaches, but research has discovered that they do share certain characteristics. These include: a belief that all children can learn, but not all in the same way, a belief that are children learners and teachers as well. Teachers are encouraged to develop value — related capabilities with a high level of respect for all students; teachers have high expectations for all students, but not the same for all and they are humanistic rather than custodial approach to classroom control. They discuss disagreements that arise from differences in values, and negotiate solutions, to make ethical decisions Inter–faith talks are organised by different organisations, lectures by different religious leaders from the various faiths of Hinduism, Christianity, Islam, Buddhism and Jainism will promote religious tolerance and reverence. Teachers can teach their students the values, as John Wesley says, "Do all the good you can, By all the means you can, In all the ways you can, In all the places you can, At all the times you can, To all the people you can, As long as you can". To promote the values Teachers will help the students to "Watch their words, Watch their actions, Watch their thoughts, Watch their character and Watch their heart" so that they do not hurt any one and adhere to human values.

Conclusion

Sathya Sai Baba and Mahatma Gandhi said that "Politics without principles, Education without character, Science without humanity and Commerce without morality are not only useless, but positively, dangerous."

As teachers we have to play a very crucial role to inculcate value system in the youth of today who are otherwise involved and engaged in many other activities that take them away from the realities of the world. Unless the present generation is cared for and guided in the right direction their future will be uncertain in the globalised and highly competitive world.

22

Ethical Values and Accountability of Engineers

"Engineers, in the fulfillment of their professional duties, shall up hold the safety, health, and welfare of the public and shall, regard the practitioner's duty to public welfare as paramount."

India has a powerful battery of missiles today. Now we are capable of producing our own tanks and aircrafts. A state of the art aircraft carrier is being built. Nuclear submarines and air breathing hyper planes are on drawing board. Light combat aircraft-Tejas would go on production line in a few years. Fast breeder reactor technological, magneto hydrodynamic, superconductivity, nano-technology and nano materials research is booming. Chandrayana 1 mission was a successful attempt and now it is in the orbit the moon with a payload of advanced technology. There are now ambitious plans to explore the solar system. Very soon India would dominate the commercial satellite launch market. Within 60 years of India's independence at a very low cost Indian space engineers have achieved spectacular success. Indian oceanographers would be soon conquering the North Pole and get involved in some serious research, to bring out the secrets of North Pole.

Today Indians are dictating terms to global IT industry. Many NRI venture capitalists are well established in the Silicon Valley. IT firms like TCS, INFOSYS and WIPRO are global brands dictating terms with many global companies. There is a huge demand for skilled Indian IT professionals in the world as their performance excels others. This is natural for our country because Indians invented and the game of Chess and the concept of Zero to the world. Besides pursuing the nuclear energy option, India has also boosted research in alternative sources of energy to solve the energy crisis. Several hundred-wind power generation farms have been established. Within next ten years. India may emerge as top five countries in the world in wind power generation and solar energy India may rank second to China in biogas generation as well. India was one of the few countries to recognise the potential of biotechnology in 1982. Within 25 years the biotechnology industry has seen an unprecedented boom in India. The business has crossed more than a billion dollars, thanks to technology that now. We are able to compete with the whole world in this area.

The most amazing revolution in India after Independence is in telecommunications. In 1947, it was considered a miracle to get a long distance trunk call booked within half an hour. In 1957, the waiting list for landline telephone connections had millions of names.

In 1977, there was uncertainty over colour television. Now, every house has a colour TV set. There are tremendous change acceleration in telecom sector. Global telecom giants consider India as one of the top five fastest growing market for mobile telephony. The number of mobile handsets in India may soon cross hundred millions. Mobile phones are now penetrating deeper in rural India and has become inevitable in everyday life.

India's Remote Sensing Satellite programme and the INSAT series of satellites have shown to the world that we have finally arrived as equals to the superpowers in this sector also. The launching of a powerful Military Satellite would be a force multiplier for Indian defense forces. Future wars would be fought electronically and in cyberspace, though India is a Peace loving country.

India's all round scientific progress was possible because of services and sacrifices of thousands of scientists and technicians day and night. Indian government has announced a large number of incentives to attract young students join science, technology and engineering courses. Hence the future of Indian science, 60 years after Independence is very bright, with full of young scientists and technocrats. That's why many IITians are returning from abroad to serve their country India. The brain drain of the past would be brain grain of the future. Indian scientists and the technocrats will go abroad to help and guide them but will not stay back. Their footing will be in India and their thoughts will be shining India'.

There is a growing awareness that professional engineers need a substantial acquaintance with a variety of subjects traditionally taught within the humanities. The solution proposed is the creation of formal intellectual alliances between humanists and engineers to foster the reflective discourse needed to impute humanistic concerns into the problem-solving strategies of engineers. The argument is often made that engineers need more exposure to the humanities. This position reflects the claim put forth on many fronts that modern, scientific technology poses many questions of a highly value laden nature that can be addressed only by using the methods and insights of the humanities.

Engineering ethics is the field of applied ethics and system of moral principles that apply to the practice of engineering. The field examines and sets the obligations by engineers to society, to their clients, and to the profession of engineering. As a scholarly discipline, it is closely related to subjects such as the philosophy of science, the philosophy of engineering, and the ethics of technology. As engineering rose as a distinct profession during the nineteenth century, engineers saw themselves as either independent professional practitioners or technical employees.

When the nineteenth century drew to a close and the twentieth century began, there had been series of significant structural failures, including few bridge failures, notably the Ashtabula River Railroad Disaster (1876), Tay Bridge Disaster (1879), and the Quebec Bridge collapse. Concerns for professional practice and protecting the public highlighted by these bridge failures, as well as the Boston molasses disaster (1919), provided impetus for another movement that had been underway for some time: to require formal credentials. In the United States, the National Society of Professional Engineers released in 1946, its Canons of Ethics for Engineers and Rules of Professional Conduct, which evolved to the current Code of Ethics, adopted in 1964.

Principles of Codes of Conducts and Obligation to Society

Professional Ethics are concerned ones with conduct of behaviour and practice when carrying out that professional work. The institutionalisation of Codes of Conduct and Codes of Practice is common with many professional and business bodies for their members to observe. As Mahatma Gandhi says that, "The things that will destroy us are: Policies without principles pleasure without conscience, Wealth without work; Knowledge without character, Business without morality; science without humanity; and worship without sacrifice". A code is adopted by a community and society because its members accept the adherence to these rules, including the restrictions that apply. Apart from codes of ethics, professional ethics also concerns matters such as professional indemnity. Furthermore no two codes of ethics are identical. They vary by cultural group, by profession and by discipline.

Codes of Ethics for Engineers are Concerned with the Following of Issues

Academic honesty, Adherence to confidentiality agreements, Data privacy, Handling of human subjects, Impartiality in data analysis and professional consulting, Professional accountability, Resolution of conflicts of interest, and a Software piracy.

Code of Ethics enables us to live as if we were to due tomorrow; learn as if we were to live forever.

Set out the ideals and responsibilities of the profession and life exert a *de facto* regulatory effect, protecting both clients and professionals improve the profile of the profession through your conscious contribution to it. Motivate and inspire practitioners, by attempting to define their *raison d'être* Provide guidance on acceptable conduct required in the profession. Raise awareness and consciousness of issues relating to the profession. Improve quality and consistency of the profession leading to happiness in life.

Codes of engineering ethics identify a specific precedence with respect to the engineer's consideration for the public, clients, employers, and the profession. Many engineering professional societies have prepared codes of ethics.

They shall hold paramount the safety, health and welfare of the public and shall strive to comply with the principles of sustainable development in the performance of their professional duties.

They shall perform services or engaged only in areas of their competence and don't engage themselves any other activities in which they don't don't have expertise.

Issue public statements only in an objective and truthful manner.

Engineers shall act in professional matters for each employer or client as faithful agents or trustees, and shall avoid conflicts of interest by giving Engineers shall build their professional reputation on the merit of their services and shall not compete unfairly with others any statements against the objectives of the profession in which he is involved. Besides this they act in such a manner as to uphold and enhance the honor, integrity, and dignity of the engineering profession and shall act with zero-tolerance for bribery, fraud, and corruption.

Engineers shall continue their professional development throughout their careers, and shall provide opportunities for the professional development of those engineers under their supervision by maintaining good. Relationships with clients, consultants, competitors, and contractors by ensuring legal compliance by clients, client's contractors, and others without any Conflict of interest Bribery and kickbacks, which include: Gifts, meals, services, and entertainment.

Engineers should remember that they have to keep confidential and proprietary information to themselves without letting out at any circumstance. And try to avoid outside employment or activities so that you could keep professional secret as much as possible.

Ethical Issues

While engaging in Engineering they face certain issues such as Public Safety, Bribery and Fraud, Environmental Protection of being fair and Honesty in research and testing and conflicts of interest both individual and professionals.

The study of Engineering Ethics helps and creates.

Increased awareness of importance due to publicity surrounding high profile engineering failures. Engineering decisions can impact public health, safety, business practices and politics Engineers are made aware of moral implications as they make decisions in the workplace.

Develop a Moral Autonomy

Ability to think critically and independently about moral issues relating to application of engineering in real situations.

Promote ability to apply this moral thinking to situations that arise in the course of professional engineering practice; Ethical problems in engineering are often complex and involve conflicting personal and professional ethical principles. Engineers must therefore, be able to intelligently resolve these conflicts and reach a defensible decision. This process involves dealing with how we treat others in our day-to-day lives

Business/Professional Ethics Involves choices regarding relationships between organizations and other organisations, government, and groups of individuals.

Our leaders and scientists in independent India have provided tremendous boost to indigenous scientific research and technological development. Nehru therefore Prime minister of India was a truly modern, progressive, rational personality. During his 17 years of prime minister ship a very solid foundation was laid down for India's scientific and technical infrastructure was laid down. A network of public sector research laboratories and industries was created to boost the moral and code of ethics of professionals. India did not produce a rifle or a tank or an aircraft in 1947. India had to beg for arms and ammunition during the Chinese incursion in 1962. Indigenous missiles, frigates, warships, tanks were a distant dream, then.

Who knows by the time India celebrates its centenary of Independence-in AD 2047, we could be world's topmost scientific superpower and see a vibrant India.

23

Inclusive Growth for Sustainable Development

"Earth provides enough to satisfy every man's need, but not everyman's greed".

— Mahatma Gandhi

"Inclusive growth means much more than poverty reduction. Issues of equity, both inter-generational and between rich and poor, regional inequities and the needs of minorities need to be factored in," said Montek Singh Ahluwalia, Deputy Chairman of Planning Commission Basically inclusive growth means, broad based, shared and pro-poor growth. It decreases the rapid growth rate of poverty in a country and increases the involvement of people into the growth process of the country. Inclusive growth by its very definition implies an equitable allocation of resources, three pillars of sustainability Economic growth, human development, social and environmental protection are there. These three pillers include all the components of human life and wellbeing. Of course our immediate concern when we think of sustainable and inclusive growth is economic growth and poverty alleviation; by enhancing the living conditions of population as a whole with emphasis on raising the standard of living condition of the poor.

"Our Common Future" a land mark report produced by the World Commission in 1987, on "Environment and Development defines sustainability as" "Sustainable development is development that meets the needs of the present, without compromising the ability of future generations to meet their own needs" This suggests that while we attempt on sustainable development we have to think of the future too. There is growing concern and anxiety about biodiversity, protection of plants, animals and community based activity.

Growth Trend in India

Growth in the Indian economy was quite low in the first 30 years after Independence from 1950 to 1980, due to increase in population and other reasons including non-judicial use of resources that led to degradation of nature. Forests are destroyed and the constructions are taking their place making the green forest as concrete forest. Though there were some fluctuations, in the next two decades, gradual and sustained improvement produced an average rate of growth of 5.7 per cent per annum for the 20 years. Building on that base, the economy have taken-off into a higher growth plane, with real GDP growth averaging 8.1 per cent per annum in the three years 2003-04 to 2005-06, and the target growth rate of 8.5 per cent over the 11th Five Year Plan period, 2007-12.

The theme of the eleventh Five-Year Plan, 2007 to 2012 was 'towards faster and more inclusive growth,' which clearly reflected a sustainable balance between growth and inclusion. To ensure an inclusive growth is a challenge for India today. It sets a direct relationship between macro and micro determinants of the economy and its growth. The micro dimension includes the structural transformation of the society and macro dimension includes the country's gross national product (GNP) and gross domestic product (GDP). By creating an environment of equality in opportunity in all dimension of livelihood by creating employment , market, consumption, production, and poor to have access to good standard of living. For the last two decades the world is focusing on long-term, sustainable, and inclusive growth in order to provide development opportunities for all sections of the society. Inclusive growth has created a platform to inclusive marketing. There is a huge consumer base in the rural market which is unexplored. This is because there is a huge competition in regular market.

Now India is ready for a new era of growth with a young workforce, an abundance of entrepreneurial skill, drive and vigour, a highly competitive international services sector, and massive untapped consumer demand in its rural populations. Growth should be considered to be pro-poor where poor people also benefit in the areas of income, consumption, expenditure, nutritious, food, literacy and other indicators of welfare.

We are worried about problem of unemployment because unemployment does mean not having the money; it also talks about the lack of skills, relevant work experience and poor health. A new social contract is needed which demands responsibility and guarantees individuals' access to the support and resources they need to make choices about their lives. There should be a paradigm shift; we need a model which better integrates our social and economic goals. Economic growth alone is not enough. It must translate into individuals' achievements and social inclusion.

Attributes of Inclusiveness

There are four important attributes of 'inclusiveness' in the context of a developing society. The economy of an inclusive society would provide many opportunities for better livelihood to its people, facilitating increase incomes. It would also provide various means for the people, to enhance in employment and their capabilities to utilise those available opportunities. Access is the third of the attributes of an inclusive society, which actually brings opportunity and capability of individuals together. If an individual has access to social needs like education and health services, can appreciate self values in society better: a sense of his or her true place in the larger community, and its obligations. The fourth dimension of an inclusive society is security, which is to be provided by the government to its citizens in a rapidly growing economy. Safety in terms of predictability and stability of livelihood to its people. In the Indian context, this dimension of security in sustainable inclusive growth must be considered as paramount importance, as majority of our population is still primarily dependent on agriculture-based livelihood activities.

Growth in Agriculture and Construction Industry

Sustainable Agriculture is being defined as environmentally friendly methods of farming that allow the production of crops and livestock without damage to the farm, soil, water supplies, biodiversity and other natural resources that preserve ecosystem. Growth in agriculture generates the highest benefits for the poorest households and the unskilled workers. Construction industry is the next best source of poverty reduction due to its unskilled worker intensity. Deforestation, deterioration of critical water sources is likely to affect water supply. The quality of land resources has been reduced by erosion, pollution, and land conversion. These resulted in decrease in agriculture activities leading to poor food production as well as less employment in agro based industries. Prosperity in India can come from rural area by building their capacities and capabilities to manufacture, value added products and remain sustained with agricultural production and agro based industries. The great resources of diversity, earth resources, knowledge and skills that rural India possess could thus be greatly enhanced.

Infrastructure and Energy

Enabling inclusive growth requires improving access for the poor, allowing them to participate in the mainstream development, eco-system through economic opportunities. Information and Communication Technology (ICT) has important role to play in economic growth of any country. An inefficient transport network and unreliable power supply are the most significant infrastructure constraints on overall growth. India has a huge problem with power generation. Rural India does not have easy accessibility to electricity. Power generations from renewable resources are the most effective methods of energy production any where in the globe. Localised energy can help India's growth much better. Pressures on India's infrastructure could be attributed to rapid growth of population, expansion of trade, priority for higher growth of manufacturing, the rapid urbanisation, modernisation, and competition in the global market due to globalisation, the revival and diversification of agriculture. These pressures created serious bottlenecks in the mobility of people and goods across the country, access to power, drinking water and sanitation for the vast majority of India's population.

Public Expenditure on Education

Literacy plays a vital role in poverty reduction as it enhances equality, employability by providing the means for people to create or enhance their capabilities and skills in order to exploit available opportunities. Hence it becomes important to provide quality education to all. There are three components that are to be emphasised in quality education; provide basic skills that the individual needs to function within his socio-economic environment such as literacy, numeracy and, in today's times, some basic IT capabilities that are relevant to the market. Productivity will increase only when the individual is able to fit into a team with the larger collective objective. Expenditure incurred an education should therefore concentrate both on quality and quantity. Therefore the emphasis on qualify education for all.

Public Expenditure on Healthcare

When we are aiming at "Health for All" India's public expenditure on health care, at 0.9 per cent of the GDP, is very low even while comparing with the standards of other developing countries in the world. Only 35 per cent of the population has access to medicines today. In India people are now living longer than a century ago and the Indian population is slowly ageing. The ageing factor plays a vital role not only in healthcare planning and healthcare delivery; dependency ratio also increases. We should also strive together to strengthen the capacity of health care systems to deliver basic health services and to reduce environment-related health risks by providing health awareness and medical expertise to people.

Security/Safety

It becomes an important component to provide adequate security and safety measures to people to protect themselves against either a temporary or permanent loss in agriculture due to un foreseen circumstances such as failure of monsoon and inadequate supply of manures and pesticides. As there is growth in science and technology, industries and machineries also become obsolete and new ones emerge. Predictability and stability of their livelihoods can be quite brutal as majority of our population is still dependent on agriculture. Weak protection to the investors and a high degree of social conflicts, natural disasters and calamities can damage physical infrastructure, directly affecting human lives and health of livelihoods, particularly the poor and vulnerable. Ensuring the security of their livelihoods is important for sustainable development. With increasing purchasing power, wasteful consumption linked to market driven consumerism is stressing the resource base of developing countries. It is therefore, important to counter this through education and public awareness.

Access to the Essentials

There is no guarantee for the basic daily nutrition needs, access to improved sanitation, medical facility, potable drinking water, school and higher education institutions. How to eradicate poverty and how to reduce the income gaps between the developing and the developed countries if we do not adopt a right development strategy and good opportunities to achieve dynamic growth and equitable income distribution in their process of development and access to education and jobs. Investment in the human resources is the important component for broad-based growth. This requires equitable access to basic social services, social safety and social protection against shocks. The major priority reforms in education have to be spelt out and implemented. It should ensure that such programme are accessible to the needs of the vulnerable groups, children of both sexes, men and women, the elderly, and the disabled. Education is critical for promoting sustainable development and improving the capacity of the people to address environment and development issues. This type of individuals alone will be self regulated, self dependent and could contribute better to a sustainable society.

How to bring Inclusive and Sustainable Growth?

As Gandhiji said "We cannot have ecological movement designed to prevent violence against nature, unless the principles of non-violence become central to the ethics of human culture." According to him the industrialisation and urbanisation have created multiple problems and miseries for the modern man. Industrialisation, modernisation and urbanisation have led to lop-sided development, rapid depletion of natural resources and danger for natural environment. The displacement of human labour is an essential characteristic of a machine today. Machinery leads to mass production, not production by masses. Mass production necessarily leads to over production, problem of storage and transportation. We have to create provision for all these to avoid lop sided development in the society.

"Mechanisation is good when the hands too are few for the work intended to be accomplished. It is an evil when there are more hands than required for the work." said Gandhiji. He was in favour of technology and development of cottage and small scale industries at village level because these industries are localised, energy saver job intensive and less polluting. Gandhji suggested building up a local economy where everybody in the area would be employed and self-sufficient. They could sustain themselves and their family with dignity with their own earning. He was for bottom up approach in growth for inclusive and sustainable growth by using Appropriate Technology in industries.

Appropriate Technology

Appropriate technology is the kind of technology that fits small-scale, grassroots, community centered economics with people as the centre. It is the contribution of the British economist Dr Fritz Schumacher, author of the book "Small is Beautiful — Economics as if people mattered", which is still the foundation for a sustainable future. Appropriate technology works from the bottom up; it is not an overlay to the situation; it is a genuine grassroots solution to economic needs. Appropriate technology fits in to the infinite variety of life on Earth, rather than forcing life to fit the technology. A developing country needs to have an appropriate strategy that guides their technology/industrial borrowing from the developed countries. For example Khadi is the symbol of unity of Indian humanity, of its economic freedom and equality. Moreover, Khadi also means decentralisation of production and equable distribution. It is eco friendly and produced locally by masses and consumed locally by masses.

Conclusion

Simple living and high thinking will lead to inclusive and sustainable growth and development. Using India's natural human resources to sustain the economy without the excessive or massive pollution of the environment is very important. Globalisation has resulted in increased competition and the drive to make more at a cheaper cost has increased our reliance on machinery leading to pollution, energy crisis, unemployment and other social evils in the society. Use of appropriate technology is an alternative to all these evils and an attempt to address the problem of resource in India and provide a sustainable growth model based on self reliance. It would be an answer to Energy crises across the world increasing food prices and inflation could be solved by going in for renewable energy sources.

Corruption, bureaucracy and resources are few major stumbling blocks for the future and growth of India. Localising production and maintenance of resources such as energy can promote inclusive growth, alleviate poverty and help in creating local self and decentralised good governance—the bottom-up approach in which each individual is an active participant in making his or her own government. The poor villages are being exploited by the city dwellers. The villagers produce the food and go hungry. They produce milk and their children have no milk to drink. They live in poverty, ignorance and with less medical facilities.

Nehruji, the first Prime Minister of India, who was for modernisation of India, if alive today, would have written to Mahatma Gandhi that "I revise my outlook on your [Bapujis'] Constructive Programme. I am seeing the havoc that modern technology and civilisation are causing to our earth. Today we speak of Sustainable Development and in doing research on this endeavour I found that the fundamental edict of this initiative is much in conformity with your concept of Village Swaraj. Forgive me [Nehru] for taking your idea, as you stated — I am convinced people will have to live in villages" Village Swaraj and Sustainable Development Mahatma Gandhi's Ideas as Seen through the Eyes of Pandit Jawaharlal Nehru Today; quoted by— Dr Rukmin Maharaj. As Muhammad Yunus says, "The poor themselves can create a poverty-free world — all we have to do is to free them from the chains that we have put around them."

We should therefore, restrict our requirements and reduce our needs to move towards an inclusive growth which will be pro poor, eco friendly and sustainable. It does not mean that we should not be modern; we should not be progressive; we have to follow what is appropriate for our country, what will make a large growing population live with dignity, with out taking a begging bowel even for our basic requirements. To achieve this let us all follow what Gandhiji wanted "Be the change you want to see in the world", by leading a simple life.

24

Environmental Education the Key to Sustainable Development

"In wilderness I sense the miracle of life, and behind it our scientific accomplishments fade to trivia."

— Charles A. Lindbergh, Life, 22 December 1967

"I believe that the great Creator has put ores and oil on this earth to give us a breathing spell. As we exhaust them, we must be prepared to fall back on our farms, which is God's true storehouse and can never be exhausted. We can learn to synthesise material for every human need from things that grow," says George Washington Carver.

Indian Saints who lived in forest, Jains and Buddhists admired and worshipped the Nature. Where as the so-called civilised modern man has become self centered and has become the destroyer of the nature with indiscriminate use of the natural resources. While talking about the environment and the nature around Lord Buddha describe that.

"A tree is unique. It has unlimited tolerance, patience, and generosity. It provides a congenial atmosphere for many living organisms to survive. It also keeps on providing shade (as long as it stands) even to the man who attempts to destroy the tree with his axe." The relationship between tree, man and animals indicates the close link between nature and culture. The value system of any society emerges only from this relationship between man and nature. Infact the Gurukulas, the petal of learning in the forests paved the way to the ancient civilisation and the educational system. They maintained a clean and beautiful environment as essential for survival. It includes unpolluted air, water and soil suitable for human survival and growth. A clean atmosphere provides mental and physical security, happiness and serenity to life.

India is a land of ancient traditions. With over a billion people and at least 17 major languages, the diversity of India in terms of culture and biological wealth is enormous. In spite of rapidly changing lifestyles, the traditions of living in harmony with nature and of environmentally sound practices underpin the lives of most people. It is against this backdrop that the country's Environmental Education strategy has been evolved. The Constitution of India explicitly makes environmental conservation as a duty of every citizen. But the environment in India faces several challenges today. With poverty and low literacy levels, over 650,000 primary schools and rapidly increasing population, the development and environmental challenges are enormous. Conservation efforts may not be successful in the absence of a general understanding of the need to integrate environmental consideration into development strategy.

Tony Blair, former Prime Minister of Britain said in the launch of "Breaking Climate Deadlock", a collaborative global initiative for successful international policy framework on climate change in New Delhi on 20th March, 8, said "India would face the worst consequences of climate change that would involve its food security, water and energy security also. Hence, transformative and revolutionary changes in the society and economy should take place.

Environmental Education—A Brief Survey

Environmental education refers to organized efforts to teach about how natural environments around us function and how human beings can manage their behaviour and ecosystems in order to have a sustainable life for the future generation. The term Environmental Education is often used to imply formal education within the school system, from primary to tertiary education. But it is a comprehensive term used more broadly to include all the efforts made to educate the public and other audiences, including print materials, websites, and electronic media campaigns.

Widespread poverty, recurring natural disasters and a dwindling natural resource, a clean and healthy environment is quintessential for the very survival of the human race. A vast country like India faces formidable challenges in the form of exploding population growth and their survival. The action of an individual or society that has an impact on other societies constitutes a global issue.

Global climate change, airborne toxins, ozone depletion, and solid waste management are a few of the global environmental issues that are of current concern for our environment. How do general public, learners and educators know which global issues are important to their lives, and from where do they acquire their knowledge and skills to deal with these environmental issues? Ecology is becoming a more and more important subject today because it scientifically studies the relationship between the nature and living organisms as well as with their surroundings. It is due to the destruction of the natural resource base through deforestation, destroying fauna and flora, and disturbing the natural environment for various development activities. Air pollution has an adverse effect on the ozone layer.

Because of the multidisciplinary and interdisciplinary nature of environmental education, it is often difficult to define. Environmental education can mean concepts in ecology, outdoor education, environmental science or instruction about issues (Ramsey, Hungerford and Volk, 1992). A primary goal of environmental education is the development of responsible environmental behaviour in citizens, both as individuals and societal groups. Every human action has an impact on the environment, both individually and globally. In a formal education setting, it would seem that incorporating environmental issues into the curriculum would be relatively easy though there are gaps between knowledge, understanding and application.

Effective environmental education brings about an increased awareness and appreciation of nature. It is only through Environmental Education we could establish the relationship between nature and development. Therefore, every environmental educator must address and motivate students into action to protect the nature for sustainability of world by preserving its natural resources. As UNESCO statement says sustainability education develops skills, knowledge and values that promote behaviour in support of a sustainable environment. It is not confined to formal schooling alone. It also occurs in a wide range of non-formal education settings at home and society.

Environmental education (EE) should be a comprehensive lifelong education and responsive to changes in a rapidly changing world. It should prepare the individual for life, through an understanding of the major problems of the contemporary world, and the provision of skills and attributes needed to play a productive role towards improving life and protecting the environment with due regard given to ethical values. (UNESCO, 1977) Australian educator believes that as environmental educators, we are teaching in the present, preparing students for the future. We must strive to create educational experiences that challenge our students' perspectives both locally and globally. Whether we use a field guide or a database, the strength of our environment education curriculum will be measured through the knowledge, attitudes and actions of our students. The impact of our methodology of environmental education will be revealed in the next generation.

The Sarvodaya model of 'Moral education for environmental protection' of Sri Lanka is based on traditional Asian cultural values and differs from isolated, unilineal, material-oriented development models. It is unique, since it is developed through people-centred activities and for people-centred activities. Thus this model is directly associated with both an individual morality and a social morality within the central value system of society. It is imperative that the development process in a community is compatible with its environment as well as with the particular culture of that community model has been applied to achieve environmental protection through moral education. Sarvodaya is defined as the awakening or liberation of one and all, and it follows the Gandhian concept of human advancement. The pioneer of the Sarvodaya movement in Sri Lanka is Dr A.T. Ariyarathna. He says that the Sanskrit word '*sarva*' means all-embracing, integrating everything pertaining to man, society and nature. The word 'environment' is used here to mean the physical, social, emotional and mental environment in which humans live. The physical environment includes the house, kitchen, latrine, well, sources of water (such as tanks, ponds, streams), garden, soil, land, vegetation, pathways leading to and from the house, neighbourhood, roads in the village, the main roads, air and all other things of physical character.

Environmental Education in India

In 1984, India initiated EE programme with the assistance of the Ministry of Environment and Forestry. As a continuation of this effort, when the National Policy of Education was formulated in 1986, importance was given to Environmental education in the formal system of education. It has been stated in NPE that "There is paramount need to create a consciousness of the environment. It must permeate all ages and all sections of the society, beginning with the child, this aspect will be integrated in the entire educational process." Environmental education has been made as a compulsory subject in all educational institutions across the country by the Supreme Court of India in 1991 following the filing of a Public Litigation. As the result of it (EVS) paper has been introduced first in class IX for the academic year 2005-2006, in keeping with the SC order extended in class X in 2006-07, when students from class IX get promoted to class X next year.

The original Supreme Court order, issued in 1991 mandated compulsory environment education to fulfill the fundamental duty of citizens to "protect and improve the natural environment," as set out in the Constitution of India. In 2004, Mehta re-petitioned the Supreme Court of India to enforce the 1991 court decision making environment studies a compulsory subject at all levels — primary and secondary within the school system and at the tertiary level as well. In its 1991 order the Supreme Court had directed the central agencies of the National Council of Educational Research and Training (NCERT), the University Grants Commission (UGC) as well as the All India Council for Technical Education to put their heads together to formulate a well-graded curriculum for schools and colleges. In response to this with the assistance of NGOs, environmental educationists and other experts in the country formulated a National Curriculum Frame works.

Appreciation and concern for the environment are values that need to be inculcated during the early years of development. Hence EE for children and youth becomes an integral and important part of the EE strategy of the country. This was emphasized and introduced at the primary level by Sarva Shiksha Abiyan. EE Science was introduced at primary and secondary levels. Universities were asked to include EE at the higher education institutions and to be responsible to create awareness among the public as well to protect the environment for future.

Goals of Environmental Education

Goals of EE at various levels may differ, but the core will be the same. Environmental education for sustainability integrates goals of conservation, social justice, cultural diversity, appropriate development and democracy into a vision and a mission of personal and social change. This involves developing the civic values and skills that empower all citizens to be leaders in the transition to sustainable future. The long-term goals of environmental education for sustainability include developing the capacities of students to:

- understand the interdependence of social, cultural, economic and ecological dimensions at local, national and global levels;
- reflect critically upon how this interdependence affects communities, workplaces, families and individuals and help to make appropriate decisions;
- develop favourable attitudes and skills which are conducive to the achievement of a sustainable future;
- appreciate and respect the intrinsic value of whole environment; and develop personal responsibility, commitment and stewardship towards all aspects of the environment; and actively participate in all activities in building a sustainable future.

Learning Objectives of Environmental Education

An understanding that humankind is an inseparable part of the ecosystem and whatever humans do may alter their surroundings is vital in EE. A basic knowledge of the natural laws which govern the environment, skills to permit solving environmental problems, and recognition of each individual's responsibility toward finding solutions to environmental problems are the essential components of the goals of Environment education. The development of a stewardship ethic toward the conservation of natural, historical and cultural heritage, and the prevention and correction of continued environmental degradation should be inculcated in the minds of the people.

Learning objectives could further be grouped as creation of knowledge and understanding (Cognitive) attitudes and values (Affective) Skills and capabilities (Psycho-motor).

Schools implementing EE with the above goals have to plan learning experiences that enable students to achieve the following learning objectives or outcomes.

Schools are to be flexible learning institutions where children learn to reflect and evaluate their values for sustainability of the future. Heads of the Schools and other teachers play the supportive, proactive role, and actively involved in implementing and growing all aspects of environmental education for sustainability; Teachers are to be enthusiastic about teaching and developing effective relationships with their students, committed to the goals of education for sustainability. They should be willing to be life-long learners, adaptable, and open to new ideas and teaching strategies. And the students are to be active, self-directed and collaborative learners and ethical and responsible citizens taking action for a sustainable future.

Promote knowledge and understandings of the nature and function of ecological, social, economic and political systems and how they are interrelated; the natural and cultural values intrinsic to the environment in relation to national heritage of socio, cultural, economic, political and ecological sustainable development. Educators recommend that environmental endeavors focus not only on awareness, but also on attitudes, skill development and citizenship participation in environmental problem solving.

In the area of development of attitudes and values promote appreciation and commitment to respect and care for the nature's growth in all its diversity, for its sustainability. Activities that promote awareness, sensitivity, positive attitude and skills to protect nature should be introduced. A basic knowledge of the ecological problems and its interdependency will encourage the people to work individually and collectively to achieve the goals and find solutions to the problems.

Attitudes and Values

Attitudes and values are reflected in an appreciation and commitment to: respecting and caring for life on the earth in all its diversity; conserving and managing resources in ways that are fair to present and future generations; building democratic societies that are just sustainable, participatory and peaceful; and understanding and conserving cultural heritage.

Skills and Capabilities

When we teach environmental concepts our concern should not be only on the acquisition of knowledge and understanding. The learners must be made to appreciate and develop concern and ability to protect the nature. The ability to engage in: explorations of the many dimensions of the environment using all their senses; observations and recording of information, ideas and feelings about the environment; identification and assessment of environmental issues; critical and creative thinking about environmental challenges and opportunities are to be promoted.

While talking about the development of skills and capabilities it is emphasised that we should help the learners to explore the dimensions of observation using all their senses and recording of information, ideas and feelings about the environment; identification and assessment of environmental issues; critical and creative thinking about environmental challenges and opportunities; consideration and prediction of the consequences. Develop skill in oral, written and graphic communication of environmental issues and solutions to others; co-operation and negotiation to resolve conflicts that arise over environmental issues; and individual and collective action to support desirable outcomes.

Curriculum Planning

Strategies of curriculum construction for an effective environmental education for sustainability should aim at providing the knowledge and understanding, attitudes and values, skills, and opportunities for participation and action that will help students create a sustainable future. Thus the basic characteristics of curriculum planning to promote environmental education for sustainability are being followed in the National Curriculum Framework for environment education and included the concepts about the environment, ways to preserve and promote the environment.

Education about the environment focuses on students developing knowledge and understanding of important components of environment such as facts, concepts and theories.

Education in the environment involves students to have direct contact and experience with the environment around such as beach, forest, street or park to enjoy and develop awareness and concern for the environment.

Education for the environment aims to promote willingness and ability to adopt Lifestyles those are compatible with the wise use of environment and its resources. It also aims at promoting skills to preserve/ protect environment for sustainability when students have the logistics of about, in and for environment they will be able to develop an inner desire to protect it without spoiling and destroying. EE will also take conscious effort to promote and preserve the nature for the future. Students' prior knowledge, experiences, attitudes and skills from their own lives and their previous learning experiences obtained either formally or informally are to be identified while planning the curriculum, as this would form the basis for building new knowledge and skills.

Approaches to Curriculum Construction

Environmental education programmes have been designed for either infusion or integrating into existing curricula or the introduction of it as new courses of study. In the infusion or inclusive approach, content and skills are integrated into existing courses/subjects so as to focus on that content without losing the identity and the importance of the courses themselves. For example, at the elementary mathematics class students might calculate the amount of solid waste that 30 students produce in a year, or the issue of airborne toxins can be learnt while talking about prevailing winds in an earth science class. Infusion is possible in elementary and middle school levels, but less in high school where classes are departmentalised and topically related EE has been considered as an additional or elective subject in traditional curriculum. At elementary school level it takes the form of Environment Science (EVS) by enriching Science curriculum, natural history, fieldtrips, community service projects and participation in out door science activities. At the secondary school level EE curriculum is a focused subject as an integral part of sciences or a part of science clubs or eco clubs.

At the undergraduate and graduate level, EE can be a specilised subject of its own fields of education, such as environmental studies, environmental science, biodiversity and policy, ecology, energy, pollution or human/cultural programmes. The students are enabled to relate the EE to their surroundings as a frame of reference and connect its importance and relevant to their own lives.

Environmental education of today makes the move from an approach of ideology and activism to one that allows students to make informed decisions on Natural Systems and Resources, Biodiversity, Pollution, Energy, People and Environment and others. Within this process, environmental curricula have progressively been integrated into education at different levels.. This trend may be viewed as a microcosm of how many environmental education programs encourage first to participate through developing a sense of appreciation for nature which is then translated into actions that affect conservation and sustainability.

Environment Education at Different Levels

A desirable period to begin Environment Education is Pre Primary School itself. As this period being a formative period any activity initiated at this stage will have a long standing effect. This will motivate them to start loving the nature and develop a desire for protecting it. Children at this level learn through direct experiences by walking in the midst of the plants and trees, observe the streams, sky, soil, trees, sun, moon and the clouds and enjoy the nature. Introducing environmental education at the pre primary level will be highly appropriate. The children have opportunities to recognise and perceive the relationship among them and nature and between them and the environment and culture.

At the elementary school level, environmental education can take the form of science enrichment programme, natural history field trips, community service projects, and participation in outdoor science activities. They could initiate and engage in tree planting, maintaining small home gardens, soil conservation, prevention of water pollution, repair of small irrigation systems and group savings. They can be encouraged to interact with other groups in the community.

In secondary school, environmental education curriculum can be a focused subject within the sciences or as a part of student interest groups or clubs. These enhance their environmental awareness. They are trained to acquire practical skills, the development of organisations, and to participate in community development programmes. They are encouraged to engage in self help activities and group activities depending on the circumstances.

At the undergraduate and graduate level, it can be considered as its own field within education, environmental studies, environmental science and policy, ecology, or human/cultural ecology programmes. This group is relatively mature, knowledgeable and responsible. It may be more active in environment protection than previously mentioned groups. Some of their activities may include collecting planting materials, tree planting, participatory environmental protection programme. Use the course as an opportunity to ensure that the core environmental studies course should reflect the four pillars of sustainable development-social, cultural, economic and environmental.

Teachers to Teach EE

Teacher educators and teachers play a crucial role in imparting EE and inculcating a positive attitude to protect the environment. It is primarily through teacher education the future teachers are to be prepared. Unless the teacher education institutions promote during the pre service training, in the teacher trainees an aptitude for loving, caring and protecting the nature and willingness the same among the students, EE efforts will not be successful. In service and refresher courses should also be organised to update the curriculum, to plan the strategies and prepare a band of future environmentalists who would devote themselves for the cause of environment. Workshops are designed to give educators the knowledge and skills necessary to implement environmental education with their students. At the teacher education every trainee must be made to acquire the theoretical knowledge as well as develop concern for the environment and develop skill to impart EE effectively.

Design the training program and train faculty to teach EE with the help of institutions such as Centre for Environment Education who have considerable experience in the philosophy, approaches, methods and practice of environmental education/education for sustainable development; Academic Staff Colleges should train the teachers to teach Environmental Studies at different levels in colleges, including teachers' training colleges Links between NSS and other social services organisations and EE should be seriously considered as they would lend synergy and meaning to both activities; Expand linkages with the community beyond the university for the purpose of promoting education for sustainable development; Provide additional funding for faculty development to teach the environmental studies course; this funding should not be restricted only to universities but should also involve NGOs.

EE for the Public

EE programme should be made available to all in the community and follow both a formal and non formal approach to environmental education. The programme for the public who are not exposed to the environmental concepts should include concepts of environment, the need to preserve, enjoy and participate in the sustainable development of the nature. On completion of each program, as an encouragement participants can receive a certificate. This will give them recognition in the community to take up the work of spreading the EE. to the public. An action group to implement

EE programme be created in all the communities. The public can be trained in child care, tree planting, moral and spiritual family nutrition, home economics, home crafts, sustainable farming practices, post-harvest newly gained knowledge with traditional knowledge and pass on their experiences to their development, children.

Community Programmes

A wide range of free public programs could be offered throughout the year in the community. Programme themes may include environmental issues, cultural/historical, natural history, ecology; environmentally sound technologies such as of animal husbandry, cooperative dairies, soil and water conservation, watershed development, energy efficient devices, alternative fuels, and field trips to places of natural interests. Special family programs are planned for adults and elementary school age children. EE should insist on first eco-development programme for implementation of various educational and developmental programmes in the community.

Strategies of Teaching and Learning EE

Teaching EE cannot be thought of an examination subject alone. It is to be thought of a subject needed to improve the personal life and society's wellbeing. The learners are to be convinced of the importance of learning about environment as an essential component of the future life of the humanities has to be multi-dimensional and multi-directional and highlight its social relevance not only to protect environment from further deterioration but also for its improvement, conservation, creation of awareness, consciousness and love for the future of the mother earth.

Principles of Teaching EE

It is a life long learning process to protect and develop a consciousness for sustainability of environment through formal non formal education. Hence interdisciplinary approach in curriculum construction and instruction should be followed. EE concepts are to be integrated into all the subjects of learning. A systemic approach to teach should be adopted. Partnership approach between education institutions and the community outside should have equal responsibility in EE. Multi-cultural approach is another important principle which emphasizes studying the perspectives and approaches of various cultures and ethos to sustain the environment.

Using the Environment as an Integrating Concept for Learning the following Goals are Incorporated

1. Break down the traditional boundaries between disciplines.
2. Provide hands-on learning experiences through problem-solving and project-based activities.
3. Create collaborative relationships among teachers to share expertise.
4. Understand individual students, adapt to their unique skills and abilities.
5. Develop knowledge, understanding and appreciation for the environment, community and natural surroundings.
6. Child-centered, inquiry-based school camping to be organised.
7. EE can be best learned in the out-of-doors, through direct experience, dealing with native materials and real life situations.
8. Developing an environmental education either by one teacher or as a collaborative approach—which could include: cross-curricular units, complementary teaching or team teaching across several subjects, special projects and theme days or weeks, performances, excursions and visiting experts and collaborative projects with other schools.
9. **Experiential learning**: 'Learning by doing' or 'hands-on', experiential learning engages students in constructing knowledge, skills and values from direct experience and in contexts that are personally relevant to them.
10. **Creative thinking:** A range of techniques is available that encourages students to explore environmental issues, generate possibilities and look for possible answers or solutions. We need to provide opportunities for divergent, multi-dimensional thinking in addition to the more convergent reductionist approaches favoured in teaching sciences. Developing students' creative thinking skills helps them develop a vision for a sustainable future.

11. Problem-solving is a strategy for helping students develop skill in environmental problem. Working through step by step can help them decide, from a futures' perspective, what can be done about the problem.

12. **Storytelling:** Learning through storytelling is highly interesting. An entertaining and interesting narrative can be used as a gateway for students of all ages to explore environmental education for understanding sustainability concepts, attitudes and develop skills. Story telling is also an important technique in imparting indigenous knowledge, and can be a strategy for understanding and exploring other ways of knowing.

13. **Inquiry learning:** Inquiry learning encourages students to respond to their own concern or curiosity and to investigate and act on an environmental issue. Students are encouraged to think through and solve problems associated with that issue. They are responsible for collecting and analysing data in order to reach their own conclusions and to decide on appropriate courses of action to preserve the eco system.

14. **Field trips:** Outdoor environmental education programs for school groups, called field learning experiences or field visits or exposure visits can be an effective way of teaching EE.

15. **Environmental Education Forum:** Selected students from high schools or colleges can choose a local environmental issue through sessions at the state park site and local community and investigate to find a solution.

Technology in Teaching EE

Technology helps us extend concepts through our senses. Since we interact with the environment through our senses, using technology seems to be a logical element of instruction about the environment. Integrating technology into our educational programmes provides students with additional tools to enhance their learning. Technology supports our efforts to appeal to different learning styles. With a variety of learning tools, students can understand their experiences through verbal, written, spatial, quantitative, and/or graphical means. Technology supports our multidisciplinary approach to learning. Integrating different disciplines helps students combine their mathematical, logical, scientific, linguistic, artistic, and social knowledge to make their lives and interactions with the world Technology aids our efforts in supporting teachers. Regardless of their disciplines, few teachers currently receive training in the use of technology. Technology allows us not only to demonstrate teaching strategies, but also to deliver training, which provides teachers with the skills and confidence to become leaders in their classrooms and schools and the community. Technology gives us a way to connect with each other and extend the learning experience.

Activities

Activities that can be organized to promote environmental consciousness/awareness among children, youths and the public both formally and informally are listed here. Educational institutions and other organisations involved in EE can periodically sponsor essay, poster and photography contests, Conduct "teach-in" local schools and colleges, participate in town meetings to encourage public about recycling, carpooling and discuss issues that affect the environment, pollution prevention, Create public awareness about proper handling of household chemicals, pesticide containers etc. Encourage the recycling habits and eliminate unnecessary packaging/storing of rarely used materials.

Other activities that could be organized for the benefit of learning EE could be environmental exhibitions, picnics, cleaning up beach and other places of public interest. Encourage planting of trees and ensure they survive through the years; Conservation of Natural Resources, save water by turning off the taps when not in use; Clean and wash vegetables in a large bowl of water instead of washing under the running faucet. Horvest rain water for watering the plants and shrubs; Use organic fertilizers instead of inorganic chemicals to provide nutrients to the soil; protect the beneficial insects (such as ladybugs, bees, spiders etc.) around the gardens; Leave the grass clippings, leaves etc. on the ground because they make excellent mulches and provide nutrition to the soil; promote the protection of endangered, threatened species and wildlife across the country and around the world will create social responsibility.

Conclusion

Biodiversity, Habitat, Carrying capacity, Conservation, Ecological footprint, Ecology.

Ecospace, Ecosystems, Interspecies equity, Natural cycles and systems, Basic human needs, Cultural diversity, Cultural heritage, Human Rights, Intergenerational equity, Participation in Peace, Risk management, Social justice, Cost-benefit analysis, Economic development Eco-efficiency, Life-cycle analysis, Natural capital, Natural resource, accounting, Steady-state economy, Sustainable consumption, Sustainable production.

Training in Citizenship, Democracy, Decision making, Tolerance, Power, Respect and Conflict resolution will make the citizens be more conscious of their duty and responsibility to the nature and the community. The discussion we had shows that there are many challenges for environmental educators in India, a large and diverse country, to find the right blend between centralised and decentralised efforts and approaches.

Effectiveness of Environmental Education in schools and higher education institutions depends on the commitment and positive attitude of the heads of the institutions teachers towards the environment and the future of the mother earth. As Gaylord Nelson says, "The ultimate test of man's conscience may be his willingness to sacrifice something today for future generations whose words of thanks will not be heard."

Always remember, 'Nature' is our most trusted friend around us. Ruthless destruction of the nature through unplanned construction activities, pollution and overexploitation of resources will continue to affect our future generations. So, let us take a vow to protect our mother earth from the perils of human negligence and carry out the tasks of "Earth-Friendly" and "Nature Friendly" activities along with our daily "rituals". The sooner we activate our protective thoughts the better would be the chances of a "pollution free" planet Mother Earth for today and a brighter tomorrow! Environmental Education should be taken up with a missionary zeal to protect the environment for a sustainable and bright future of the humankind.

25

Technology for Rural Development

The aim of development is to raise the living standards of the people in backward areas to those of the advanced and developed areas. This may be through the development of agriculture or industry, trade or commerce, education or technology.

Development does not imply the economic growth measured in terms of Gross National Product (GNP) or Gross Domestic Product only. Development embraces wider concerns of the quality of life, education attainment, nutritional status, and access to basic freedom and spiritual welfare by providing infrastructure/ such as transportation, Communication, energy and other basic services to enhance connectivity. These will help to have more employment opportunity and the mobility of people in rural areas to other places and at the same time arrest migration. Thus sustainable development is ensured, without affecting the cultural ethos of the rural areas.

Sustainable development is a positive change towards improvement of environmental and social systems on which the human race depends. This requires a coordinated approach to planning and policy making that involves public participation. Its success depends on widespread understanding of the critical relationship between people and their environment and the will to make necessary changes. Progress made by the human race in last few centuries was due to a direct consequence of the advancements in technology leading to development and progress in social institutions. Now, with the assistance of inputs from science and technology, growth and sustainability is a near reality. Care is to be taken that technology used for rural development lends itself to the rural requirement; village centered, decentralised and satisfy the test of sustainability, equity and justice. Technology should always be a servant of man; otherwise, it will become a master with disastrous consequences. They should help to improve established technologies, generate, adopt new technologies to meet local requirements and meet latest challenges in the advancement of science and technology.

Development of Rural Sector

Rural sector is the core sector of the Indian Economy. Development of rural areas and the people living there is critical for the development of the country. It is appropriate to remember Mahatma Gandhi here who said that India lives in villages and villages are the back bones of India. This requires creation of an environment to educate the rural population and enable them to join the mainstream for the day of the nation. Technology is becoming a driving force in economic system.

A convergence of information technology and communication technologies will enable us to educate the rural population and bring about changes in their living. Main occupation of people in rural areas in India is agriculture and allied services, 64.0 per cent of the labour force is employed in agricultural sector. Agriculture in the 21st century will be an extremely diverse industry, with technological inputs which will also face the nature's hazards of not having adequate rain and water for cultivation.

The opportunities presented by globalisation and new technologies on one hand and the emerging concerns for long term sustainability of agricultural production system on the other, substantially enlarge stakeholder base and vision for agriculture of the future. This implies that agriculture will no longer be simply a set of farming practices carried out in a field. It will involve a diversity of economic activities that affect a far wider range of stakeholders-consumers, farmers, government, industry and the society at large. Farming will therefore, have to be intertwined with allied farm based industries to attain pre targeted outcomes and impact. The penetration of technology in human life will definitely influence not only the growth of economic activities but also influence and modify the social attitude and behavior of people.

Agricultural research and education systems will need to redefine their respective visions and goods to reflect the new expectations of society from agriculture. Information and communication technologies (ICT) can be powerful strategic tools whose benefits can be brought to bear on all key aspects of agricultural research and education and contribute to the growth of Indian agriculture and the national economy.

Rural Development in India has been accelerated with the Indian space Research organisation's ability to provide satellite communication network and the development programmes initiated utilising satellite communication technology. This has enabled the government in extending its reach to the remotest corner of the country and to concentrate on the rural development and education. Indian National Satellite (INSAT) training and developmental Communication channel started in 1995 is being used by Government and private agencies for industrial training, training of Panchayat workers, agricultural extension workers, and others in rural development activities.

While choosing a technology for rural development it is relevant to quote E.F. Schumacher who points out, "We need methods and equipment which are cheap enough so that they are accessible to virtually to every one; suitable for small scale application; and compatible with man's need for creativity." The technology adopted for rural development should help to achieve better utilisation of locally abundant resources, development of simple processes and techniques that would reduce drudgery and fatigue of the artisans, at the same time it does not reduce the employment potentials and opportunities of the people. It should also lead to economic and social development of the people.

Technology in Farming

Infusing new technologies in the field of agriculture, small scale, cottage industries, transport facilities and housing could increase economic growth and development. In the field of agriculture, the main thrust has been to improve the skills and techniques of farmers to produce more and introduce technological innovations. The power-operated tiller, de husker, polisher, the power driver, potter's wheel, the design of an improved lime kiln, the bio-gas plant etc though technologies they will not replace the human labour force and will not make the people un employed. Even so to make these industries catch up with the progress in other areas much more technological advancement may have to be thought of. The main consideration should be to reduce the drudgery that accompanies the present method of processing which leaves the worker in poor health and with a paltry wage. This implies that agriculture will no more be a set of farming activities only. It will affect the entire gamut of life of the stakeholders, producers, consumers, government and industry. Use of technology in agriculture should project the future requirement, the demands and the capability of supply in relation to the past experiences. Whether it is appropriate to go in for mechanisation, in a country like India where there are more hands to be employed more mouths to be fed, clothed and housed, leading to unemployment in rural areas is a very big question. At the same time the need for producing more food, preserve, and distribute demand adoption of scientific knowledge and technology in agriculture and other rural industries as well.

It is not uniform technology or advanced or high technology that will completely set aside the manpower, to be introduced, but an appropriate technology that will be eco friendly and demand driven should be introduced so that people in villages also could enjoy the fruit of science and technology in rural areas. For example use of improved seeds, methods of cultivation, matnring, pest control, harvesting and preserving food materials without much waste will help the poor farmers to produce more food for every one to eat without hunger and without problem of unemployment. Technology in farming if encouraged the rich, with large area of land holding, it becomes an anti poor technology. Any technology used for cultivation should be pro poor. Indigenous methods of agriculture using the fruit of invention should be encouraged. Radio, Television and virtual classrooms with computer online learning are used effectively for better farming.

Technology and small scale Industries

More than 75 per cent of the working force lives in villages. They used simple tools to produce beautiful articles. Industrial revolution introduced modern technology even in small-scale industries including textile industry. This change is related to consumer culture. Consumers are happy when things are available at a cheaper rate. Sophisticated technology used by even small entrepreneurs gives them maximum profit; in some cases it is led to exploitation, energy crisis, pollution and unemployment to the local artisans. Judicial use of technology and energy will create more employment opportunities, which are eco friendly. For example inventions and modification in spinning charka and in looms for weaving by using little power has increased the production to get more wages, and reduced drudgery of the spinners and weavers. Computerised designing has brought more attractive designs without much effort.

Cost Effective Technology in Housing

Millions living in rural areas are houseless. We need to provide house to them which is one of the basic requirements of the mankind and it is also a social obligation, that everyone has a shelter. In this effort to provide house for all at an affordable cost, attempts are being made to reduce the cost of building materials, which form 60 to 70 per cent of the cost of house. By improving the life span of the traditional or conventional building material like soil, bamboo, timber, brick, stone and lime, along with cement and steel the cost of the building is reduced to a very minimum, saving nearly 30 per cent of the conventional methods. Stabilised mud Block, Hollow concrete Block, Rat Trap Bond, Filler slab, Pre Fabricated Roofing elements, Micro Concrete Roofing, MCR tiles, Ferro cement Door stutter and Furrow cement Water Tank are produced and used in the cost effective house construction. This technology also adds to the eco friendly way of living.

Connectivity through transport and electronic media has increased the mobility of the people resulting in change in life style. There is increased awareness among the people on the changes that take place in different dimensions in different places. They could get more profit for their products, as they are able to have good market support from the nearby cities and towns. In some villages they have established electronic connectivity centers that enable the farmers to get the latest price list from markets in towns and cities so that they could choose a market, which gives best price for their products.

Villagers are educated through virtual class rooms established in rural areas. Physical Connectivity through roads and transport; Economic Connectivity; finance, commerce and warehousing to store their products; knowledge connectivity; schools, colleges and vocational training centers; Societal connectivity; hospitals, recreation centers, places of worship; and Electronic connectivity; telecommunication, Internet and IT services available in rural area have really made villages come closer to the towns. It does not mean that migration of people from rural area to cities is encouraged. This in turn will attract more investments as they are the providers of good marketable commodities, labours and raw materials.

PURA, a scheme-providing Urban amenities in Rural Areas, conceived by former president of India Dr Abdul Kalam emphasises that high quality amenities if provided to the rural areas both cities and he villages will be benefited. It is a new paradigm shift by providing good physical connectivity to attract both the villagers to take advantage of taking their products to cities for better marketing, for better education, medical care which also slowly move to rural areas. By using minimum of everything both in cities and villages pollution could be controlled, better working space and living space is made available to all and healthy living is ensured. As Gandhiji dreamt, it is also a form of decentralisation and village swaraj. At the same time we have to be cautious about exploitation from dominating group. There should be harmonious blending partnership with the natural growth of both cities and villages.

Conclusion

Growth of science and technology and its impact on human race has become inevitable. At the some time we should be watchful that these do not replace the human power, energy, expertise leaving man unemployed and underemployed. Benefits of innovations and discoveries should enable humankind, whether living in urban or rural area and rich or poor to live in harmony, and dignity without one exploiting the other, without any kind of monopoly. A new legacy of interdependence, and co-existence in spite of introduction of science and technology any where, should be encouraged and ensured. It is therefore suggested that there should be a harmonious blending of science and technology to the rural development without determental to humankind.

26

Millennium Development Goals and Education

We are living in a knowledge era where there is knowledge explosion every day. Along with imparting to our students we need to preserve our ethical values, principles and pass on to next generation keeping in mind the changes that demand in the new Millennium. Teacher has to display excellent behaviour in the society so that the society gets new dimensions and it progress in the right direction according to the changes. To understand the changing pattern in the New Millennium teacher should continue to be a learner. As Rabindranath Tagore says, I quote "A teacher cannot teach unless he is teaching himself. A lamp cannot burn another lamp unless it continues itself to burn".

Education is beyond learning literacy or 3 Rs – Reading, Writing and Arithmetic'. Education can no longer be considered as schooling alone. It should be seen from development perspective. True education should aim at creating an environment in which the child's full and complete innate potential is unfolded. It should equip the individuals to lead their life with meaning and purpose. Education should provide the courage and skill to face the changing world with conviction. The teachers and the educational institutions play vital role in building and shaping the future of tomorrow's citizens–the leaders, scientists, doctors, advocates, artisans and others. Education helps us to expand our ability to improve our life. I would like you to be exposed to a new concept called "Millennium Development Goals". Your are going to play a major role to achieve these goals, by 2015.

Millennium Development Goals

Millennium project was launched in July 2002 by UN. Secretary General, Kofi Annan with the support of UN Development Group, with the objective of reviewing innovative practices, prioritising policy reforms, identifying means of policy implementation and evaluating financing options.

Millennium Devlopment Goals has a framework of 8 Goals, 18 Targets and 48 Indicators to measure progress made by each country towards achieving the MDG. This expects the nations, especially the developing and under developed to evolve and adopt their own strategies, on the basis of their conditions and the requirements and dowtail into their planning and implementation. The countries should decide the priority, policy and strategies and incorporate them in their budgets at different levels National, State Panchayats and other service organisations. "The achievement of the goals is not optional, but an essential investment in a fairer, safer and more prosperous world" says Kofi Annan.

Goal 1 of the MDG aims at eradicating poverty and hunger; with the target to bring the proportion of people whose income is less than one dollar a day by half between 1990 and 2015, so that there could be reduction in poverty and hunger and the second target aims at bringing down by half the proportion of people who suffer from hunger.

Indicators describe that proportion of population below $1 per day, Poverty gap ratio, share of poorest quintile in national consumption, prevalence of underweight children under five years of age and proportion of population below minimum level of dietary energy consumption. They have not only provided indicators and direction in national plan and in international co-operation; they have also indicated measurable results. But still we are far away from achieveing these MDGs, though now we are in 2013.

Efforts are being taken in India to achieve this goal by 2007 and make successful completion of agenda of a hunger free India (M.S. Swaminathan 2004). He also suggests action plants to set out in terms of measurable, realistic and achievable goals. He hopes that Mahatma Gandhi's dream will come true, and no Indian will have to go to bed hungry and more, when we celebrate the 60th independence day of India. UNDP Resident Representative and Resident co-ordinator said, "in India, per capital growth averaged a robust four per cent, annually from 1990- 2000 and it is on track to halve the number of people living in poverty by 2015".

This will be possible only when our education system is tailored to make our children/youth to work towards this goal by making education career/job oriented with dignity of labour, improve the agriculture practices and produce more food to growing population. At the same time tries to reduce the family size.

Goal II of MDG is to achieve Universal Primary Education and Goal III is to promote gender equality and empower women Targets 3 and 4 of these goals insist on ensuring by 2015, children everywhere, boys and girls alike, will be able to complete a full course of primary schooling and eliminate gender disparity in primary education, preferably by 2005 and in all levels of education no later than 2015.

Indicators describe that net enrolment ratio in primary education proportion of pupils starting grade 1 who reach grade 5 Literacy rate of 15-24 years – old Ratio of girls to boys in primary, secondary and tertiary education Ratio of literate women to men, 15-24 years old share of women in wage employment in the non-agricultural sector and proportion of seats held by women in national parliament.

Education is Key to Development

Education is essential for development as it creates opportunity for men and women. Poverty, problem of unemployment, and child labour are the result of not having proper education. If we Invest in education of our children, it is a great asset and worth the effort. It has been estimated that one rupee spent on child promotion and prevention from unwanted atmosphere is worth more than six rupees spent on interventions or solving the social problems.

Education is a key to development. Ignorance and lack of education is a threat to development. It helps in eradicating poverty. There is a link between, especially the education of girls and women and poverty reduction. Illiterates will not be able to take advantage of public services available for their betterment. Where as, the educated women and men, even if they are poor they demand their rights to secure and use public services.

Participation in Democracy and Decision-Making– Role of Education

Democracy depends on educated people – men, women and youths who take part in decision – making process that affect their lives. Better

–informed person is a catalyst for change that leads to development, in the political arena too. When the educated people actively take part in the decision making process in politics, there will be better governance and sustainability of democracy and development could be ensured. Education removes the vulnerability of girls and women as they could have a say in decision making at all levels from the home to State and National level and participate in development process. It is therefore essential that we ensure the gender equality in education. Economic Survey of 2003 -04, indicates that the literacy rates increased from 18.3 per cent in 1951 to 65.38 per cent in 2001 – males 75.96 per cent and females 54.28 per cent. There is faster growth in female literacy of 14.9 per cent compared to 11.7 per cent of males in the last decade. Rural, urban gap in literacy is reduced from 28.4 per cent in 1991 to 20.9 per cent in 2002. Number of primary school increased from 6.39 lakhs to 6.64 lakhs and upper primary schools increased from 2.06 in 2000 – 2001 laksh to 2.19 laksh in 2001-02. Of the estimated population of 193 million in the age group of 6-14 years in 2001-02 nearly 82.2 per cent were enrolled in schools. Enrolment ratio in primary school is 90 girls per 110 boys, which indicates that still there is gender disparity.

Investments in Education in Recent Years

In 1998, expenditure on education in India was 3.8 per cent of GDP. During eight plan there was an expenditure of Rs. 8,522 crore, where 9th plan allocation for education was Rs. 24,908 crore. Of this, over 95 per cent of money is used for teacher's salary and very little for qualitative improvement. It is estimated that additional financial resources of Rs. 1,40,000 crore are required for Universalisation of Elementary Education over the next 10 years; Rs. 3609 crore for elementary education, Rs. 350 crore for Sarva Shiksha Abhiyan Rs. 969 crore for District Primary Education Project, Rs. 120 crore for Adult Education, and Rs. 400 crore for Operation Black Board Scheme. We are hopeful that India will be able to achieve the goal of Universaliation Elementary Education provide equal opportunity to all irrespective of gender, caste and religion as stated in our constitution. This scenario indicates that India is progressing very fast towards a learned society and the percentage of literate population is on the increase. We aim at achieveing 100 per cent universalisation of Elementary Education by 2010.

Goal IV and V of MDG emphasise on reduction of child mortality, and improving maternal health, with the following targets: reduce by two thirds, between 1990 and 2015, the under – five mortality ratio and maternal morality ratio by three quarters between 1990 and 2015.

Indicators of these Goals and Targets are Described as Follows

Under – Five mortality rates Maternal Mortality Ratio Infant Mortality Rate proportion of one year – old children immunised against measles and proportion of births attended by skilled health personnel.

Infant Mortality Rate (IMR), is said to be most important human development indicator of a nation. Infant Mortality Rate fell down from an average of 146 to 70 per 1000 live births between 1951 and 1999, and Maternal Mortality Ratio, (MMR) has also come down 437 in 1992 -93 to 408 in 1997 per 100,000 live births (The Indian Child – A profile). IMR below 10 indicates a high level of development and only in Kerala it is 14 as kerala has high literacy rate.

Prevention of Infant Mortality, Maternal Mortality and death due to diseases is possible among the educated people. Children born to educated women are less likely to be malnourished. With literacy, women's death rate could also be brought down, as they know how to keep their homes and the surroundings clean and provide healthy and nutritious diet and clean drinking water to their children, for themselves and for their family members. Educated women will also approach only the skilled health personnels for safe delivery and care of infants.

In achieving these goals of reducing child mortality and improving maternal health especially women's reproductive health it is education that plays a vital role. It becomes the responsibility of the teachers to provide adequate knowledge to their students about adolescent health, nutritional requirement, communicable diseases, immunisation, clean drinking water, sanitation etc., in order to prevent the death of infants and mothers.

Goal VI Emphasises on Combating HIV/AIDS, Malaria and other Diseases

Target 7 and 8 aim at reducing these deadly diseases by 2015 and begun to reverse the spread of HIV/AIDS and the incidence have to reverse the incidence of malaria and other major diseases.

This is indicated by HIV prevalence among pregnant woman aged 15-24 years use of condom, rate of the contraceptive prevalence, Condom use at last high-risk sex, Percentage of population aged 15-24 years with comprehensive correct knowledge of HIV/AIDS, Ratio of school attendance of orphans to school attendance of non–orphans aged 10-14 years prevalence and death rate associated with malaria, proportion of population in malaria – risk areas using effective malaria prevention and treatment measurers, Prevalence and death rates associated with malaria and proportion of tuberculosis cases detected and cured.

Goal VI of MDG emphasizes an important and urgent action to combat fatal disease HIV/AIDS. People with HIV/AIDS suffer not only with this disease but also the social stigma they meet with is unbearable. Children born to HIV/AIDS infected parents are not admitted in the school, Doctors hesitate to give them treatment, and they are isolated from the family and the community. This discrimination and cruel treatment by the society make the patients to hide or go underground. So AIDS/HIV is not only a public health challenge it is also a social issue. Women and girls who are in the age group 14-49 are more vulnerable to this fatal disease as they have little night to have control over their own body. It is spreading very fast and killed so far nearly 20 million people and it is estimated that 34-46 millions are living with HIV/AIDS.

It is the responsibility of the educational institutions along with other social agencies to give right type of education to the students of the age group 14-24 who become easily susceptible to this deadly disease. Proper awareness is to be created by the teachers and they should think that it is one of the social responsibilities of teacher to provide their students proper guidance and counseling so that they don't become prey to this disease. Awareness is the greatest weapon to prevent HIV/AIDS.

Efforts are being taken by the educational institutions to create awareness among the students so that the age group 14-24 which is in schools and colleges gets comprehensive and correct knowledge of HIV/AIDS and prevent it, which is the only cure for this disease.

Proper health education and sanitation will reduce communicable diseases like Malaria, Tuberculosis etc. This component should form part of the curriculum.

Goal VII insists that sustainability of environment should be ensured by integrating the principles of sustainable development into country policies and programmes and reverse the loss of environmental resources. Indicators described are proportion of land area covered by forest, Ratio of area protected to maintain biological diversity to surface area, Energy use, Carbon dioxide emissions per capita and consumption of ozone – depleting, Proportion of population using solid fuels, halve, by 2015, the proportion of people without sustainable access to safe drinking water and sanitation and by 2020, to have achieved a significant improvement in the lives of at least 100 million slum dwellers, proportion of population with sustainable access to an improved water source, urban and rural proportion of population with access to improved sanitation, urban and rural, and Proportion of households with access to secure tenure.

To achieve the VII goal of ensuring environmental sustainability, the education on environment should start from the very early years. They should develop love for nature and an instinct to protect nature. In ancient period men lived with nature and worshipped nature. Today we have become more materialistic and no time to even think of nature, which was lead to environmental degradation and environmental challenges. Unplanned developmental move is the main reason for environmental degradation.

Most of the natural calamities like earth quakes, floods, land slides and forest fires are due to our unplanned development move only. These pose graven concern and problems to environmental preservation. Similarly excess use of energy results in depletion of energy sources. Percapita consumption of energy is on the increase. We aim at 8 per cent growth rate in our economy which means we require additional energy.

Education can have a strong influence on sustainable production and consumption. Education institutions should create awareness among the students to love nature and preserve it. Among the public to initiate new action for sustainable development. The educated mass can easily be motivated to participate in monitoring the use of environmental resources around them. Young people are the agents of change and determine the type of environment to be handed over to future generation. Environmental education at all levels of education will create awareness to preserve and protect environment for future.

Through VIII goal of developing a global partnership for development the MDG expects every individual, state, nation and the world to take part actively in promoting and achieving the MDG. Those who have more and the rich should help the have nots, the poor and share their resources and promote the concept of partnership. The developed countries should share their resources with less developed countries. Globalisation will become more meaningful only when this is achieved where in the developed countries will come forward for promoting the development of the less developed countries by promoting employment opportunity, education and sharing of the expertise. India's decision to utilise the "India Development

Initiative" for extending project assistance to developing countries in South Asia, Africa and other parts of the world, had further enhanced India's leadership role in the developing world.

Key Principles to be Taken into Account in MDGs

We live in a fast changing world. The MDGs was developed in 2000. Our experience and exposure has made us realise the need for change and a need based approach to MDGs. It has been identified that these goals should be Universal, rights-based goals, emphasising human rights as fundamental to all the goals, through out the world, not fragmented as developing, under developed and developed countries. This will ensure equity and sustainability with differentiated responsibilities to attain those goals.

Social exclusion: We need to address the bottom 20 per cent of population who are in utter poverty and inequality. This group of people are socially and economically excluded due discrimination of the basis of caste, religion, ethnicity and gender. This needs to be tackled at the policy level rather than just focusing on secular and economic level.

Combating inequality: We need to analyse the causes for inquality and the relationship between the rich and the poor–the top 20 per cent and the bottom 20 per cent to tackle the issue, of bringing in equality, among the people to have a happy and contended life, world wide. The gap between haves and have robs should be bridged to promote disprortionate development of rich and poor.

Promoting Gender Equality and Women's Rights

Women form 50 per cent of the total population of the world. But there is no equality among the men and women. Efforts are to be taken to bring gender equality to reduce discrimination against women, ensuring women's economic, social and political rights for a balanced development in all the dimensions in the world. This could be materialised and achieved only when there is equal ownership of property, including land, a violence free life, and equitable representation of women in policy making bodies like Panchayats, State Legislative Assemblies and the Parliament.

Combating Inclusiveness and Sustainability

An open Working Group of 30 members has been constituted in R10-20 Conference held in June 2012, to propose sustainable Assembly.

The aim is to combine the new SDGs with MDSs to have both inclusiveness and sustainability in the new millennium.

Introducing Monitoring and Accountability

Nisha Agarwal also points out the need for proper monitoring and ensuring accountability. The present MDGs have no monitoring mechanism, and accountability. There is need for every country to have a group to monitor the achievements, progress difficulities faced so that each country could take an alternate measure to achieve MDGs.

Conclusion

In spite of the efforts taken by under developed, developing and developed countries we are facing great challenges, and not able to achieve even our basic requirements. There exists poverty, hunger, poorly nourished sick, non development of children in the school, fulfill basic rights to protect. The environment, to have effective and conducive international relationships even with the neighboring countries for providing the development of co-operation in sharing the goods and services. Only when we achieve these goals there can be technological changes and progress to produce more and reduce poverty, hunger and other deprivations which our fellowmen in our own country as will as in the globe.

This is what Mahatma Gandhi described "Trusteeship" where in he insisted that the wealth of the rich should be shared to promote the poor and the needy. If our education institutions could promote these virtues and value system among the young the whole world will live in peace, happiness and will lead to Universal brotherhood. Let us pray that the world moves towards that direction so that our future generation enjoys a very bright future, the world which will unite every one on the globe and live in harmony. But attending the MDG's is just a step ahead. We need to take the MDGs to the next level after 2015, the dead line prescribed for attending MDG our goal to see that every one has food to eat, place to live, clean drinking water, health care, education and employment for all to lead a dignified life. Let us all dedicate ourselves to make our students responsible citizens who will be the contributors to achieve the Millennium Goals with our guidance and support.

As it is said in let us prahy the Almighty to lead us to the light.

ASATO MAM SADGAMAYA
TAMASO MAM JYOTIRGAMAYA
MRITYO MAM AMIRTHAM GAMAYA

LEAD ME: FROM THE UNREAL TO THE REAL
FROM DARKNESS TO BRIGHT AND
FROM DEATH TO IMMORTALITY

27

Status of Women in India to be Redefined

"My opinion is that, just as fundamentally man and woman are one, their problem be one in essence. The soul in both is the same. The two live the same life, have the same feelings. Each is a complement of the other. The one cannot live without the other's active help".

— *Mahatma Gandhi*

The Constitution of independent India provides equal rights to women in socio-economic, power/energy and knowledge to all. Article 16(1) and Article (2) prohibits discrimination in general and also discrimination on the ground of sex in employment. In our mythology female Goddesses are attributed for wealth, for power/energy and for education. Where as it is a paradox of modern India that very poor percentage of women wield power and hold positions at the top levels but large number of women are underprivileged and unrecognised.

Women constitute 48 per cent of the Indian population, but they are not given equal rights. Even after 59 years of independence women in India, still continue to face the negligence. There is gender discrimination in thought and action. Gender equality seems to be in preaching, not in practice. The society rarely recognises the women's contributions to the society, politics and economy of the nation. This in turn builds a poor self-esteem and self confidence in them.

The concept of "status of women" has no precise definition and hence difficult to measure precisely. However, status can be perceived in different ways on the basis of women having authority or power in society, politics, religion, economics, education and the decision making. According to Krishnaraj (1986) status connotes the notion of equality. According to Mukherjee (1975) status can be self perceived status, group perceived status or objective status, a situation which can lead to status inconsistency, where a person is very high in one type and very low in another. There are clear indicators that Indian women are still discriminated against sex ratio, mortality rate, literacy, their participation in politics, availing health facilities, employment opportunities and their status in the society. It is said that roots of discrimination in India are from religious and cultural practices from ancient days. In the Vedic period (2500 B.C to 1500 BC) patriarchy family system prevented women from coming out of home, though a few women had the opportunity for education. After 300 BC, when the Brahmins dominated there was decline of the women's status, prevalence of child marriages, women to be the slaves of men and worship them; barren women and widows had a very low status in the society.

Other religions that have their origin in India, like Buddhism, Jainism, Sikhism or Islam started questioning certain practices of Hinduism But, even these religions kept women under certain restrictions. It was Bhakti cult which tried to restore women from all these religious practices and questioned some of the oppression women met with. When English education was introduced during the colonial period there was a change in attitude towards women. Arya Samaj and the Brahma Samaj and social reformers like Raja Rammohan Roy and Ishwar Chandra Vidyasagar inspired women to fight against social evils and some forms of oppression against women. In 1917, the first women's delegation supported by National Congress met the Secretary to the State and made a demand for political rights. When India was declared as independent nation, its constitution gave equal rights to women. This made them participate in people's movements, for their rights for land, environment, and anti-price rise and anti liquor movement.

Gender disparity can be seen through the lens of the Gender related Development Index (GDI) and Gender Empowerment Measure (GEM) developed by UNDP. The GDI attempts to measure inequality between men and women in the fields of educational attainment, life expectancy and income. The GEM measures gender equality in key areas of economic and political participation. These indices reveal that in no society women enjoy the same opportunities as men.

Indicators of Women's Status

Indicators of women's status start with sex ratio in the society. There is decline in the birth of girl baby, as it is destroyed at the womb of the mother itself. The latest census of India 2001 indicates that the ratio is 933 female per 1000 male population. The sex ratio of the age group 0-6 sharply declined from 945 in 1991 to 927 in 2001.

Health

The health status of women is another indicator which could be easily observed. Poverty, early marriage, mal-nutrition, and lack of health care during pregnancy have resulted in both maternal and infant mortality. Nearly one-third (1/3rd) of all girl babies born are with low birth weight. Maternal mortality is estimated to be 385 to 487 per one lakh live births. Nearly one lakh twenty five thousand women die, during pregnancy related causes each year, which indicates the availability of poor anti-natal services.

Women are deprived of food. Hence the nutritional standards are also poor with fewer intakes of calories and female suffer chronic energy and nutrition deficiency. Nearly 50 per cent of children under five are mal-nourished and 70 per cent suffer due to nutrition deficiencies Social restrictions on women's mobility, Poverty and lack of awareness hinder mothers from giving adequate care for their children. Women's health care services are viewed narrowly as reproductive health, giving less importance to other health care services, like communicable diseases.

The access to safe drinking water is another problem for women. It is estimated that 62.3 per cent of India house-holds have access to safe water 81.5 per cent in urban and 55.5 per cent in rural areas. This makes women to devote large part of their time and energy in fetching water and it's a burden to them. Sanitation facilities are another special problem for women and girls both in rural and urban areas. Public toilet facilities for women are very few. In spite of many schemes introduced to provide sanitary facilities we do not have toilets for girls and for women teachers in some schools.

Education

India has the largest number of non-literate people in the world. Women's literacy continues to be low, at only 54.16 per cent as per the 2001 census. Further discrimination reveals that the literacy level of Dalits and Tribals is as low as 5 to 7 per cent only. Immediately after the dawn of independence, the first census was taken in 1951, revealed that only 25 per cent of men and 7 per cent of women were literate. Female literacy has risen to 39 per cent in 1991, and the 2001 census indicated that 54.16 per cent of women are literate. Still nearly 250 million Indian women cannot read and write. Education is one of the crucial aspects to empower women with knowledge, skills and self confidence necessary to participate in the development process and nation building activities.

In spite of Government's efforts through DPEP (The District Primary Education programme) adult literacy programme, the World Bank funded programmes-SSA, we are not able to increase the literacy rate in India especially of girls/ women. The causes attributed to girl's drop-outs are, their responsibilities of taking care of young-ones at home and social restrictions. Mid-day meals, free books and uniforms, other health care services and child-care services like day care centers provided may increase the literacy rate and bring more girls to school system.

It has been urged by the women's group that the government should invest more on education, but actually the budgetary provisions made for education and real expenditure fall far short. Expenditure on education was 3.4 per cent of GDP in 1989-90, and 1995-96, it was only 2.8 per cent.

However, there is visible change from 70's onwards. The National policy on education of 1986 emphasized the need for educating women for their empowerment. The five year plans state that education of women is essential in order to improve health and nutritional status and to control population explosion. The plans have also recognized women as partners in development. It has stated that women's education, as education for women's equality. It was identified that the growth of economy of our country was poor due to its negligence of women's contributions to the development of the nation. It was felt that women must be equipped with capabilities to take up new responsibilities in nation-building for which women's education is imperative.

Religion and Women

Women's role in all the religions seems to be highly deplorable. In the past decades, religion has continued to establish a strong hold on social and political spheres. Migration of people as inmigrants and refuges has created complex and multi religious societies. In these societies women started having alliance with, Theology, Ethics and rituals in different religion.

Women had equal status during Vedic and Rigvedic periods and the degradation started since the patriarchal joint family system change in property ownership, early marriage, self immolation of widows (*Sati*) or permanent widowhood, customs, traditions, religious beliefs and life style changed the women's role in religion and religious activities. There is inequality in gender in the name of rituals and traditions in different religions. In front of God all are equal. He doesn't have any discrimination. Then why should these rituals, traditions and customs? Why should women be made untouchables in religious practices and their involvement in performing rituals?

Economic Status of Women

Remunerative employment is considered to be one of the major status deciding factors. Man is given higher status in the family and the society due to his earning and his position as bread winner. Majority of women are employed in informal sectors, with low wages, poor working conditions and lack of security. Woman will also get higher status if she is given the opportunity to earn more and stand on her own legs without depending on the male.

The discriminatory approach towards women is still deep routed in our society. We have failed to recognise the extensive contributions of women to house-hold and National economy as an active worker and producer of goods. Gender difference is linked with unequal distribution of resources, rewards rights and responsibilities. Approximately 80 per cent of women are employed in primary sector of economy. Female participation in the economic development activity especially in agriculture and house-hold industry is higher. About 47 per cent of women workers are agricultural labourers. A significant section of working women in agriculture is under most oppressive working and living conditions with no legal protection. Women are involved in hard work like breaking lumps of earth, manuring the land, planting or sowing the seeds, watering plants, weeding, tending cattle, poultry keeping, collecting fodder, harvesting, transportation, storage and processing of products which are not only strenuous but also time consuming, whereas men do only ploughing. But the female wage varies from 70-80 per cent of male wage though the Article 39 of Indian Constitution calls for equal pay for equal work irrespective of sex. There are also Equal Remuneration Act 1976 and 1982, which emphasis equal wages. In spite of all these the discrimination prevails.

There are cultural and religious constraints which restrict women participating in the production and technology activities. The primary reason do not support the viscous plot to keep women in a sub-ordinate position to men, but because men make the policies and do not understand and recognise women's role in economic development and productivity. It is also felt that, women would displace men and provide undue competition for male bread winners.

All women irrespective of their status in the society and employment outside devote their energy and time to different house-hold activities like fetching and trans porting water collecting fuel, cooking and food processing, managing the house and taking care of children which are unpaid work. For all these activities she is not being paid and her contributions to economy of the family are not even recognized. Whereas, when a man goes out and spends 6 to 8 hours a day in wage earning he is considered as bread-winner, and not expected to take part in any house-hold activities.

Women as professionals, administrators and in other jobs are not in very significant number, though there is a marginal increase in a service sector such as personal and domestic services generated by increase in population especially in urban area. Now employment opportunity in industries and other sectors are available only to technically trained and qualified women. But they are very few in number, as opportunity for training is also less. A few enter self-employment by getting credit, either from banks or co-operative society.

There is a myth that women are not capable of becoming equal to men. But in reality, men are afraid that they have to forge their jobs or employment opportunity if there is a competition between men and women. Employer prefers a woman to a man because of her sincerity and hard work. The feeling of insecurity on the part of men folk would like the women to be always sub-ordinate to them and suppress their progress in lives.

Social Status of Women

The Social status of women varies by class, ethnic group, caste, culture, education and religion. The position of women at home, society and at the national level decides the social status. The promise of equality of opportunity and status through the right of equal participation in all spheres of national life has not been translated into reality except for minority women. A large number of women virtually remain invisible to everyone, from common people to policy makers and administrators. There is unjust discrimination in rewards for their contribution to the economic and national development. Hence the oppression of poverty and inequality in the society wage more heavily on woman.

In the family woman is subordinate to man. About 2000 years ago the position of women in the Hindu society was cogently enunciated in the laws of Manu. It is stated in his book that "a woman should never be independent. Her father has authority over her in child hood, her husband has authority over her in youth and in old age her son has authority over her".

Caste is a system of hierarchical, social relations in Indian society. For untouchable women, untouchability prevents their access to vital necessities in daily life, starting with getting water and confined them to separate living spaces. There is little protection from harassment and attacks by upper caste men. The lower caste, particularly Dalit women represent the poor women. In spite of the reservation policy, Dalit and minority groups are poor and have less access to formal education employment, and health care. The limited impact of reservation policy has mainly benefited men on the social sector, women from these groups fair worst. But now Dalit women started organising themselves against the oppression on the basis of caste, class and gender and are trying to assert their rights.

Political Participation

India got its independence in 1947. The constitution of India firmly affirmed the equality of all citizens before the law. It said that women, as weaker sections of society were discriminated against for generations, that they deserve special facilities and support for growing up in every sphere including their participation in politics and ruling the country, opportunities for women to represent in politics and have influence in political matters are the important parameters of democracy and thus an integral part of political development of any democracy. Increasing the active participation of women in politics and the representation of women in legislative assemblies, Lok Sabha, Rajya Sabha and Panchayats with powers is a crucial step towards achieving gender balance in politics.

Women's political participation and representation, traditions, and change in women's political roles, women and political leadership and women and section of power are the essential components of the women's position in politics. The political status of Indian women remains very poor, although Indian woman played a major role in freedom movement it did not continues participation in public life in the post-independent era. It is observed that after independence many women withdrew from public life. Representation of women in the legislative bodies and Parliament is very low. In 1999 elections 6.5 per cent of candidates were females and now it is 5.9 per cent only in Lok Sabha.

Since 1996 women are pressing for passing of the 81st Amendment Bill that proposes the reservation of one third reservation in these bodies as the 73rd Amendment to the Constitution of India has given 33 per cent in Panchayats. Though this was made possible after five decades of struggle by women's organisations it has brought women to the forefront and enabled them in policy framing and decision making. Where as in passing the 81st Amendment the political parties have sabotaged the attempts even in the last session of the Parliament It is high time that the Government tables the women's Reservation Bill in the Parliament to reserve 33 per cent in the Assembly and Parliament. This will enable large number of women participate in policy level decision making and implementation at the National and global level in the globalised world.

Strategic Plans to Redefine the Status of Women in India

On the basis of the above discussion the following suggestions and plans could be drawn to improve the status of women in India:

1. Women must be made visible by providing equal opportunity to take part in the nation building. Economic independence of women will create the environment to emancipate them by making them come of their traditional bonds. FAO's Plan of Action for Women in Development (1996-2001), aims at giving women equal access to and control of land and other productive resources, increase their participation in decision and policy making, reduce their work loads and enhance their opportunities for paid employment and increase income.

2. Steps should be taken to reduce their drudgery of women by providing them with opportunity for generating means for improving their health, sanitation, education and environmental conditions and find out the ways and means of protecting women from occupational hazards.

3. Owning the property jointly both by husband and wife should be emphasised.

4. Women are to be trained in science and technology which are of direct help in enhancing the farm-production. Appropriate technology is to be introduced in cultivation to reduce their drudgery in farming activities.

5. Instead of treating women as receivers of dole and a few welfare schemes they should be recognised as producers and economic asserts of the nation.

6. Women should be paid equally as men for the amount of work they put in, whether it is organised or unorganised sectors. The time taken and energy required should be taken into consideration for deciding the wages.

7. Effort should be taken to replace the traditional value system which is based on in-equality of sexes, where women play a subordinate role. Women should be encouraged to perceive their role positively in the society.

8. Efforts should be taken to identify unemployed and under employed women both in urban and rural areas in order to arrest the increasing displacement of women.

9. Women should be given equal opportunity for education, employment and other positions in the society, if required reservation for women should be emphasised till a sizable number of women get employment opportunities. Selection for employment should never be based on the sex. It should be based on the competency and capability.

10. Local level women's organisations are to be set up in order to enlist potential women and to serve as a "Think Tank" and linking agency with other developmental organisations.

11. Women should find place in all the decision making bodies, so that male, domination can be reduced.

12. The government and all the organisations which employ women should see that they provide childcare facilities in their work spots, so that mother's with children can be relieved of their anxiety and worry, while working.

13. Other supportive services such as provision to offer housing, transport facilities, security arrangements, and health facilities should be provided to the employed women.

14. There should be adequate budget provision for improving the maternity and health care services to the women, in their own vicinity.

15. Health education programme should be given to women both in primary health centers and in the non-formal and adult education centers.

16. To improve the education of girls and to reduce large number of girls dropping out from the school, we should try to bridge the gap between female and male enrolment and retention rates.

17. Education and training for girls should be directed towards the acquisition of practical and vocational skills needed for making the women self-reliant.

18. Education for girls should build the positive attitude towards development and life. Sex based curriculum and text-book should be eliminated, so that a positive attitude towards development and life could be built.

19. Women oriented researches should be undertaken by colleges, universities and voluntary agencies to throw light on the practices of different social evils and atrocities on women, so that the strategies could be evolved to eliminate them.

20. Women should be given equal right for performing religious rituals.

21. Women entrepreneurs, doctors, lawyers, teachers pilots, athletes, artists, journalists, writers, professionals, house wives and women in other walks of life should meet as often as possible and exchange ideas on matters of concern and expand the horizons of knowledge and share other facilities available for them to upgrade their status.

Conclusion

Exclusion of women from economic, social, educational and political opportunities is a continuous indictment to human progress. All these efforts and programmes to raise the status of women will prove futile, if women themselves do not assert their individuality and claim their rights. Those who are already in work force should look up for development programmes to facilitate upward mobility in their existing status. Those who are waiting to enter the workforce should try to qualify themselves.

The challenge before every Indian woman is to take measure to increase self-confidence, leadership quality and to become capable of joining the skilled workforce organised sectors, participate in politics and boost their image. They should further receive all the social development measures to increase their participation in development programmes of the nation. We could feel happy and be proud only when many parents think that they have a daughter to perpetuate their family. Let us all strive hard to make the new millennium be the Millennium of the Women and redefine their status.

I would like to conclude by quoting again Mahatma Gandhi who had high regard for women and inspired them to come out of their homes to participate in freedom movement and welfare activities.

"Woman is the incarnation of Ahimsa. Ahimsa means infinite love, which again means infinite capacity for suffering". "Woman is the embodiment of sacrifice and suffering and her advent to public life should, therefore result in purifying it."

28

Gender Justice, Development and Rights

Women constitute 50 per cent of the world population, still global picture of women is most ignoble and inequality exists in every aspect, in economic, politics, education, and employment and in cultural life of women. Though women do 66 per cent of the work, their income is only 10 per cent. Women are deprived of even basic needs like nutrition, education, health, and sustainable living which are the indicators of the Women Development Index (WDI). When there is a move to achieve the Millennium Development Goal which insists on eliminating gender disparities in primary and secondary education by 2005 and achieving gender equality in education by 2015, with a focus on ensuring girl's full and equal access to and achievement in basic education, health care services. This neglect of women and deprivation of her rights, leads to human deprivation. Allowing women to enjoy their legitimate rights alone can help them empower. Empowerment of women is ensured only when there is enhancement of economic power which is essential for realising and achieving gender equality, prestige and freedom.

The Indian Constitution has the following provisions for women, to enjoy equal rights in Article No. 14, 15, 39, 42 and 51 A and E. These provisions emphasis that there should be equal rights and opportunities in political, economic and social spheres (Article 15); avoiding sex determination tests before birth, enable affirmative discrimination in favour of women (Article 15-3); equal means of livelihood and equal pay for equal work (Article 39); just and humane conditions of work and maternity relief

(Article-42) and fundamental duty to renounce practices derogatory to women (Article – 51(A) (e)).

To achieve these provisions, the legislation has made policies such as National Empowerment of women 2001, as well as in 7th, 8th, 9th and 10th Five Year Plans. Though there are policies and programme brought by the Government, the struggle for gender equality and justice is a continuous one. The discrimination against women seems to be never ending phenomena not only in India, it is world wide. It is therefore suggested that we should evolve a comprehensive reform to protect the right to dignity autonomy and freedom in every dimension – Social, economics and political.

Causes of Gender Injustice

The causes for gender decimation and gender injustice are the creation of human being only. The main cause is male chauvinism found in different degrees in the society since the origin of human being. Even in developed countries only after a very long struggle women could get the right to vote. To combat male chauvinism attitudinal changes in value system are needed. Without this change the battle cannot be won. In this world of consumerism, with utilitarian approach many do not aspire to have a female child thinking a girl means a "financial liability", as they have to give fabulous dowry for the daughters' marriage, and the other rituals which is deep rooted social evil in India. Another reason is that girl child means she has to leave the parents' house one day and if there is any earning by her it will not be useful to the parents. But they forget that it is their own daughter who is going to be responsible for bringing up another generation. Our culture and social believes are the other forms of obstacles for gender equality hence, women do not enjoy the same rights and opportunities as men, both at the home where they are born and the home to which they shift after their wedding. Women are to be recognised as dynamic factor and valuable assert for the total development of humanity.

Parity and Equality

Women work longer hours but are paid less than the men; their life chances and choices are restricted than for men. Achieving gender parity in education is another dimension of the issue. Parity in education implies that same proportion of boys and girls enter the education system and complete full primary and secondary education. When it is said equality, it means that same chances to go to school have same type of education without any stereo type. Girls should also have the liberty to have same length of schooling or higher education which will in turn lead to same employment opportunity as men with same qualification and same remuneration could be the law. The right to education is enshrined and accepted internationally by all organisations, which also eventually insists on achieving gender equality. More and quality female education has a positive impact on labour supply and productivity. Women work for longer time with much concentration and produce more. Though there seems to be more preferrnce for women with required qualification for the same job, still they are paid less in unorganized sectors, as the qualification is not considered to fix the salary.

Investing more on the education of girls/women increases the personal and social well-being which is the essential components of all development activities. When the mother is educated it is said that it is equivalent to the education of the entire family. She takes care of the health of the children. They are fed with quality food; good health habits are inculcated and will have greater chance of her children attending school as she knows the value of education. Investment in education of girls/women ensures that future generation will be better educated and liberated in every aspect of life.

When World Education Forum in Dakar in 2000 pledged to eliminate gender disparities in Primary and Secondary education by 2005, 104 million girls were out of school two third of the 860 million illiterate were women. So ensuring the right to education is not just a question of numbers. It is to achieve as per the millennium Goals by 2015, gender equality so that girls and boys, women and men enjoy the same learning opportunities and outcomes, personally, socially, professionally and politically. This will also reduce the women's fertility rates resulting in small families; lowering infant and child mortality rates, as the educated women will ensure that their children are properly fed, immunised, practice improved sanitation and health habits; lowering maternal mortality rates by following proper health care practices; protecting against HIV/AIDS infection which reduces the vulnerability of girls/women becoming victims; increasing women's labour force participation rates and earnings leading to better economic growth of the country and creating intergenerational education benefits. Mothers' education is a significant variable in the educational attainment of their children.

Strategies and Actions Towards Gender Justice and Human Rights

The Platform for Action of United Nations Fourth World Conference of Women reaffirms that all human rights civil, cultural, economic, political and social, including the right to development are universal, indivisible, interdependent and interrelated. Human rights of women and girls are an inalienable, integral and indivisible part of universal human rights. Full and equal enjoyment of all human being including girls and women is the fundamental right and freedom of women and girls. To achieve all these goals the following actions are to be initiated :

- Government should enact and implement the laws and policies to prevent the human rights violation relating to women and protect them by eliminating all forms of violence and discrimination against women. These laws are to be fully recognised and effectively protected, applied and reinforced in national law as well as in practice in family, civil, penal, labour, commercial and administrative regulations.
- Draw national action plans to implement international, regional and national human rights treaties.
- Eliminate all forms of discrimination against women.
- Create and strengthen independent national institutions for protecting and promoting the rights of women.
- Develop and popularise Human Rights education at all levels to raise awareness among women and the public.
- State parties should be encouraged to review and implement the laws, policies, practices and procedures to ensure that they meet obligations with regard to human rights and gender justice.
- Strengthen the implementation of relevant Human Rights instruments in order to combat and eliminate organised and other forms of trafficking in women such as sexual exploitation, prostitution and sex tourism. Provide legal and social services to the victims and prosecute and punish those who are responsible for this organised exploitation of women.
- Give full, equal and sustained attention to the human rights of women to exercise and promote universal respect for and

protection of all human rights like civil, cultural, economic, political, and social and the right to development.

- Develop comprehensive policy and programme for mainstreaming the human rights of women and play an active role in implementation of the programme.
- Ensure the integratation and full participation of women as both agents and beneficiaries in the development process.
- Disseminate information on gender based human rights and their violations in the developmental activities.
- Integrate and strengthen the activities of various commissions which are involved in human rights of women and their development.
- Promote the equal rights of women to be the members of trade unions and other professional and social organisations.
- Ensure that women have the same right as men to be judges, advocates, police officers, and prison and detention officers.
- Establish either free or at the affordable cost, mechanism and legal aid programme to women in distress and in violation of their rights.
- Involve non governmental and women organisations to protect and promote all human rights and gender justice.
- Ensure equalisation of opportunity for persons with disabilities paying special attention to non discrimination and equal enjoyment of all human rights of women and girls.
- Encourage the development of gender-sensitive human rights and legal literacy programme.
- Take appropriate measures that refugee, displaced and migrant women be aware of their rights and mechanisms available to recourse them.
- Bring legislative changes and reforms needed in property and inheritance rights to women to establish gender equality.

If these actions are initiated by both Government and Non Government organisations gender justice could become a reality.

Conclusion

Gender injustice is a problem prevailing through out the world. But development of a nation depends on the Gender Development Index. The battle for gender justice has a long history in the world. In India social reformers initiated the movement to change the mind set of orthodox, tradition bound society to usher women's decision making and be equal in the social, economic cultural and political spheres. But it is the duty of every human to protect the human rights and establish gender justice by providing female role model to promote gender equality and justice.

Any society committed to improving the lives of its people must also be committed to full and equal rights for all, including women with out any marginalisation and discrimination. Women now started getting a taste of economic independence due to the employment opportunities either in the organised or in the unorganised sector. This needs to be still systematised and women should feel that they have equal rights for a moment of triumph in their life like the other partner–men.

29

Challenges before Women Graduates

When I see young graduates a big question before me is "What Next?" Are they going to follow the conventional career designed solely for women? Or are they going to prove their individuality. Are they going to be satisfied merely to be shut down inside the four walls of domesticity or are they going to prove that women are capable of combining marriage and a chosen profession successfully.

Gone are the days when Women were thought of as 'objects', 'the other', 'secondary'! This is an era of Woman, a fully liberated woman who retains the virtuosity of a wife, affection of a mother, compassion of a woman, also proves her capability of being an administrator, a teacher, a doctor, a lawyer, an engineer, a police officer, a pilot, a politician – the list is endless. The traditional roles assigned to men and women based on biology and custom, nature and culture have been revolutionised and revamped from time to time. Many have evinced an interest to find out the roles women are playing. Among ardent feminist, the basic biological difference is accepted, the doubt is cast whether this difference should be extended to aptitude? The assumption that women are more naturally the tenders of home and children is now challenged and it is suggested the innate patience and endurance of a woman would go a long way to make her adaptable to social stresses and that a woman is a natural leader.

Through out Indian history there has been a stream of social consciousness urging and encouraging liberalization of attitudes towards the status of Women. Women's participation in the national movement and nation building activities though meager in early days later on gained momentum. The first Indian woman to enter into active politics and live to see India attain freedom was Sarojini Naidu. The entry of a woman of such eminence into active politics was a real inspiration to the hesitant womanhood of India. The fact that she left home, husband and children to identify herself with the movement for independence had a tremendous impact on women in determining their future participation in national movement in recent years. We have the distinction of having had a dynamic Prime Minister Smt Indira Gandhi who was the epitome of courage and determination. The world witnessed the regime of Women Prime Ministers simultaneously – Mrs Margaret Thatcher in England, Smt Indira Gandhi in India and Mrs Golla Meyer in Israel. These women proved that they were in no way lesser than men.

We have examples of women potential in the fields of education and social welfare. We need not go far in search of them. Sister Subbualakshi and Dr Muthu Lakshmi Reddy of Madras were actively associated with educational and social work. Both were born in orthodox families and have had traditional upbringing. Inspired by Mahatma Gandhiji they came out of the self-imposed isolation of women. Their sincere interest in the welfare of women has brought about a silent revolution and a good deal of the services have come to the women of India through the unrecorded efforts of these great women. I have had the good fortune of personally knowing Dr T.S. Soundaram, the Founder of Gandhigram who was inspired by sister Subbulakshmi and Dr Muthulakshmi Reddy to establish Gandhigram and dedicate herself to the cause of welfare and development of women and children. Dr Muthulakshmi Reddy has the distinction of the first South Indian woman to receive education abroad. When these women had the courage to educate themselves in those days when women were not even allowed outside the house, why can't we, the women of today, take up a career? and do some service to the society.

With remarkable foresight and with the experience he gained in South Africa, Gandhiji assessed the strength inherent in women. He realised that the only way to arouse them from their traditional role of domesticity was to awaken in them national consciousness and social responsibility Gandhiji's message offered to the women of India an opportunity to break away from the past with all its frustrations. Later on this paved way for the social and economic rehabilitation of women.

When we talk about Bapuji's foresight, when we talk about economic independence for women and when we talk about the imperativeness of a career for women I stress the positive aspect of women's development and I do not speak negatively of the domesticity. Whereas some feminists deplore of women as solely reproductive machine, I view the sanctity of motherhood as a unique privilege conferred on women by God. Marriage gives security, partnership to women, to some extent marriage is a necessity. But it is not an entity by itself.

Many women think of education as a passport to marriage with a groom settled abroad. I deplore this attitude in some of the young, modern women. Education is for all round development. It gives knowledge, self-confidence, individuality and above all social identity. The Government spends public money so much on education, because, education is the only healthy vehicle of social development and national development. The education women receive should broaden their outlook; inspire them to take social responsibilities through a career; motivate them to face the challenges of life with courage; instill in them the moral courage to resist social evils like dowry and corruption, inculcate the ethical values of individuality; and sharpen their sense of justice and integrity; in short education should make them ideal women who can take care of their home and at the same time upkeep their identity as a person who can make use of education to choose a suitable career.

Women's education should be geared towards inculcation of qualities of self-respect, fearlessness, self-confidence, spirit of enquiring and ability in decision-making. Women have to remember that they are not merely 'second sex'. They are full-fledged individuals with potentials and education they get at college level is not a culmination; and women should not let it be a culmination. When women were denied the rights to education, we insisted on women's education; now that ample opportunities are offered for women's education, we should look one step ahead and think how best this education can be utilised.

I am not for male superiority or female superiority; I am an advocate of complementarily of male and female. A woman's education serves her in her development. Development is a progressive change in an individual, continuously directed towards a specified condition; it is not merely a quantitative increase in output, but it envisages an in-depth qualitative progress. The education received should help in qualitative development. It should enable every woman to say with confidence that she is a compatible wife, a loving mother, an efficient manager of the house and above all a woman with identity, a woman who can channel her potentials in a suitable career and prove to the world and herself that she is educated in the true sense.

All those who are educated, should remember that before opportunity knocks at their door, seek opportunity, grab it, take up a career, find herself, her identity, and her individuality. It is marriage to all women as it gives them social security and it is also advocate that a suitable career for them as it ensures individual identity.

30

Empowering Women Through Teacher Education and Teaching Profession

"Intellectually, mentally, and spiritually, woman is equivalent to a male and she can participate in every activity."

— ***Mahatma Gandhi***

Women Empowerment refers to the provision, availability, and accessibility of opportunities, services, and observance of human rights which enable women to actively participate and contribute to the political, economic, social, and cultural development of the nation as well as those which shall provide them equal access to ownership, management, control of production, and benefits in the family, community, and society. According to Cambridge English Dictionary empowerment means "to authorise". In this context it means the people have to be authorised to have control over their lives. When applied in the context of development the particular segment of population, the poor, the women, the vulnerable, the weak, the oppressed and the discriminated have to be "empowered" to have control over their lives to better their conditions in every walk of their life. But who empowers them and how to empower them? Ideally speaking no one empowers any one, the best way is 'self empowerment'. They should empower themselves without any outside help. Empowering may be understood as enabling people, especially women to acquire and possess power resources, in order to make decision on their own or resist decisions that are made by others that affect them. A person may said to be powerful when he/she has control over a large portion of power resources in society.

Women's development and empowerment can be attained by improving their status and bargaining power in the economy. The National Policy on Education (1986) suggested certain strategies to empower women. Accordingly, women become empowered through collective reflections and decision making enable them to become agency of social change. Though women constitute nearly 50 per cent of the world's population, as far as their social status is concerned; they are not treated as equal or at par with men in all the spheres in the society. Empowerment of Women through creating an enabling environment for women to exercise their rights, both within and outside home, as equal partners along with men. Empowerment of women is mainly related to their participation in decision making with regard to raising and distribution of resources i.e., income, investments and expenditures at all levels.

The Parameters of Empowerment

The following parameters have been identified as empowerment of women

Empowered women will have a positive self-image and self-confidence by ensuring equal participation in bringing about social change. They will have the ability to think critically and creatively. They will also exhibit the ability to build group cohesion, foster decision-making and act with self confidence and encourage group action in order to bring about change in the society by providing the wherewithal for economic independence through employment. The work participation rate of woman has increased from 22.3 to 25.7 per cent during 1991and 2001. This increase in the work participation of women during the decade 1991-2001 is mainly due to the increase in the proportion of marginal workers as paid or unpaid labour especially in agriculture, agro based industries sectors and as domestic servants. At the same time it is felt that a women's job just not interfere or compete with her primary role of wife and mother.

Empowerment has four components-cognitive, psychological, economic and political. According to Ms Stromquist, the cognitive component would include the "women's understanding of their conditions of subordination and the causes of such conditions at both micro and macro levels of society. It involves acquiring new knowledge to create a different understanding of gender relations as well as destroying old beliefs of structure of gender ideologies." The psychological component, on the other hand, would include the "development of feelings that women can act upon to improve their condition". "The economic component" believes that women be able to engage in a productive activity that will allow them some degree of financial autonomy, no matter how small and hard to obtain at the beginning. Access to work increases a woman's economic independence and with it a greater level of general independence is created. As Hall (1992) notes, economic subordination must be neutralised for women to be empowered. The political component of empowerment entails the ability of women to analyse the surrounding environment in political and social terms; it also means the ability to organise and mobilise social change in the political arena.

Provision of educational opportunities to women has been an important programme in the education sector since independence. The literacy rate has increased from 7.93 during 1951 to 51.10 per cent during 2004-05. Still women comprise 49 per cent of the illiterate population. In spite of the efforts made so far, the education system has not been able to make sufficient contribution towards women's equality. The National Policy on Education (NPE) envisages that education should be used as a strategy for achieving a basic change in the status of women. The National education system should play a positive interventionist role in the empowerment of women; contribute towards development of new values through redesigned curricula and text-books, and women's studies to be promoted as part of various courses. The concept of empowerment has been linked to the range of activities undertaken by and for women in different areas. Self-confidence and self-esteem-the indicators of women's empowerment cannot be taught, one must provide the conditions and opportunity and the women have to imbibe it. Empowerment requires involving women by participating in planning and implementation of the programmes. Activities that seek empowerment must involve women in all stages of any project. Only through direct participation we could eliminate illiteracy; develop self-esteem and self-confidence. Creating knowledge about their bodies and sexuality; by developing ability to make their own decisions and negotiate; raising their awareness on civil rights; promoting skills for income generation; making them participate in community/society more effectively will prepare them to be good women leaders.

Towards Empowering Women

Gender equality and women's empowerment are the heart of development and the achievement of the Millennium Development Goals. The principle of gender equality is enshrined in the Indian Constitution. The Constitution not only grants equality to women, but also empowers the State to adopt measures of positive discrimination in favour of women. However, there is a wide gap between the goals enunciated in the Constitution, legislation, policies, plans, programmes, and related mechanisms on the one hand and the situational reality of the status of women in India, on the other. Gender disparity manifests itself in various forms, the most obvious being the declining female ratio in the population in the last few decades. Social stereotyping and violence at the domestic and societal levels are some of the other manifestations. Discrimination against girl children, adolescent girls and women persists every where.

Efforts are to be made in the following dimensions to empower women to play their role effectively in nation building activities as equal partners. The State should institute policies and programmes that seek to reduce the poverty and vulnerability to risks and enhance the social status of the marginalised women by promoting and protecting livelihood and employment, protecting against hazards and sudden loss of income, and improving their capacity to manage risks. Providing equal rights, opportunities and responsibilities to women, will go a long way in removing the existing gender discrimination. Employment, education, health and media images, place of residence, household chores, their participation in social and political activities, and their legal status in terms of marriage, divorce and inheritance of property decide their status in the society. Efforts are also being initiated to finalise the draft 'National Policy for Empowerment of Women' to legislate reservation of not less than 1/3 seats for women in the Lok Sabha and in the State Legislative Assemblies which will ensure adequate representation of women in decision making; to adopt an integrated approach towards empowering women through effective convergence of existing services, financial and human resources, and infrastructure in both women-specific and women-related sectors; to adopt a special strategy of 'Women's Component Plan' to ensure funds/benefits flow to women from other relevant sectors; and to organize women into different organisations like Self-Help Groups that will mark the beginning of a major process of empowering women.

Involving the male is equally important for the empowerment of women and for stabilisation of population. Reproductive decisions are taken within the family and hence promoting gender equality within the family has to be based on partnership and not on relationship of domination or subordination within the family. To achieve better understanding, every effort must be made to involve men in the promotion of reproductive rights. This is vital in order to change the societal perceptions about the contribution of women. This can happen only when women are seen by men-and society - not as 'better halves' but as 'equal halves'.

Facilitating Factors

As Gloria Steinem says "Power can be taken, but not given. The process of taking is empowerment in itself." Creating an environment through positive economic and social policies for full development of women to enable them to realise their full potential, equal access to participation and decision making of women in social, political and economic life of the nation, equal access to women to health care, quality education at all levels, career and vocational guidance, employment, equal remuneration, occupational health and safety, social security and public affairs will facilitate empowerment of women.

Women empowerment could also be promoted by encouraging formation of women's organisations; by providing support systems for women; by making available women-specific data and other relevant information; adequate funds; women leadership; networking; favorable media coverage and making available favorable policy climate. But there are constraints such as heavy work load of women; isolation of women from each other; illiteracy; traditional views that limit women's participation, internal strife/militarisation/wars; disagreements/conflicts among women's groups; structural adjustment policies; discriminatory policy environment; negative and sensational coverage of media in implementing these which do not allow women to proceed further.

Empowerment through education is ideally seen as a continuous holistic process with cognitive, psychological, economic and political dimensions in order to achieve emancipation. "Education remains the key to both economic and political empowerment". (Barbara Jordan) Gender sensitive curricula need to be developed at all levels of educational system in order to address sex stereotyping as one of the causes of gender discrimination.

Women and Teaching

"A woman is the full circle. Within her is the power to create, nurture and transform." Diane Marie child says. Hence women are highly suitable to be the teachers. Children are to be made creative thinkers, they are to be nurtured and transformed into worthy citizens and be able to compete in the fast changing world whether women or men. But teaching needs not only the skill of teaching or imparting mere knowledge but dedication, commitment, an affectionate approach to children and be a mother substitute. Education is not instruction. It is intellectual, moral, and physical development, the development of a sound mind in a sound body, the training of reason to form just judgments, the disciplining of the will and affections to obey the supreme law of duty, the kindling and strengthening of the love of knowledge, of beauty, of goodness. Women have these qualities by virtue of having motherhood in them. Women were by nature nurturing and maternal, as well as of high moral character. Teachers must be moral exemplars, the models and instructors of upright living.

In our society, there is gender discrimination in employment which dictates the kind of education and training one should undergo. If one talks about women's empowerment, it is important that women have access to the different training opportunities previously denied to them. Teaching became a source of income and self-sufficiency for women in the early nineteenth century. Women began teaching in rural schools I n the same years that the manufacture of cloth, spinning and weaving moved from the home to factories. The feminisation of teaching evolved piecemeal. Beginning in the late eighteenth century, women proved their intellectual abilities. This became apparent at the public examinations of female and coeducational academies where they were high achievers.

From colonial times and into the early decades of the 19th century, most teachers were men. The more educated and ambitious schoolmasters were young men who made the school a stepping-stone on their way to careers in the church or the law. The connections they made with local ministers and school committees in securing teaching jobs often helped them when they moved on to their real professions. Henry Barnard and Catharine Beecher saw that the schools needed not only more teachers, but better teachers. Most promising young men continued to be siphoned off by more prestigious professions, as well as by new industries that will fetch more income. At this juncture came the option of involving women as an alternative to engage women teachers and the public has to accept it. The reformers often had doubts about women's intellectual capabilities.

Yet women were becoming better educated than ever before, teaching was feminized in the nineteenth century and attracted more women towards teaching profession. The feminisation of teaching changed not only how society perceived women, but how women perceived themselves in the male dominated society.

Before 1800 when academies for women became popular, few women had an education that would qualify them to teach. Female education was a luxury for the well-to-do or a privilege of daughters whose fathers were highly educated. Because women in general had little opportunities to learn, there were few women with the necessary education to provide leadership in women's education. At the same time people were worried about maintaining the discipline and order in the classroom and disciplining unruly children. But now there is realisation that women could be motherly at the same time lead the children in the right direction and administer well. The increasing number of new schools across the country demanded greater numbers of educated teachers. In order to staff the schools, communities turned to women, spurring the feminisation of the teaching profession. But they had the doubt whether women need to be paid equal to men as women were paid only one third of what men received. Convention on the Elimination of All Forms of Discrimination against Women demanded that the State shall accord women equal rights, protection, and opportunities available to every member of society. The State affirms women's rights as human rights and shall intensify its efforts to fulfill its duties under international and domestic law to recognise, respect, protect, fulfill, and promote all human rights and fundamental freedoms of women, especially marginalised women, in the economic, social, political, cultural, and other fields without distinction or discrimination on account of class, age, sex, gender, language, ethnicity, religion, ideology, disability, education, and status. Thus the number of female teachers increased to nearly 75 per cent during the 20th century. Though it took time, the women teachers was largely successful. They gained better (and eventually equal) pay, pensions and tenure today. They started assuming the administrative positions like the Principals, Vice chancellors and mange more efficiently.

Conclusion

To day it is seen in every walk of life in the history of women as icons of successful woman power, as pioneer who stormed the male has excelled in every assignment Honours, awards and medals are nothing new for the woman who exemplifies how there is no stopping a woman with grit and guts. Women will continue to be excelling and leading the globe as they have dedication, perseverance, courage, commitment and conviction in their thinking, feeling and doing. Let me conclude my key note address by quoting Gillian Anderson who says.

"Be of service. Whether you make yourself available to a friend or co-worker, or you make time every month to do volunteer work, there is nothing that harvests more of a feeling of empowerment than being of service to someone in need."

31

Empowerment of Women—A Realistic Approach

"Woman must not accept; she must challenge. She must not be awed by that which has been built up around her; she must reverence that woman in her which struggles for expression."

— ***Margaret Sanger***

In an ever challenging and changing society, empowerment of women has been a matter of great concern to every one. When we are observing the 100th year of International Women's Day we are still talking about women empowerment and try to find a balance in gender equality. Article 1 of Indian Constitution says "all human being are born free and equal." Article 2 provides "freedom without any discrimination." Article 3 assures that 'every one has the right to life, liberty and security" Article 5 of the Constitution proclaims that "no one shall be subjected to torture, cruel, inhuman or degrading treatment" and Article 6 states that "every one has the right to recognition everywhere as a person before law." But discrimination seems to be a never ending phenomenon. Prejudice is the cause of this ignorance and injustice.

After observing Women's Day for a century, 9th March 2010 has been made a memorable day in the history of India by introducing in Rajya sabha the Bill of Reservation of 33 per cent to women, both in Parliament and in State Legislative Assemblies with lot of objections. "Media say that it was a historic and giant step". Of course it is a great move after 73rd and 74th amendments in the Indian Constitution which brought the women to politics by contesting in Panchayat elections, winning and discharging their duties with efficiency and commitment as Presidents and members. And made people now feel not to underestimate the power of a woman, through their functioning with all the inputs they had in the capacity building training programme.

"There will never be a true democracy until every responsible and law-abiding adult in it, without regard to race, sex, color or creed has his or her own inalienable and unpurchasable voice in government," says Carrie Chapman Cattti. Though Women comprise of the fifty percentage of the world population there is still denial in many aspects of their life quoting the culture. It is not gender which is destroying our culture. . . it is our interpretations of culture which has destroyed gender equality. A woman from Madurai recalls and says that "in our culture we never allowed our women to go out and sudy. But we have to work ourselves and depend on ourselves" As Jane Galvin Lewis says "you don't have to be an anti-man to be pro-woman". To feel and make women equal we have two ways either we have to be like the candle that spreads the light or the mirror that reflects the light.

When there is realisation that a woman is the full circle and within her we find the power to create, nurture and transform it will make every one to have the feeling of gender equality justice and live in harmony. Peace and contentment in life comes only when we look at what we have in our life, we will always have more. If we look at what we don't have in life, we will never have enough. We must learn to respect each other and we must learn to listen to each other to live together. It is the time that every woman realises that our own words are the bricks and mortar of the dreams that we want to realise; our words are the greatest power we have. There is a growing strength in women. All are capable of achieving what they desire and decide for which there should be encouragement and support.

Indicators of Women Empowerment

There are women activists through out the world who articulate and voice their concerns and issues so that the issues of women could be heard loud and made clear. It is not just raising the voice that will bring about change and empower the women folk. Systematic efforts, though sporadic, has brought changes in the life of women and empowered them which could be observed in their behaviour pattern.

The following are some of the indicators of the empowered women:

A positive self-image and self-confidence, ensuring equal participation in bringing about social change, ability to think critically and creatively, exhibition of the ability to build group cohesion and be leaders, courageous and commitment to foster decision-making and encourage group action in order to bring about change in the society by providing the wherewithal for economic independence through employment and the right to property are considered as the characteristics of empowered women. Men and women should play complementary roles in the process of empowerment, and they cannot be separated.

Empowerment has four components — cognitive, psychological, economic and political. Cognitive component involves acquiring new knowledge to create a different understanding of gender relations and destroying old beliefs of structure of gender ideologies. The psychological component stresses on development of feelings and emotions that women can develop to improve their conditions. The economic component stresses that women should be able to engage in any productive activity that will lead them to financial autonomy. Access to work increases a woman's economic independence and with it a greater level of general independence is created. As Hall (1992) notes, economic subordination must be neutralised for women to be empowered. The political component of empowerment promotes the ability of women to analyse the political and social environment and mobilize social change in the political arena. Only when a woman gets up and comes out of the shackles of the traditions and belifs she can assure of her empowerment.

All these will lead to a complete and comprehensive development of women, enabling them to be active participants in development activities in the society. Female work force and their participation is needed for empowerment. In General now a days the gender gaps in labour force participation have been shrinking and women's entrepreneurship development has been impressive. This participation helps women to build up positive self and confidence in them. Women, therefore require education to acquire skills and knowledge to increase their value in labour markets and to get social status.

Action Plan

Discrimination against girl children, adolescent girls and women persists every where, that need immediate attention to make them have equal participation. Providing equal rights, opportunities and responsibilities to women, will go a long way in removing the existing gender discrimination.

The principle of gender equality enshrined in the Indian Constitution should not be only a constitutional provision; it is to be ensured that there is really gender equality in all the dimensions of life of the women: education, employment, political and social. The critical mass should be in a position to understand, feel and act to achieve their goal in life.

Gender disparity is seen in various forms, the most obvious being the decline in female ratio during the last few decades both in urban and rural area. Social stereotyping and violence against women at the domestic and societal levels are some of the other manifestations that are very obvious in the society. To empower women to play their role effectively in nation building activities as equal partners, efforts are to be taken in the following dimensions The State should formulate policies and programmes that will reduce the poverty and vulnerability to risks of women. Social status of the marginalised women should be enhanced by promoting and protecting livelihood and employment, protecting against hazards and sudden loss of income, and improving their capacity to manage risks.

Employment, education, health, media images, place of residence, household chores, women's participation in social and political activities, and their legal status in terms of marriage, divorce and inheritance of property decide their status in the society. The recent move of reservation of 1/3 seats for women in the Lok Sabha and in the State Legislative Assemblies will ensure adequate representation of women in decision making; to adopt an integrated approach to both women-specific and women-related sectors; to adopt a special strategy of 'Women's Component Plan' to ensure funds / benefits flow to women from other relevant sectors; and to organise women into different organizations like Self-Help Groups and Federations that will mark the beginning of a major process of empowering women.

Women should be made to realize as Gloria Steinem says "Power can be taken, but not given. The process of taking is empowerment in itself." Creating an environment through positive economic and social policies for full development of women will enable them to realise their full potential. Equal access to women to health care services, quality education at all levels, career and vocational guidance, employment, equal remuneration, occupational health and safety, social security and public affairs will facilitate empowerment of women. Women empowerment could also be promoted by encouraging the women to form have their own women's organisations; by providing support systems for women; making available women-specific data and other relevant information; adequate funds; women leadership; networking; favorable media coverage and making available favourable policy climate.

Education remains the key to both economic and political empowerment. Empowerment through education is an ideal action as it is a continuous holistic process with cognitive, psychological, economic and political dimensions in order to achieve emancipation. Gender sensitive curricula need to be developed at all levels of educational system in order to address sex stereotyping as one of the causes of gender discrimination.

IFAD supported Tamil Nadu Women's Development Project in 1999. Identified as the main processes that could lead to women's empowerment: changes in women's mobility and social interaction; changes in women's labour patterns; changes in women's access to and control over resources; and changes in women's control over decision-making. The study also has suggested the action programme and key initiatives for bringing about these changes.

Women are to be considered as key change agents. Women bear all the responsibilities at home for meeting basic needs of the family, yet there is denial in providing adequate and needed resources, information and freedom of action to fulfill this responsibility. Equally women also take up jobs outside to earn their livelihood or to supplement their family income. When women are denied adequate nutrition and health care facilities, the children are also born mal and under nourished. When women are not provided with the opportunity for education the children also suffer of illiteracy. Hence it is said that if a man is educated and individual is educated when a woman is educated the whole family is educated, as the mother is the first teacher. When women are empowered and are supported it leads to a healthy family and empowered nation.

Conclusion

As stated in Beijing Platform for Action, Fourth U.N. World Conference on Women, 1995 "The advancement of women and the achievement of equality between women and men are matters of human rights and conditions for social justice and should not be seen in isolation as women's issue. They are the only way to build a sustainable, just and developed society. Empowerment of women and gender equality are prerequisites for achieving political, social, economic, cultural and environmental security among all peoples."

In the goals of National Policy for Empowerment of Women it is stated that we should Create an environment through positive economic and social policies for full development of women to enable them to realise their full potential and encourage them to be equal partners in nation building activities. As Mahatma Gandhi says: "Intellectually, mentally, and spiritually, woman is equivalent to a male and she can participate in every activity." This approach towards women empowerment will enable a prosperous and progressive world to emerge. Let the world move towards that direction and show a new and bright dawn to the generation to come.

32

A Perspective Development Plan for Women

Development is a process at the individual, group, social, local, regional, national and global levels, for the economic social and cultural enhancement in the quality of the human life. Development strategy is said to be of bringing in structural changes in the achievement of development in every perspective, in order to find a coherent and lasting solution to the problem which the society faces and of which it has become aware.

Women's Development

Gandhiji says, "My opinion is that, just a s fundamentally man and woman are one, their problem must be one in essence. The soul in both is the same. The two live the same life, have the same feelings. Each is a complement of the other. The one cannot live without the other's active help".

Our mythology and constitution of independent India give equal rights to woman in socio-economic and cultural life, by defining all economic prosperity power and knowledge–flowing from the female Goddess Lakshmi, Durga and Saraswathy, whereas in reality the condition of women I different. In spite of the constitutional gruarantee for equal rights of participation in all spheres of life, such as political process and equal opportunities and rights in educational employment women are not enjoying this. The large majority of women are not benefited by the development. On the contrary a steady, decline in the position of women in the society is observed. There is excessive mortality among women and female children, glaring disparity between men and women in access to health care and medical services, decline in sex ratio, increasing gap between men and women in literacy, education and training for employment. An accelerated decline in women's employment is observed. The laws by themselves cannot bring any desired results, unless the socio-economic fabric of women is recast. Unless traditional attitudes are changed and women are provided access to independent income and property right, efforts to improve their status will remain a mere dream.

Women are given little representation in decision making bodies at the lower level as well at the higher levels from local to national levels. This phenomenon is extended to almost all aspects of women's lives such as employment, health, socio–economic and cultural status and education. Women in our society suffer from inequality and discrimination based on sex in addition to poverty and injustice caused by the social, political and economic system. Women's oppression, inequality and discrimination are manifested through social structures, institutions and irrational attitudes and values about women's role in development.

The development plan has not sufficiently reached he women folk in our country. We have facts and figures to show the deterioration in the status of women. They are poorer among the poor. They are least educated among the less educated. They are the more ill physically and mentally among the ill. They are without rights and freedom. There are development programmes and policies in India which neither involve nor allow participation of women. Women have been suppressed under custom and law for which man has been responsible and in the shaping of which she had no hand.

Development Plan for Women

A development plan for women should try to focus the attention of the people on their socio-economic and cultural status, rights and privileges available to them and how to enable them to achieve a better position or an equal status in the society. The recognition of women's development must constitute a priority for both women and nation. This should include the role of women in the society in bringing about changes in the following areas of development:

1. Women and food production
2. Women and economic development

3. Women's access to health care
4. Women and education and
5. Women and employment

A development profile for women should envisage the attainment of cent percent literacy for women, full health coverage for women, grater electoral participation and access to position of decision-making, application of scientific and technological innovations to their daily lives and subsequent promotion of socio-economic development of women.

Women and Food Production

Women play a vital role in agriculture and farm development. About 47 per cent percent of women workers are agricultural labourers. A significant section of working women in agriculture are under most oppressive working and living conditions with no legal protection. They are involved in breaking lumps of earth, manuring the land, planting or sowing the seeds, watering the plants, weeding tending cattle, poultry keeping, collecting fodder, harvesting, transportation, storage and processing of farm produces which are not only strenuous but also time consuming, whereas men are involved mainly in ploughing. But when we compare the wage structure women are poorly paid. The female wage varies between 70-80 per cent from the male wage. They also do not hold the rights of the land. Invariably it is the main who is the owner of the land.

Even though women are more active than men in agricultural and marketing activities, they have to do all the household work without much help from men. The house will starve and the village economy will come to a halt if women ceseased working even for a few days.

A Developmental Strategy for Improving the Status of Women in Agricultural Sector

Women play an important role in agriculture and could play an even more important role through the transfer of improved technology in farming, and by improving their wages. The women are to be trained in Science and Technology which are of direct help in improving the farm production. The courses which are planned for women agricultural workers should include improvised and improved techniques of preparing the lands for cultivation, selection of good varieties of seeds and seedlings, quicker method of planting and sowing, improvised method of irrigation, weeding and harvesting. Appropriate technology is to be introduced in cultivation, so that women need not spend much of their energy in farming activities.

These schemes will mark and bring about a qualitative change in development programmes for women. Instead of treating them as receivers of dole, charity, and a few welfare schemes, they will be recognised as valuable, economic assets of the nation.

They should be given training in horticulture, raising kitchen gardens, food and fruit preservation, growing trees and better animal and crop husbandry. They should be taught to conserve our land and water resources.

The women should be paid equally as men, for the amount of work which they put in farming. The time taken and energy required should be taken into consideration for deciding the wages.

Economic Status of Women and Development

The discriminatory approach towards women is still deep-rooted in our society. We have failed to recognise the extensive contribution of women to household and national economy as an active worker and producer of goods. Sex difference is linked with unequal distribution of resources, rewards, rights and responsibilities. Women are largely employed in primary sector of economy, constituting about 80 per cent. Female participation in the economic development activity is increasing, especially in agriculture and household industries as compared to their participation in industry, transport and communication.

Women are not permitted to participate in economic development programmes, especially in rural areas. There are cultural and religious constraints that restrict women in the production and technology. The primary reasons do not support a vicious plot to keep women in a subordinate position to men, but because men make the policies and do not understand women's role in economic development and productivity. It is also felt that women would displace men and provide undue competition for male breadwinners.

All women, irrespective of their status in the society and employment outside, devote their energy to different household activities such as fetching and transporting water, cooking and food processing, collecting fuel, managing the house and taking care of children. For all these activities she is not being paid; and her contribution to the economy of the family is not even recognised. Whereas when a man goes out and spends 6 to 8 hours a day in wage earning he is considered as breadwinner and is not expected to take part in any household activities.

Development Programme for Economic Self-Sufficiency of Women

An effort must be taken to remedy the present situation. Political, cultural and educational problems of women's position in the society should be elevated. This is possible, when a national policy is framed for improving women's economic status and image based on proper perspective of issues in which they are involved by realising the immense potential that a woman has in national development. They can easily take part in small scale energy production system and other small scale industries.

Efforts should be taken to replace the traditional value system which is based on imequality of sexes, where women play a subordinate role. We must bring about betterment in the quality of life for women. Women should be encouraged to perceive their role in society and in the economic front.

Very little attempt is being made to encourage women entrepreneurship in our country. If we prepare a profile of women and their potentialities in income generating activities they would come forward for taking up small units in villages. Banks should come forward to giving loans to women entrepreneurs as being done through Self-help Groups.

Women and Employment

Women form the larger section of the unemployed in both rural and urban areas. Women a professionals, administer and in other jobs are not a significant number. There is a striking observation that women are being displaced from employment at an alarming rate, not only in agriculture but also in the formal and informal industrial sectors in both rural and urban areas, though there is a marginal increase in the service sector such as personal and domestic services generated by increase in population especially in urban areas.

Now employment opportunity in industry is available only to technically trained and qualified women, who are very few in numbers. Opportunity for training is also less for women. Attempt to create facilities for self-employment for women is gaining momentum to get credit and supply of raw materials, either from banks or co-operative societies. There is a myth that women are not capable of becoming equal to men. But in reality men are afraid that they have to forge their jobs or employment if there is a competition between men and women. Any employer will prefer a woman to man because of her sincerity and hard work. The feeling of insecurity on the part of men folk would like the women to be always subordinate to them and suppress their progress in lives.

Development Plan for Priorities in Employment for Women

Efforts should be taken to identify the employed and underemployed women both in urban and rural areas in order to arrest the increasing displacement of women. Contribution of women in almost all fields including those that were taken to be men's exclusives should be brought to light. Women are breaking the shackles of traditionalism and are proving to be an asset to the developmental process, occupations being no exceptions. They are found equally competent in offices, industries, hospitals and such institutions and places where employment of man power is required.

Women should be given equal opportunity for employment, if required reservation for women should be emphasised till a sizable number of women get employment opportunities. Selection for employment should never be based on the sex; it should be on the basis of the competence and capability.

Local level women's organisations are to be set up in order to enlist potential women and to serve as a lilnking agency with other developmental organisations at every level so that employment opportunity for women be enlarged.

Women should find place in all the devision-making bodies so that male domination be reduced. In all the co-operatives and credit societies for economic development there should be women representatives.

By virtue of their physical and mental make up women are more suited for health education and social services. Efforts should be taken to give priority to women while selecting workers for these services.

The rules and regulations for recruitment for different services should suitably be modified by raising the age of women for appointments.

The Government and all the agencies which employ women should see that they provide child care facilities in their work spots, so that mothers with children can be relieved of their stress and worry while working.

Needed other supportive services such as provision after in service training, housing, transport facilities, security arrangements and health facilities should be provided for employed women.

Consultation services are to be provided so that women could get further qualification and employment potential.

Exploitation of women by employers should be curbed. Payment of low wages should be curtailed.

Women's Access to Health Care Services

Women constitute half the adult population in our country. If the goal of health for all is to be achieved more attention must be paid to women's health and their roles in health and development. Women's health is being affected by her work inside the home and outside, and her role in the family as child bearer and rearer affect her health. Woman due to the societal norms is conditioned to self-suffereing. Her health is neglected. While the incidents of diseases caused by malnutrition is higher among women, admission in hospital and treatment formen for these disease is larger. In spite of heavy toll of lives of women every year during childbirth maternity facilities available in the hospitals is less.

Because of early marriages and early, frequent childbirth there are more cases of maternal mortality. When a mother is seriously ill or dies as a result of child birth it is not only a personal tragedy but also a family and national tragedy. The early weaned and uncared children might become sick or die. Even in controlling the size of the family it is only the women who have to undergo the operation not the men. Women have less role in any decision regarding the size of the family.

Health Care Programme for Women's Development

Health is a new conception which can serve as an entry point to an integrated socio-economic development. It is well-recognised that healthy people are in better position to contribute to the economic and social development of the country; people in that country suffer less illness. This interrelationship between health and development aim at the creation of human conditions which allow for a maximum level of self realisation and social development. Improvement in health and nutritional status of women will raise the health status of the country. Good health is the foundation of human welfare and productivity. Health status of any society is a complex concept that cannot be measured easily. It reflects the life expectancy and infant mortality rate. Along with sound living this could be done only with the economic and educational status of women, ie. by improving the nutritional status, maternal and child health facilities, sanitary conditions, improved water supply, medical facilities for controlling the communicable diseases and integrated approach for improving the environment.

Improved health and increase in income are possible only through increased literacy level of women. Hence, there should be adequate budget provision for improving the maternity and child health services. Women should be adequately provided with maternity and child health services in their own vicinity or locality.

Improvement in the health status of women have a favourable effect not only women but on the whole community. Healthier mothers give birth to healthier children. Hence, every society should strive hard to improve the health status of women. Women must be provided with adequate knowledge of nutrition and health. Health education programme should be given to women both in the primary health centres and in nonformal and adult education centres. This in trun will improve the health and nutritional status of women. Women are the chief nutritionists, health workers and educators. In many developing countries they are also responsible for food production. Proper nutrition of mother and the pregnant women is an extremely important factor in human resource development.

Literacy and Women's Development

Why should women be educated is a simple question for which the answer is simple. That is to ensure better health and nutrition for themselves and their families and for better economic development. The quality of life of women shows the performance pattern of country. In India women are at a serious disadvantage in the educational system. Human resource development demands knowledge and skills to help people in their economic performance. It also helps to develop the right type of values and attitudes towards environment and development towards society, home and the work spot. Improved health and increase income are possible only through increased literacy level of women. In terms of population planning education of women delays marriage for women and increases their chances for employment.

The crude female literacy rate has increased from 7.93 per cent to 54.28 per cent between 1951-2001. But the number of illiterate females in India increased due to increase in population. The percentage of literacy in rural area is very poor.

A Perspective Plan for Women's Development and Education

While talking about universalization of education there is a problem of large number of girls dropping out from the school. We should try to close the gap between male and female enrolment and retention rates. The girls should be encouraged to enroll and continue their education. Women should be provided with skills for appropriate employment and should aim at proper socio-economic development. Education and training should be directed towards the acquisition of practical and vocational skills needed for making the women more self-reliant. Education must be improved in quality and should have social relevance to reflect the local conditions and requirements.

In the modern wcrld of knowledge, scientific and technological explosion the contribution of education to the total development of women can hardly be under estimated. Only by educating the women one could encourage them to use technology for reshaping and transforming the traditional society. Education of women should also aim at providing adequate basic inputs for the acquisition of information, skill and training about work opportunities and job openings, thus, increase the female participation in economic development of our country.

Vocational and technical education should be provided to women based on their aptitude and interest.

As the educational policy has rightly pointed out there should be sensitisation of teachers, trainers, planners and administrators to women's issues. Education for women should build a positive attitude towards development and life. Sex biased curriculum and text-book should be eliminated so that women have equal opportunity along with the male population.

Girls should have access to higher education, technical and professional education. There should be reservation in all these institutions until such time they have attained equal status with men.

One of the most important objectives of education for women should be that of changing the women's attitude and the training of the skills so that they can increase their own capacity to be effective economic agencies.

Social Status of Women

The social status of women varies by class, group, caste, culture, education and religion. The position of women at home, society and the national level decides their social status. The promise of equality of opportunity and status through the right of equal participation in all spheres of national life has not been translated into reality except for a minority of women. A large number of women virtually remain invisible to every one from common people to policy makers and administrators. There exists unjust discrimination in rewards for their contributions to the economic and national development. Hence, the oppression of poverty and inequality weights more heavily on women and children.

In the family woman is subordinate to man. About 2000 years ago the position of women in the Hindu society was cogently enunciated in the laws of Manu. It is stated in his book that "a woman should never be independent. Her father has authority over her in childhood, her husband has authority over her in youth and in old age her son has authority over her". This state of affair will continue if we do not raise the standard of life of women in our society. Economic independence of women alone can create an environment which will emancipate women by making them come out of their traditional bonds.

A Perspective Development Plan to Raise the Social Status of Women

Steps should be taken to reduce the drudgery of women by providing them with opportunities for generating means for improving their health, sanitation, education and environmental conditions and finding ways and means of protecting them from occupational hazards.

Committees consisting of women members to plan women's imancipation, to evolve laws and to protect the interest of women should be constituted by the planners and administrators. Decision-making should never be the monopoly of men. Women should have equal opportunity in policy-making and decision-making.

The concept of owning the property jointly by both the husband and wife should be emphasised. Even in a landlord's family a woman is a landless labourer. Only if a man decides to be considerate, the wife may feel that she is part of a joint enterprise. If not, she has no economic, social or political power to resist maltreatment. This state of affair could be avoided only when the property and wealth is owned by both husband and wife.

Women oriented researches should be undertaken by colleges, universities and voluntary agencies to throw light on practices of different social evils and atrocities on women. The mass should be enlightened with awareness of equality for women. Women should be given equal right for performing religious rituals. Protection of traditional rights should be accompanied by positive measurers to enhance the well-being of the women in ways appropriate to the life style of the community.

Broader measures are to be taken by the human resource development ministry to promote health and nutritional status of women; educational facilities and institutions should also be made available to them. By making the best use off these, they could improve their socio-economic status.

Reservations for women in educational institutions and places of employment will help women claim equal social status. Women entrepreneurs, doctors, lawyers, teachers, athletes, pilots, artists, journalists, writers, housewives and women in other walks of life should be able to meet often and exchange ideas on matters of mutual interest and expand the horizons of knowledge.

Conclusion

All these efforts and programmes will prove futile if women themselves do not assert their individuality and claim their rights. Those who are already in work force should look upto development programmes to facilitate upward mobility in their existing status. Those who are waiting to enter the workforce should try to qualify themselves.

The challenge before every Indian woman is to be take measure to increase self-confidence, leadership quality and to become capable of joining the skilled workforce and organised sectors. They should further receive all the social development measures to increase their participation in development programmes of the nation.

33

Road to Success

"Success is a journey, not a destination."

Unless teachers and students of today are convinced of the great virtues and ethos of this country, practice them in their life, they cannot expect the next generation to adopt them in their life. Good virtues and value system are passed on from teachers to the students, as the great teachers inspire and make the students imbibe them.

All those who are educated are fortunate, who are one among the 10 per cent of youth of our country, who enter the Higher education in India. If every educated person is able to educate at least one, as the saying goes "Each one catch one and teach one" India will soon become a "Knowledge Super Power", and a guiding star to the whole world. In this great venture the young students and teachers have a greater role to play. Dr D. S. Kothari, the Chairman of Education Commission—1964-66 as the opening sentence of the report says "the future of India is being shaped in her class rooms", it is the responsibility of teachers to make it true. The future of India is in your hands of the youth. To realise the dream of making India a Super Power youth have to work very hard, with a vision and social commitment.

Grab the Opportunities

Opportunities will not come in search of any one. We should go in search of it. Opportunities might lack but what is needed is courage in heart – courage and confidence to excel in life and be of use to the society. Just grab any opportunity on the way, to be successful in life. Don't miss it.

A journey of thousand kilometers begins with the first single step! The ascent to greatness begins with understanding oneself especially of what one is capable of. We should develop our personal skills: promote the ability and skill to move with others, without any inhibition and hesitation. If this is done systematically through positive thinking, the skills to deal with the world will develop, leading to success in our life. Positive attitude and skills to deal with situations are the tools for success.

We should not be afraid of criticism and failure, fight against conflicts, evils and confrontation, and at the same time problem-solving and decision-making skills are to be enhanced for you to be successful. This will enrich and empower us with self confidence and courage to face any eventuality in life for the cause of welfare of the society. This will give us great satisfaction in our life.

What we think we become; thought is the instrument for action. So always be positive in our thinking. Right thinking blesses all without exception and helps every one to realise the self and shows what we are and where do we stand in the society. As it is said:

"If you think you are beaten, you are

If you think you dare not, you don't!

If you think you'll lose, you're lost;

Success begins with a fellow's will."

So always try to be positive; think positively and act positively to create a society with happiness and contentment.

What is Success?

Success is not something that comes to us by accident. It requires hard work; takes a lot of preparation and perseverance. Everyone likes to win but how many are willing to put in the effort and time to prepare to win? It needs sacrifice and self-discipline. There is no substitute for hard work. Henry Ford said, "The harder you work, the luckier you get" Running away from problem is not going to help you to find any solution. Face the problem and will solve it. Success comes to those who do not hurt others, even in our words, be loyal to the duty, and be calm and patient in despair and happiness are the keys to success in life.

Face Boldly; do not give up

As every mountain has a peak, every valley has its low point, so also life. Life has its ups and downs, its peaks and its valleys. No one is up all the time, nor they are down all the time. Problems do end. They do go away. They all will resolve in time. Here are a few tips to solve the problems:

Never try to avoid the problem, but face the problem.

Consider every problem as an opportunity for growth.

No problem is permanent. It passes away.

Approach every problem with positive thinking.

We should find the various ways of solving the problem before taking the decision. Once the decision is taken, whatever might be the consequences, we must be able to stand firm to realise the decision in life and make it a reality.

Risk Taking

Learn to take risk for achieving success. Greater the risk; greater will be the achievement. If we don't dare to take a risk, we will never get ahead. The people, who risk nothing, do nothing, have nothing, and are nothing to achieve in their life.

We should dare to proceed even when there are hurdles on the way. Risks must be taken, because the greatest hasard in life is to risk nothing, we will be inactive and our identity and mobility will be lost if we are not ready to take risk in our life. Only when we are active, we are alive. An inactive person is a dead wood.

Time Management

Efficient management of time is another skill which everyone should acquire in our life. The management of time is the Management of our life. When we waste time we are wasting our life. Punctuality is a problem for many people. When we are late for classes, appointments, meetings or work, we show a lack of respect for other people's time as well as our own.

Loneliness

Loneliness is a common experience among the youth and feel as if they are isolated. They can overcome. Much of the emotional pains we experience, as loneliness come from our negative interpretation of present life situation. We are part of a group or crowd for some time, when they leave we feel lonely without realising that we may join the same group or some other group tomorrow. To overcome loneliness, take positive decision, rather than defensive action. Avoid withdrawing from any such situations by challenging our irrational self-thoughts, take time to develop personal interests and self-awareness, and seek contacts with others through a wide range of personal and social contacts. Maintain a balance in enjoying our time when we are alone.

As the following verses indicate do not quit the tasks when things don't, go as we wish; take everything as part of the game and go forward that will lead to success When things go wrong:

As they sometimes will,

When the roads you're trudging seems all uphill,

Rest if you must, but don't you quit.

Don't give up though the pace seems slow

You may succeed with another blow.

Success is failure turned inside out

So stick to the fight when you're hardest hit

The Power with in

Every one should realise the power with in us to achieve the best in the world. If we are able to realise and bring out the innate potential within us immense power will be generated and there will be happiness in our life. Wisdom and thought start penetrating into every action of our life. It is the wisdom which forms the essential part of everyone's biography, irrespective of caste, creed, religion, age and sex. Afterall it is we, we and we alone. Who can give it to anybody? Just grab it and, that is the game one has to play to be successful in life. As Sri. Aurobindo says, "When we have passed beyond willings, then we shall have power. Effort was the helper; effort is the bar." It is our duty to set our own goals and devise a path to walk along to reach it. Let us sharpen and train our mind and body to accompany us in our effort to achieve the success in our life.

We have to decide what is needed for us; on the basis of our own capability and interest; no one can take a decision on our behalf as no one could shoulder our cross. We have to draw your own conclusion; during the process try to question all our actions, beliefs, education and achievements; that will guide us to achieve what we want to.

The society has extended this opportunity to us and now it is our turn to commit our self to the society, be accountable and repay it. Serve the people who are disadvantaged and make them also reach our height as they too have the equal right to enjoy the best in life. Our service and contributions will go a long way in growth and development of our country and our people. Try to be apostles of change and bring progress in our life, our family, our society and the great nation-India.

Above are some of the clues we should keep in mind to go ahead and overcome any problem or hurdles on the way, in our life so that we are able to win the race in this high competitive world.

Let me conclude by quoting Merilyn Jemimah.

"On the journey to success, the goal you set becomes the roadmap. To succeed you have to move constantly towards the goal. And setting goals is the best way to ensure success."

34

Changing Perspective in Home Science Education

From Domesticity to Moderately

Industrialisation, modernisation, mechanisation and emancipation of women have changed the value system in the society and the individuals irrespective of gender. Women in equal number have started coming out of homes to take up jobs in offices, hospitals, schools and colleges. They take part and perform better in non traditional areas of business, self employment and entrepreneurship. At the same time they have to perform the traditional home making activities such as to be an efficient housewife, a lovable caring mother, an in–law and a grandma. Though men also now share the responsibilities in home making and child care still women have special responsibilities at home, which no one could deny and replace.

Women and Development

Development is not possible without the active participation of women who constitute 50 per cent of the population. They have to participate in promoting economic and social activities for the total development of the nation. Spread of education has created awareness among women and society and in general there is a gradual change in the attitude of the people. Women are breaking the shackles of traditionalism and proving to be an asset to the developmental process, occupations being no exceptions. That is why it is aptly said that "The education of a girl is the education of a mother and through her education of her children". "A literate woman is far better and surer guarantee of education of the coming generation than a literate man".

Brief History of Home Science Education

The introduction of Home or Domestic science or Home Economics or in every name as a subject of study for both girls and boys has great relevance in the modern world. Home science with its concern for personal, family and social living provides an unusual opportunity by offering a programme which is a vital concern to the development of individual, the community and the whole nation. Decades back Home Science was started as Home Economics mainly to encourage and attract young women to apply scientific principles to child rearing, cooking and house keeping along with liberal education. Some people started cooking schools to train women to be professional cooks to prepare healthy and low cost meals. Later "Land Grant schools" were started with an emphasis on providing scientific training to the wives of farmers on cooking, house cleaning, sewing, laundry, care of the sick and sanitation and called it as "Domestic Science". Those who studied this course besides being good and efficient parents and home makers, started entering the jobs outside the home as wage earners. Many pursued careers in businesses, like food industry, textiles and clothing, hotel management, interior design, public health, social work, and education.

In India, Home Science was started as an off shoot of All India Women Conference held in 1927 that emphasised the need for starting Home Science for women. It was Lady Irwin College at Delhi which introduced Home Science as a subject of study in 1932 and University of Madras was the first University to start Home Science at the undergraduate level. Very few women only opted for Home Science. As the parents and the public were under the impression that why should their girls be sent to schools and colleges to learn cooking and sewing, when these could be learnt at home.

At the same time a few thought that learning home making will help them get good grooms to their daughters as it was concerned with daily living-the food they eat, the clothes they wear, care of home in which they live, maintain good family relationship, health and bring up children. In the modern world, home making activity has become inevitable for boys and girls. Hence, Home Science education has been introduced to both boys and girls, keeping individual, family and the community as the focal points, with arts and science of living with.

Goals of Home Science Education

Home science Education is considered as an education for living and the study of every thing that pertains to home and the family life. It is an application of all branches of science and arts leading to better health, and happy family life. "Home economic stands for the ideal home life of to-day, unhampered by the traditions of the past and the utilisation of all the resources of modern science to improve home life". (Ellen Swallow Richards (1904).) Home Science is not a single speciality; it is a multidisciplinary subject, which includes consumer's science, nutrition, cooking, parenting, human development, interior decoration, family economics, textiles and resource management.

Study of Home Science helps to create clean quick thinking minds and decision making capacity in the charming and honorable women by building self-confidence in them. This promotes efficiency to deal with personal and social life. Home makers to-day live in a complex society with different patterns of living and have to assume a wide variety of responsibilities. Basic needs of individuals, the family and the community, for food, clothing and shelter remain the same but in a very different form. So a home maker has to have the knowledge of the changing pattern of life so that she builds forces which would promote physical, mental and social well being of the members of the family and society.

Trying to make a good home in the modern world has to be concerned with making the community better, safer and healthier than before. Problems of human relationships and adjustments are different to day. The home maker, thus, cannot confine her activities to the four walls of the home. She should be prepared to pierce the veil and come out, build capacity to stand alone and fight against any odd eventuality both in personal and social life. This is possible only when women are empowered to play their complimentary roles efficiently and effectively both at home and in the society as wage earners.

Study of Home science prepares the youth for the vocations as well as home making. It promotes right values and helps them to apply their knowledge in everyday life. Home Science provides experiences that enable a woman to form desirable habits, broaden mental vision, deepen the understanding of her status in society and enables her to acquire skills to meet and solve problems encountered in everyday life. By broadening her social outlook beyond home as the champion of social causes she readily plunges into action for changing roles. It is therefore said that study of Home Science enables families both as individual units as well as a social institution, to build and maintain systems of action which leads to maturity in individual's self formation and to enlightened, co-operative participation in formulating social goals and ways of accomplishing them. This will make a woman a moving spirit, performing and perfectionist in the society.

As Home Science is the application of scientific principles and skills in home making, child rearing, preparing healthy, nutritious and low cost meals, common household textiles and clothing, housing consumerism, and resource management, it lays a strong foundation for a balanced happy home, and prepares for career, profession and industries outside the homes without burning the candle at both ends.

Home Science education also provides guidance and opportunities to grow in social graces, managerial ability and competence in home making skills. It helps to find solutions scientifically to the problems faced by the members of the family as well as the community by applying their presence of mind, reasoning and quick decision making. Home Science provides scientific methods and techniques in developing individual and community relationship and the development of personal, family and social value system.

Home Science in Changing Scenario

There is a paradigm shift from traditional home making to universal application of science, technology and social sciences in making a family, a society and nation peaceful, happy and progressive-from domesticity to modernity. Home making to-day should have a background of scientific training to compete with an ever growing world with challenges both at home and in work spots. There is a shift from restricted, traditional domestic care and maternal roles to a wider role outside the home. A home maker wants to maintain her house with the least possible strain as she has to play the double role for which she needs good training and preparedness. This is possible only through a well formulated, updated Home Science curriculum, revising as often as possible.

Living style is constantly changing; hence change is needed in role performance and role expectations of a home maker. Cooking, house keeping, sewing, laundry, care of sick and sanitation are modernised by applying scientific theory and technology which expect the home maker to have the knowledge of applied as well as basic sciences and its application at home. Women have started playing equal role in agriculture, administration, business, management of restaurants, professions, as executives, economics, scientists, designer and decorator of house, dress and environment, nutritionist and dietitian, curriculum planner and executor, teacher, researcher, extension worker, development and welfare activist, leader and nation builder. So, Home Science can not be exclusively for women alone. It should be taught to both boys and girls without gender discrimination. Women are no more home makers only though it also involves all these roles to be played by them at home for which payment in cash is not made. A recent study shows that if a home maker is to be paid for her services at home it will be the highest paid profession in the world.

Need to Restructure the Curriculum

There is an urgent need to revamp and restructure the Home Science curriculum to suit the demands and the changes, so that it could attract both boys and girls to opt for this course. It is the responsibility of the curriculum planners and the teachers to understand the changing trends and scenario in life style, the role expectations and performance at home, in the community and the nation. It is thus important to modify the curriculum to suit these changing trends. Promoting life skills in food industry, textile technology and apparel, beautician, advocacy and standardisation of hospitality, human development, care and education, services, reading labels and advertising should become the focal points while restructuring the curriculum. Curriculum development Committee of UGC for Home Science reviewed the present curriculum followed in various Universities and updated by incorporating multidisciplinary skills, linking the general studies with professional courses and allowing vertical and horizontal academic mobility.

UGC's model curriculum envisages the need to go along with the tide so that the students are able to the earn their livelihood. Home science should also teach how to manage in emergency and in crisis like flood, famine, earth quake war and Tsunami which we never experienced before. These situations demand a new approach in designing the houses, food to be consumed, type of clothes to be worn, conservation, preservation and rationing of various commodities-food, clothes, and other things. Patterns of consumerism, farming and processing of farm products and their distribution along with appropriate education should also be aimed at. If we have the right type of knowledge and the ability we can raise to the occasion by providing knowledge, and skills to deal with all these situations, enable them to be not only employable but also social activists, sensitive, and responsible entrepreneurs.

Technology is introduced by incorporating applied science into different activities like clothing, food preparation, food storage, home marking, energy saving, power generation, computer and telephone. Home scientist should develop competence in maintaining these equipment. It should also address population growth and its impact on food, housing, health care, effect of science and technology on quality of life, care of dependent persons, role expectations and performance, position of women and men at home, special care of high risk groups at home and society, education for all age groups, balance between technology development and the environmental stewardship by using resources without destroying future supplies. As Dr Green says Home science should work predominantly in a preventive educational and developmental mode rather than a remedial mode.

Curriculum revision should also be based on the needs of students, the society, nation, changing trends in other disciplines, research findings, advancement in science and technology and their applicability in modern life. A participatory approach in curriculum planning by involving the stakeholders—the students, teachers, the consumers and the community will be more helpful to have a paradigm shift from domesticity to modernity.

Strategies of Teaching Home Science

Depending on the audience-the learners, objectives, the topics, duration and infrastructure facilities available we should choose diverse methods of teaching. The audience learners who learn Home science, purpose of their learning and the topics vary. It is a subject taught to people with varied background illiterate, literate, farmers, homemakers, public, parents, students and teachers. We cannot follow particular technique or strategy to teach all the units or topics in the subject. We have to choose the technique to different groups depending on the nature of topics. As far as Home science is concerned it is taught to improve their living conditions and disseminate new concepts and skills for adoption.

Though there are conventional methods of teaching like lecturing, demonstration exhibition, discussion, debate and dialogue, there are the latest techniques of print and electronic media that could be used to teach Home science more effectively. Electronic, media-ICT sucha as Radio,

Television, Video, films and computers could be used to disseminate new knowledge in Home Science, But what ever technique be used to impart the new knowledge, we should ensure that hands on experiences are provided so that the learners can develop the skills. Effective and efficient teachers with aptitude for teaching and faith in the subject alone can make Home Science more interesting and useful.

Areas of Research in Home science

Home Science being a recent discipline comprising various components from bacteriology to human behaviour we have vast scope for multifaceted researches in Home science. Inter disciplinary researches in Home science will be highly socially relevant, need based and the results could be applied directly in everyday life.

It is found that more than one third of malnourished children 57 million out of 146 million children are in India. It is therefore; felt that we may not be able to achieve the Millennium Development Goal of halfing child hunger by 2025. Six lakhs deaths every year could be averted with simple health interventions along with correct feeding habits. One out of every 3 adult women is underweight with a risk of giving birth to lower weight babies. All these could be reverted if Home Scientists take action researches with advocacy on importance of nutrition and low cost diets. If mothers are educated on importance of giving colostrums to new born with 6 months breast feeding infant mortality rate could be reduced. It is just one example to show how interdisciplinary researches in Home science could be of highly valuable to the society.

There are other areas Home science that lend themselves to need based Human development researches-child care services and education, consumerism-consumer behaviour in relation to food, clothing and housing, food conservation, preparation, distribution, handling and marketing, micro nutrient supplementation choices and planning in food, clothing and housing, mass production and proper distribution of nutritious diet at lower cost, running a well planned restaurant, planning human resources etc.

Unlike other disciplines where the choices of researches are limited, Home Science is open to wider application oriented areas of researches. Home Scientists should come out to take up researches of interdisciplinary and multidisciplinary nature so that the fruits of these studies will be directly useful to the society.

Career Options in Home Science

In the modern world the occupational choices have become wide and certain jobs require specific and specialised knowledge and skills that are promoted by subjects students. Especially at the higher education level, students of Home science, feel that their future in the employment market is not very bright when compared to the other areas of specialisation. Home scientists could have a wider choice in the job market. He\She can play a crucial role in nation building activities as her\his specialisation has a wide range of subjects which are directly related to the life both traditional and modern. Emerging areas in Home Science would attract many careers, provided we excel and prove our efficiency. Career need not always be an employment under some one. There are many areas in which Home scientists themselves could become job providers by becoming entrepreneur and self employed.

During the early years Home Science education prepared women to become efficient home makers and teachers. Many joined careers in welfare programme, extension services, industries, have started beautician clinics, hospitals, hotels, hostels and restaurants as managers and executives. When there was a critical bridge in 20th century by restructuring Home Science curriculum from domesticity to modernity, the emerging areas have adopted and become a discipline of its own like textile technology, food industry, interior decoration etc. and started attracting students as they could get employment in these fields easily. Hotel industry has become highly popular where in what is learnt in Food and Nutrition and Resource or Home management the core components are. If these subjects are suitably restructured employment opportunities in hotel industry will also be more.

People are highly health conscious today. Nutritionists could start Nutrition Clinics to guide and counsel by preparing and selling appropriate diets for various age groups, and health conditions. By starting Nutrition clinics they could also give employment to many. Specialisation in mass production of nutritious and low cost diet would also attract self employment. Small and big business houses to day require people with intelligent, quick thinking and decision making capacity. Home Science promotes these qualities among students thus they will be in great demand.

Talented and committed Home Scientists can also become scientists and economists and play vital role in building the economy of the country. They can design houses, dresses and curriculum to suit various sections of the society. Teaching and research attract many even to-day. Many are employed in social welfare departments of the Government and Non Government programmes and many started welfare programmes and schools to the needy and deserving population.

Home scientists should therefore, feel that they have a pivotal role to play in different spectrum of activities in the society. Home science can attract the youth by providing challenging programmes which will help them get not only a degree but also the competence to earn their livelihood.

Conclusion

Every one of us who are in Home science education should feel that we should not be conservative; we should have progressive positive thinking and action to make the course more meaningful and attractive. Home Science curriculum, teaching strategies followed and researches undertaken are to be periodically revised and updated to suit the changing scenario so that it becomes need based and popular among the youth and the parents. The goals of teaching Home Science should be broadened and achieved through our untiring efforts. We should take a vow that all of us will work to achieve these goals and make Home Science education inevitable for sustainable development.

I would like to quote Dr Armaity Desai, former Chairperson of UGC, who stated in her inaugural address at the Biennial Conference of Home Science Association of India in 1995, "The quality of life of society and family determines positive functioning. Home Science has a vital role to play in increasing role to play for a better quality of life through the competences they develop as graduates. Not only are they empowered through such competence based career development, but in turn they can extend it through their work to the community and vulnerable groups, thus leading to social and economic development."

35

Parenting Practices and a Conflict Free World

To maintain a joyful family requires much frcm both the parents and the children. Each member of the family has to become, in a special way, the servant of the others.

— Pope John Paul II

Parenting practices refer to the methods and styles of parenting followed to control and socialise children including disciplining tactics, supervision and monitoring of the children. Certain parenting practices and parent child relationships can increase the conflict among children leading to youth violence. It has been identified that one of the strongest predictors of youth violence is early childhood conflicts and aggression. It is therefore important to address family factors related to the learning of aggression in childhood to effectively prevent youth violence, and a conflict free world.

Conflict and violence among the children and youth is a major social issue in the modern world causing anxiety in the world. The prevalence of violence among youth gives concern to everyone in the world, whether developed, developing or under developed. The tendency of youth to become violent has the relationship with child upbringing or parenting, behaviour/style. Violence is a behaviour which is unacceptable and condemned everywhere around the world. However, it occurs almost every day and everywhere. The outcome of violence is broader than physical injury or causing disability; violence is a psychological and social problem.

The childrearing lays the foundation for adult personality. If children see the parents disapproving of the use of violence to solve interpersonal problems then they are more likely not to engage in violent behaviour. Studies show that 40 per cent of the parents indicated that they would permit their child to hit back if another person pushes him or her; some parents, advise their child to fight back when they are provoked is the best way to make their child safe. Using corporal punishment as a disciplining method by parents increased the youth violence. Seeing parents using corporal punishment may suggest to young children that the use of physical force in dealing with a problem is normal. Parents should therefore, clearly communicate to their children how to resolve conflicts without resorting to violence and display these skills themselves by avoiding the use of physical punishment.Un acceptable Parental behaviour results in cheating others or telling lies, bulling or is cruel or mean to others, not feeling sorry after misbehaving, breaking things deliberately, disobedient at school and has trouble in getting along with teachers.

Quality of the Parent-Child Relationship

Oscar Wilde says "Children begin by loving their parents; as they grow older they judge them; sometimes they forgive them."

Children need more models than of critics, to shape themselves. Within these family contexts, children gradually internalise social standards and expectations, which facilitate, in turn, greater self regulation skills and responsibility. Families are the primary setting in which children's lives are shaped and determined. The parenting behaviours and discipline processes are central to the process of the socialisation of children at home environment. Within these family contexts, children gradually internalise social standards and expectations, which facilitate, in turn, greater self regulation skills and responsibility.

Children who experience rejection, neglect, or indifference from parents are more likely to display aggressive behaviour. Psychological aggressive strategies such as shouting, yelling or swearing at a child are commonly used by many parents; they hit a child and call a child stupid or lazy. Neglectful parents are unresponsive to the needs of children and demands. If children are neglected they show higher levels of conflict and violent behaviour than physically abused children. One reason for engaging in violence is to gain attention from their parents. In contrast, parents who are warm and supportive have children with less conflict and less aggressive. Thus the quality of the parent-child relationship also influences child aggression and violence. Consistentancy in discipline practices have been linked to lower levels of aggression and violence. In contrast problematic discipline practices and erratic expressions of anger promote aggression in children. Children who do not feel attached to their parents fail to internalize the parents' values, bonds and those of the society resulting in poor self control. High parental monitoring is associated with lower levels of aggression, conflict, violence, and delinquency among children and adolescents. Monitoring refers to parents knowing where their children are, with whom they are associating, and what they are doing. Good supervision allows parents to respond appropriately to antisocial and delinquent behaviours.

Physical force by the parent provides external controls to which children can attribute their compliance and therefore can avoid misbehaviours to avoid future punishment, but physical force does not teach children the responsibility to behave independently in morally and socially acceptable ways. The cultural context of parenting plays a role in determining the impact various parenting practices have on children. Cultures also have a vital role to play in disciplining behaviour of parents. Certain cultures accept and follow different types of discipline methods. Corporal punishment generally is viewed less favorably and may send the message that the parent is rejecting the child. Parental warmth is also expressed differently in different cultures. Therefore, how messages are communicated by their parents to the children at their early years may differ according to the cultural context in which the child is reared.

The Impact of Parenting Styles on the Personality of Children

As Margaret Mead states "Children must be taught how to think, not what to think." This is being executed parenting and parenting styles followed at home. Parenting styles, characterised as Authoritarian, Permissive, Democratic or Neglecting. It describes parental involvement and plays a role in the development of cognitive and social competence of children. Parental values and needs are associated with variations in child-rearing styles and the discipline responses of parents to their children One of the overarching goals of effective parenting is to support children's development– from dependency and external control to internalisation, the ability to take initiative and to be socially responsible. Children gradually internalise social standards and expectations, a process that facilitates greater self-regulation skills and responsibility for their own behaviours from the family setting.

Authoritarian Parenting

Authoritarian parenting styles generally lead to children who are obedient and proficient, but they rank lower in happiness, social competence and self-esteem. The authoritarian style of parenting is characterised by a dominating attitude rather than a nurturing attitude. Threats, yelling and punishment are the tools of communication by such parents. Consequently, it is assumed that children may imbibe such methods of communication which may dispose the child to violent behaviour. Authoritarian parenting styles generally lead to children who are obedient and proficient, but they rank lower in happiness, social competence and self-esteem. There is a common saying that if a child is constantly being beaten even for the slightest mistake, the child gets used to beating.

Authoritative Parenting

Authoritative parenting styles tend to result in children who are happy, capable and successful (Maccoby, 1992). Authoritative parenting style designated as was found to correlate well with successful socialisation of children. Authoritative parenting is characterised by warmth and reasoning, compared with authoritarian parenting, characterised by high levels of control. Maccoby, (1992) says that Authoritative parenting styles tend to result in children who are happy, capable and successful. Authoritative parenting recognises the child's need for control and individuality, views the rights and duties of parents and children as complementary, and is characterised by sensitivity to children's capabilities and the developmental tasks they face in happiness and self-regulation. These children are more likely to experience problems with authority and tend to perform poorly in school.

Permissive Parenting

Permissive parents, sometimes referred to as indulgent parents, have very few demands to make of their children. These parents rarely discipline their children because they have relatively low expectations of maturity and self-control. Permissive parenting often results in children who rank low in happiness and self-regulation. Permissive parents are generally nurturing and communicative with their children, often taking on the status of a friend more than that of a parent. These children are more likely to experience problems with authority and tend to perform poorly in school. Permissive parenting often results in children who rank low.

Uninvolved Parenting

Uninvolved parenting styles rank lowest across all life domains. These children tend to lack self-control, have low self-esteem and are less competent than their peers. An uninvolved parenting style is has few demands, low responsiveness and little communication. While these parents fulfill the child's basic needs, they are generally detached from their child's life. In extreme cases, these parents may even reject or neglect the needs of their children.

The parenting style adopted by a parent determines his or her child's disposition to violence. Every child has a tendency to engage in one act of violence at a time, but effective parenting puts it at a minimal and allows the child to develop social competence of the child. The goals that adults set for themselves as parents on one hand and the methods employed in reaching those goals on the other decide their child rearing practices. Some potential causes of these differences in parenting include culture, personality, family size; parental background, socioeconomic status, educational level and religion. Children of un involved parents tend to lack self-control, have low self-esteem and are less competent than their peers.

The four parenting styles and their characteristics could be summed up as:

Authoritative (high-control, high-responsive);

Authoritarian (high-control, low-responsive);

Permissive-indulgent (low-control, high-responsive) and

Permissive- neglectful (low-control, low-responsive).

Domestic Violence

Domestic violence is a big social problem that impacts every segment of the population. Since parents and the entire family setting are a major influence on the child it is imperative to find out how their styles of parenting dispose a child towards conflict and violence, in order to curb or reduce its occurrence. The threat and enforcement of physical punishment has been a tried and tested method of preventing violence. Children who live with domestic violence face increased risks: the risk of exposure to traumatic events, the risk of neglect, the risk of being directly abused, and the risk of losing one or both of their parents. All these may lead to negative outcomes for children and may affect their well-being, safety, and stability.

Childhood problems associated with exposure to domestic violence fall into three primary categories: Behavioural, social, and emotional problems. Higher aggression, anger, hostility, oppositional behaviour, disobedience; fear, anxiety, withdrawal, depression; poor peer-sibling, social relationships; and low self-esteem. Lower cognitive functioning, poor school performance, lack of conflict resolution skills, limited problem solving skills, pro-violence attitudes, and belief in rigid gender stereotypes and male privilege are also responsible for domestic violence. Higher levels of adult depression and trauma symptoms, increased tolerance and use of violence in adult relationships also lead to domestic violence. The following factors are linked with youth violence hyperactivity, impulsiveness, poor behavioural control, attention problems, history of early aggressive behaviour and low educational achievement. Some of the key family factors associated with adolescent violence are:

(1) Poor supervision of children by parents and harsh physical punishment to discipline children, (2) parental conflict in early childhood, (3) low level of attachment between parents and children, (4) a mother who had her first child at an early age, (5) experiencing parental separation or divorce at a young age, (6) a low level of family cohesion and (7) low socioeconomic status of the family.

The following Social, political and cultural factors could be attributed for youth violence: Gangs, easy availability of guns and drugs; low levels of social cohesion within a community; The quality of a country's governance its laws and the extent to which they are enforced, as well as policies for social protection. Factors such as inequality in income, rapid demographic, changes in the youth population and urbanization have all been positively linked with youth violence. Cultures that do not provide non-violent alternatives for resolving conflicts appear to have higher rates of youth violence.

Children who witness domestic violence and are physically abused are at risk for increased levels of emotional and psychological maladjustment than children who only witness violence and are not abused. Reduction or elimination of corporal punishment could have major benefits for children and for reducing conflicts and antisocial behaviour in society. If a child is spanked after the more likely the child will display antisocial behaviours like cheats or telling lies, bullying or is cruel or mean to others, does not feel sorry after misbehaving, breaks things deliberately, disobedient at school and difficulty in getting along with teachers. It has also been linked to low self-esteem, depression and low educational attainment.

Prevention of Violence

"Violent behaviour is defined as intentional physically aggressive behaviour against another person." Violence is a behaviour which is unacceptable and totally condemned everywhere around the world. However, it occurs almost every day and almost everywhere. It is inherent in humans. The tendency of youth to become violent may have to do with child upbringing, which is embedded in parenting behaviour. Violence by young people is one of the most visible forms of violence. Youth violence deeply harms not only its victims, but also their families, friends and communities. The outcome of violence is broader than physical injury or disability, but identifies violence as a psychological and social problem. Violence is the use of physical force or power, threatened or actual, against a person, or against a group or community that either results in or has a high likelihood of resulting in injury, death, psychological harm, mal development or deprivation. Violence, however, is preventable. Its causes are complex and occur at different levels. Evidence shows that there is a strong relationship between levels of violence and modifiable factors such as poverty, income, and gender inequality, use of alcohol, and the absence of safe, stable, and nurturing relationships between children and parents. Poverty increases violence by causing a sense of desperation. In other words, hunger is a powerful force that can drive a person to violence.

It is also deserved that the life skills acquired in social development programmes can reduce involvement in violence, improve social skills, boost educational achievement and improve job prospects. Promotion of life skills such as social, emotional, and behavioural competencies help children and adolescents effectively deal with the challenges of everyday life.

World Health Organisation defines youth as people between the ages of 10 and 29 years. Youth violence refers to violence occurring between youths, and includes acts that range from bullying and physical fighting, through more severe sexual and physical assault to homicide. Youth violence has a serious, lifelong, impact on a person's psychological and social functioning. Youth violence greatly increases the costs of health, welfare and criminal justice services; reduces productivity; decreases the value of property; and generally undermines the fabric of society. It is also observed that religious and political ideologies have been the cause of interpersonal violence. Life skills and social development programmes and proper parenting helps children and adolescents manage anger, resolve conflict, and develop the necessary social skills to solve problems; schools-based anti-bullying prevention programmes; and programmes to reduce access to alcohol, illegal drugs and guns.

Parenting Education

Teaching parents effective methods of parenting has been found to reduce child and adolescent, conflict, delinquency and aggression. Teaching parents to use consistent disciplining method and to monitor their children reduces behaviour problems. A more responsive, warm style of parenting has also been associated with lower levels of aggression in children. Preventive efforts in early childhood are generally more effective than later interventions in reducing aggression. We must help our children break away and free from negative cultural and media conditioning that creates aggression and conflict. It is necessary to provide them the skills, an effective conflict education curriculum that is developmentally appropriate; and key issues including raising a peaceful male child in a violent world; the effect of media violence on children; school bullies; dating violence; and empowering adolescent girls to refuse to be the victim of rape.

Children are like sponges. What ever they take in has to do with moral values and character. Books, songs, TV, the Internet, are continually delivering messages that are moral and immoral to our children. As parents we must control the flow of ideas and images that are influencing our children they should not quarrel or make nuisances before children; do not encourage them to pick up argument, and abuse other children. Train them to be polite, kind and tactful. Punish with a loving heart. Unnecessary and unwanted punishment results in guilt-ridden parents and self-indulgent, Children must understand what punishment is for and know that its source is parental love. Parents should learn to listen to children. Influencing their lives is one of the greatest things we can do. Helping our children become good students also builds strong character. Make a big deal out of the family meal at the dinner table is not only a place of sustenance and family business but also a place for the teaching and passing on of our values a process of socialisation of children. Manners and rules are subtly absorbed over the table. Family mealtime should communicate and sustain ideals that children will follow throughout their lives. Do not reduce character education to words alone. We gain virtue through practice. Parents should help children by promoting moral action through self-discipline, good work habits, kind and considerate behaviour to others, and community service.

Conclusion

To conclude, to reduce conflict and violence among children and youth we need to strengthen families, enhance positive relationships with adults, encourage a sense of connection with school and improve academic performance of children. We also need to reduce weapon carrying, school problems and emotional distress. Parents and the environment they provide at the home can make or mar the child in terms of behaviour. Child welfare advocates and service providers should share areas of common ground that can bridge the gap between them–parents, children and the community. To end violence against adults and children, ensure children's safety and protect them so that they are not harmed by the violence. In order to promote parents' strengths in their parenting behaviour we should not concentrate only on organising programs for students in the school but should also organise preventive counseling programs for parents, to promote a healthy environment at home and, a positive parenting will lead to a violent free and peaceful world at large. It is essential to know and accept what Dorothy Law Neite said: "Children Learn What They Live":

If a child lives with criticism, he learns to condemn.

If a child lives with hostility, he learns to fight.

If a child lives with ridicule, he learns to be shy.

If a child learns to feel shame, he learns to feel guilty.

If a child lives with tolerance, he learns to be patient.

If a child lives with encouragement he learns confidence

If a child lives with praise, he learns to appreciate.

He a child lives with fairness, he learns justice.

If a child lives with security, he learns to have faith.

If a child lives with approval, he learns to like himself.

If a child lives with acceptance and friendship, he learns to find love in the world.

36

Opportunities and Challenges before the Youths

"The ultimate measure of a man is not where he stands in moments of comfort and convenience, but where he stands at times of challenge and controversy."

— Martin Luther King

Dawn of a New Life

Plato, a great philosopher and an eminent educational thinker who says "By education I mean that training in excellence from youth upward which makes a man passionately desire to be a perfect citizen, and teaches him to rule, and to obey, with justice. This is the only education which deserves the name". "Young men have to spring into sphere of action and strive to the best for building up of a resurgent India and a happy peaceful world." Baba.

As Sir Roger L. Esrange says "It is not the place, nor the condition, but the mind alone, which can make anyone happy or miserable." Make every opportunity to your favour and every obstacle as a stepping stone to progress. There is nothing in world witch comes without challenge. Challenge is the core of all human activity. If there is an ocean, we cross it, if there is disease, we cure it, if there is a record we break it and if there is a mountain we climb it. Only when we realise that true happiness lies in enjoying the present, without having anxiety about the future, it will be a real joy.

Hope on the Youth

India is the great country of youth and it is fully dependent on them. If the youth of India is strong, our country need not be afraid of other world power. If youth will become unhealthy and weak they can not safeguard our nation. If all youth will do all work with co-ordination and co-operation, then that day is not very far when whole world will see us with the eye of honour and respect. As Swami Vivekananda during his true calling to youth said "with patriotism must be associated with a real feeling for others that will make our youth to shine in the world".

The Nation recognises the vital role of the youth in nation-building by promoting and protecting their physical, moral, spiritual, intellectual and social well-being. It is to inculcate in the youth patriotism and nationalism; and encourage their involvement in public and civic affairs. The role of the education system, as the cornerstone is of paramount in the development and progress of youth and will continue to utilise their energy and wisdom in nation building activities. As Swami Vivekananda said we must produce men with character, muscles of iron and nerves of steel, gigantic wills which nothing can resist, which can penetrate into the mysteries and secretes of the universe and accomplish their purpose in any fashion.

The Government through various agencies provides opportunities to youth to be active partners in nation-building through youth programmes and projects that will develop and harness their potentials and enable them to be of great service to their country. They have to challenge the social mores such as untouchability, economic and social inequality that mar the mass in the country. The government spends a lot on the development of youth annually to get all the modern facilities and to provide best form of education to make every youth to be sure that his/her future is safe and bright.

Today's education system is alienating the youth from the world around. Education, instead of being a force for liberation, often turns into an instrument of oppression, suppression and binds them to be the slaves of money, position, power and make them shut their eyes from the realities of life and their responsibility to the society. The antidote for this has to be an alternate education, a humanising, liberating the mind, power, moral, and social with commitment to their society. We have to pull down the walls of alienation and facilitate the community and the educational institutions getting seamlessly woven together into a fabric of unity. The education system today divides, discriminates and fragments the society. It alienates the youth from his/her own family/community. The seeds of a better world, of love, friendship, compassion, beauty, creativity, freedom, equality and democracy should be sown and nurtured in the minds of youth by improving and training the senses, mental and logical faculties of the young and emergetic youth. We have to take up the monumental task of placing before the young students the world of raw reality and empower her/him to understand, analyse, challenge and finally transforming this world into an egalitarian world. Thus the education of human being should begin at his/her birth and continue throughout, life till the last breath. Infact education begins with education of mother who carries the could. Her thoughts are beautiful and pure, her feelings always noble and fine; her environment is simple and harmonous so that the child in the wombs is developed as a harmoniously as possible, with all the divine qualities.

In a few years' time all of us will have left behind the potholed roads, blocked drains, century-old houses and will have moved onto some other place. Many of us will be living outside India in some "developed country" or in "posh areas" of this country with no concern about the places that we all will leave behind. But many will be working not for themselves but for the country, leaving most of the luxuries aside. Going by the new age mantra, rural areas, which are generally backward, can provide a huge market to serve for the weelleesing of humanity for many who are young today.

Plan for the Future

So the new plans for are development designed not only for the ever-rising global, urban rich and middle class but for the rural folk who constitute nearly 75 per cent of India's population. Information technology has been taken to every corner of the country by youth who want to see their childhood town developed and to gain something out of it. For many, it is a paradox that a country so rich in history, culture and talent could have been under-performing economically, and Brain drain is no longer. Ask children today about their dreams for the future and they want to be engineers, doctors, pilots, fashion designers, architects, sports persons and businessmen. This was unthinkable a few years back. It underlines the increasing number of options available to youth today. But does our education make them think of the masses who are deprived of many of these luxuries available to the people in rural area from where many of them would have come from.

There is a huge urban/rural divide rich/poor, employed/unemployed and developed/non-developed. This has led to the problem of anxiety and violence. It has been identified as the single largest problem the country is facing today and it is most widespread with unemployed youth. The origin of this owes to the penury that stems from all pervasive poverty in India. This is fueled by the exploitation of a section of the officials, the peasants, poor tribal and the educated, unemployed, youth are the victims to these.

However, these violent actions don't pave the way for peaceful rule and life because after securing freedom through violent means they don't live in peace. So today's youth face more challenges and threats than any generation before them. We have to set long-term goals of community-based Youth development initiatives to improve the long-term life chances of young people so that they become economically self-sufficient, be healthy, have good family and social relationships, and contribute to the growth and development of their community They must learn to be productive by doing well in education, development of positive attitude, interests in welfare of others and acquire basic life skills needed to lead peaceful, productive and useful life.

Creating career paths for the Low-Skilled students and under achievers will help them get the confidence that they could stand on their own legs in future by receiving skill based education that will secure a job for them and earn their livelihood A statewide networking of such educational institutions will help to evolve strategies, insights and experiences across the state/country which will be a morale booster for the youth. Making available the opportunity at an affordable cost focusing on increasing productivity within higher education, particularly in colleges and universities will build the confidence in youth It will also make them use taxpayer's money properly and be accountable to the society.

Every Problem has a Solution

By providing adequate nutrition, health services, shelter, and multiple supportive services/relationships with adults and peers, challenging activities and learning experiences will be more meaningful opportunities for the youth for their involvement and membership in the society. Physical and emotional safety provided by parents and families will encourage the youth to have social commitment. Never try to avoid the problem, but help them to face the problem. Consider every problem as an opportunity for growth and development.

Never be afraid to try something new. Remember, amateurs built the ark. Professionals built the Titanic. Begin now to do some thing that will lead you to a great destiny; don't hesitate, and don't be afraid of criticism from any corner. Similarly as Jack Handey says "Before you criticise someone, you should walk a mile in their shoes. That way when you criticize them, you are a mile away from them and you have their shoes." "The obstacles you face today are mental barriers which can be broken by adopting a more tactful techniques". "The block of granite which was an obstacle in the pathway of the weak becomes a stepping-stone in the pathway of the strong."

Face the challenges boldly and be an optimist as there is nothing which is "impossible." You can make everything possible with your will power. There are no great people in this world, only great challenges which ordinary people rise to meet.

"If you think you are beaten, you are.

If you think you dare not, you don't!

If you think you'll lose, you're lost;

Success begins with a fellow's will."

As Abraham Lincoin says "Determine that things can and shall be done, and then we shall find the way". Always try to be positive; think positively and act positively to create a society with happiness and contentment. The giver of this life gave it to be happy, not for suffering. You must always remember that "you are born to be happy, enjoy life to full and be an optimist always. What ever you can doer dream you can begin it which will lead to action. Boldness has genious, power, and magic in it. So begin it now itself without wasting time, making every minute as precious as possible to contribute to the world. It should be a continuous effort till you reach your goal as swami Vivekananda gives a clarion call to the youth."

"Araise, Awake, and stop not till the goal is reached".

37

Structural Violence and Society

"Violence can be overcome only through Non- Violence Training in Ahimsa requires purity of heart and soul force. A votary of Non-Violence will not let the slightest hint of violence to enter into his heart."

— ***Mahatma Gandhi***

Gandhiji said "if we want to bring about peace in the world, there is no other way except that of non-violence". This requires universal acceptance. Gandhiji chalked out the plan to use this weapon of non-violence and non-cooperation, not only for India but the whole world to follow. His approach became true many adopted this method in the world to attain freedom, solve communal and racial issues even in the western part of the world and in South Africa. His concept of non-violence was not only merely a theory, it was put into practice during the struggle for independence in the political arena and to carry on the struggle for realisation of achieving social and economic causes like, from imperfection to perfection, from ignorance to enlightment and from oppression to liberation.

The world to-day faces multidimensional crisis such as multi-nationlisation, proliferation and global arms race, uneven development, poverty, hunger, environmental degradation, communal race and religious clashes, degradation of moral values and internal or personal violence are competing to take the world to the edge of annihilation, due to selfish infests of individuals. Unless there is united effort and action from all corners of the globe this will become a grave issue and difficult to save the world from these crises. "We should remember that be the change you want to see in the world". Before we preach others to follow. There can be real change and happiness only when what you think, what you say and what you do are in harmony".

The Structural Violence and Causes

"Direct violence is horrific, but its brutality usually gets our attention: we notice it, and often respond to it. Structural violence however, is almost always invisible, embedded in ubiquitous social structure, normalised by stable and regular experience". (Deborah Du Nann Winter and Dana Lerghton 1999). It occurs when the people do not get what they require or eligible to get in politics, social, legal or cultural traditions. This structural inequalities also lead to suffering and death as in direct violence, but it is slow, more subtle but more difficult to get it repaired.

John Gatlung defined structural violence as any constraint on human potential due to economic and political structures. Unequal access to resources, to political power, education, health care, or to legal standing". We could observe unequal distribution of these resources in structural violence, which may lead to direct violence-physical and psychological. This structural violence, which is invisible, will result in social injustice leading to poverty, hunger, infant morality, diseases, unemployment, low wages, war, deaths, destruction of neighbourhood and ecosystem. Especially girls and women are denied their access to resources when there is structural violence in these areas.

Global economy that concentrates more on production of weapons and strengthens its army will lead to structural violence. If growth of global market creates a just society where every one will have an access to their requirement the market economy, social justice, personal satisfaction etc. will grow. Or else it will result in structural violence and every body will follow mono-culture. People will start thinking that good life means, having all comforts, conveniences, following western style of living, western values of individuality and consumerism. Inadequacy, if felt and there is poverty and hunger, physical and psychological structural violence will result in exploitative, unjust social, political and economic systems.

Forms of Structural Violence

All forms of violence-physical, economic, racial, religious, social, and ideological and others that block the progress of human race is called structural violence. Violence also has other forms between groups (social violence) and between individuals (interpersonal violence).

Physical Violence

When some one causes physical injuries or inflicts pain or disturbs vital function that leads to death is called physical violence. Physical violence occurs in the forms of war, terrorism, assault, aggression (physical) rioting, torture, rape, physical punishment, death due to hunger, pollution of natural resources, adulteration of food and suicide by individuals or groups. Hunger is a kind of violence against current and future generation. Environmental degradation is a form of violence against nature, and future as well.

Racial Violence

If any one damages others due to racial difference, customs, appearance, community etc. it is called racial violence. It may be due to ego as superior or inferior of race, caste, or community, discrimination due to colour, appearance, slavery etc.

Economic Violence

When there is inequality in distribution of resources the society denies economic rights, rising unemployment, poverty leads to economic violence. This is reflected in monopolisation, exploitation, bonded labour, fraud, bribery, over pricing, adulteration of consumer goods underemployment, robbery, hoarding things in demands etc.

Religious Violence

Religious violence occurs when some one is assaulted or beaten or spoken ill of an individual or group due to religious difference where there is religious violence; there is religious intolerance, fanaticism, fundamentalism, defamation, untouchability, discrimination, holy wars, excommunication etc. On many occasions religious violence hurts the freedom, happiness and development of individuals, through blackmail, threat, and violence, individuals, some time specific religious groups are the suffers.

Psychological Violence

When an individual harms others psychologically, mentally, morally or emotionally there is psychological violence. Threats, promotion of terror, hate, forced imposition, brainstorming through false or negative propaganda, promoting false values through mass media, biased education, censorship in certain areas of knowledge or information or culture are some of the forms of expression of psychological violence.

Moral Violence

Any person who does not prevent the occurrence of violence is also responsible for moral violence to occur. Those who are indifferent, selfish, self centered, lack communication, sensibility, egoism and to 'mind one's own business,' are responsible for inducing moral violence. People with solidarity, communication, voluntary action, interested in welfare of others and society is able to create moral values.

Internal Violence

Internal or personal violence means the violence that is experienced by any individual internally which leads to unhappiness, tension, mental disturbances etc. It has the following three main sources within the individual also 1. Past frustrations and negative memories, 2. Present disorientation, uncertain priorities, values, behaviour difficulties, poor self image or attitude and 3. Uncertainties and fear of future.

Internal violence is expressed through hatred, mistrust, frustration, negative memories, disorientation, insecurity, self enclosure, lack of communication, fears of losing things, of sickness, of old age, of death etc. lack of faith, purpose and actions. These sufferings of internal violence appear in two ways: (1) physical disturbances and illness and (2) external violence, in the form of aggressive behaviour on others.

Bronfenbrenner classifies structural violence into three systems; the socio-political (the macro system), the socio-environmental (the mesosystem) and the psychological (the micro system). These are found in individuals, in the state and its institutions.

Victims of structural violence: Everyday, innocent men, women and children mostly it is children and women are the invisible victims of structural violence. They are denied of their access to resources like health care, food, education, legal assistance and right to have access to political power as compared to boys and men. But this is not noticed by people as it is a sex biased society where males enjoy more power, prestige, and status than females. This patriarchy based structural violence will not be brought down unless women are given equal opportunity to make decisions about how to distribute resources equally. Thanks to the efforts taken by Mahatma Gandhi, Raja Ram Mohan Roy. Swami Vivekananda and others for bringing women to the fore front by fighting against the injustice done to them.

Economic and psychological structural violence impair at risk children. (Milton Schwebel and Daniel Christie). Children living in poverty have less opportunity for intellectual development as the parents of disadvantaged homes, are not able to provide adequate experiential content, learning atmosphere and intellectual mediation. It is therefore suggested that parents are provided with, better employment opportunities for better earning, good prenatal and medical care to the expectant mothers and high quality child care services along with education so that the next generation will develop into an intelligent, and caring citizens who are needed to create a peaceful world by reducing the expenditure on production and distribution of arms. If young children do not experience this structural violence we can be sure of a peaceful world.

People in developing countries, with low per capita income less than $1 a day (Millennium Development Goals) suffer more, the invisible structural violence, as they are under paid for their labour. This injustice to the labours in the global market economy leads to invisibility of injustice to the poor and the needy. The elite and the rich are least affected by any such structural violence. Wealth can not only buy a higher standard of living, it also buys life itself.

Towards a Peaceful Society

In order to establish a peaceful world as it is quoted below:

"Assemble, speak with one another

Let your minds be of one accord

May your prayer be common,

Common be your assembly,

Common the mind, common the thoughts,

Common be your aim, your heart be united,

Your mind be one, so that all live peacefully in harmony"

(Rig Veda X, 191-2 4 cf. Atharvanaveda VI – 64. 1-3)

Peace is not the mere absence of war but the full institutionalisation of violence free democratic and human rights based system where everyone has equal opportunities and access to development resources. We have forgotten that any kind of progress and growth should be based on humans and humility. Chronic, structural violence directly affects the children. Katheeri Kostelny and James Garbarino describe that chronic violence experienced by children due to war, suffer from environmental risk factors, including family violence, parental depression. Media violence and accessibility to fire arms produce violent environments to children. They become battle weary, numb and hopeless we need to build a strong community support system. The society should come forward to provide family visitation and early child hood care and education to all children, especially those who are poor, and in distress. This community intervention mechanism will reduce the effects of structural violence.

Steps to Reduce Structural Violence

Reduction of arms and race after weapons will ensure reduction in structural violence and provide adequate food, health care service, education, living wages, social and cultural protection, alleviate sexism and build lasting peace on earth. Hunger and poverty are the major two indicators of structural violence which are visible. A proper food and development policy with human consideration, framed will create a hunger free world, a new society in which people will live in peace and harmony and as Mahatma Gandhi said no one will go to bed with empty stomach. Deaths due to starvation and malnutrition will be reduced and there will be a society with peace.

Aspiration for material wealth has resulted in rich countries un certainly and depression. What is needed to day is the opportunity to live in peace. Gandhiji fought to come out of colonialism and oppression. Gandhiji's approach was civilisational, civilisation against modernised, western civilisation of industrial revolution. While fighting for independence, Gandhiji strived hard to open a new vista to the oppressor and the oppressed. He wanted both, to learn new lessons of peaceful co-existence. Gandhiji's spiritual life was searching and longing for an enriching spiritualism which will lead to a peaceful and better world. Gandhiji's faith and approach of struggle for realisation of imperfection to perfection, from ignorance to enlightenment and from oppression to liberation, holds good even today to move towards a world with peace and justice. Man today has command over science and technology that could be positively used to create a better, enlightened, peaceful future which is within our reach. At the same time man is in a fix. There are two signposts, one leading to destruction and annihilation and the other leading to peace, co-existence and non violence. It is the society to choose either of the two, for the future generation.

For Gandhiji exploitation of any kind, of man, woman and the child as well as of the nature is a violent action. Alarming disparities in incomes, over development and underdevelopment, denial of individual and societal needs, corruption, criminalisation communalism and consumerism are also considered as various forms of violence. These are to be mitigated to have a peaceful society. Modern peace researchers consider Mahatma Gandhi as a farsighted, sensitive and man of peace (Devarat N. Pathak).

The concept of structural violence is the product of social exploitation. According to Gandhiji a society will be a non-violent society if there is no exploitation including nature. He considered a society as non-violent, peaceful society where there will be no both, actor–oriented direct violence and system oriented structural violence. Gandhiji wanted to create a just social order where there will be freedom, justice and equality among various groups and individuals where substantial issues of conflict could be resolved peacefully through reconciliation and compromise with strength of human spirit and self suffering.

When Gandhiji wrote his famous book 'Swaraj' in 1908 he wrote that western civilisation was a short lived phenomena which exploited natural resources as well as mankind. Over production and over consumption are centered around the selfishness of man. Over use of earths' resources he felt that will lead to destruction and said "if free India would follow England, the natural resources, would be exhausted in 25 or 30 years." This has become true to day. Now we are starving for natural resources in India due to excessive consumption of natural resources. Gandhiji wanted to have a simple life without exerting pressure on earth. To day over pressure has made the nature furious resulting in earth quake, flood, deaths due to hunger, diseases etc. destroying the mankind. What Gandhiji said 60 years ago is true even to day and will be true for ever.

Today no nation can stand alone. Grave issues are posing threats to the human kind not in a particular country; they are global in nature. These issues cannot be solved by using violence, violence will lead to violence only. All the nations should come together to settle the issues in an amicable way, without using force or power. There should be international co-operation, interdepence and peaceful co-existence to save our human race and mother earth from disaster. Gandhiji was convinced that duty to be respectful towards all lives created by God. A strong ethical pulse of universal brotherhood he got from Christian commandment "Thou do not kill", further strengthened his conviction. He believed that a society that is built upon ethics, justice and non-violence will have more sustainability with strong network of social relationships.

Conclusion

In our attempt to create a peaceful world without violence, war, injustice, exploitation, inhuman activities and behaviour we may end up with a society which is either positive or negative. But it is to be remembered that to save human kind and the mother earth, it is the duty of everyone to adopt non-violence means, which is the only alternative to solve all the problems and save our mother earth:

> "Let the shalom spread to all your creature
>
> Let there be an end to hatred, jealousy,
>
> Competition between people
>
> Let there be only great love and Shalom between us all
>
> So that we can all gather together
>
> Everyone with their fellow
>
> Speaking to each other
>
> Learning the truth from each other".

38

Youth and Conflict Resolution

"When evil men plot, good men must plan. When evil men burn and bomb, good men must build and bind. When evil men shout ugly words of hatred, good men must commit themselves to the glories of love."

— Martin Luther King

The Youth of India which forms nearly one third of 91/3) of our Population is going to determine the future of the country. They are the key agents of social, economic and technological changes, development, innovations and torch bearers of change. The dynamic role played by the youth in the growth and prosperity of any country is extremely vital. They are to be aware of cultural, social, economic and political value system so that their contributions to uphold the ethos of the country will be made possible. They are to be directed and guided to channalise their energy and aggressive impulses. The law of love and the law of aggression which are responsible for a peaceful society should be properly defined.

Conflict–Meaning

"Since the first manifestation of creation of peace and harmony have been sought by human kind of the earth. Man has dreamt of to lead a peaceful life, yet conflicts and warfare have stained human life and brought the world at the threshold of disaster and risen (Kala Acharya 2003).

Conflict is an inevitable part of any relationships and emotions. It is the natural result of differences beet wear people on any issue. Conflict, though thought of a negative feeling, it has the potential to contribute positively to both relationship quality and personal development. Inter-personal conflict is charatersied by transmitted into constructive indignation." They should learn compassion and self-control to move towards to achieve the virutes and value system. When the youths are not guided and provided with a role model it will result in aggressive behaviour leading to conflicts and conflicts resolution. Opposition and disagreement with each other's cognitive, affective and psychomotor domains. Conflict arises when there are disputes and struggle for land, water, oil and other resources and disputes and over a religion or some ethnic issues or problems relating to one's pride, self-conceit, prejudice, jealosy, obstinancy stubbornness, delusion, greed, selfishness, intolerance and inability to forgive. Most of the conflicts emerge from political, ethnic, economic social and religious disputes. A regional disparity in terms of resource utilisation and human development also leads to conflict. If we want to build a strong and harmonious nation, it is inevitable to provide good model devoid of vested interests and formulate policies keeping in mind the ground realities.

Conflict Resolution

Conflict resolution is a formal procedure for settling problems in a way that let the youth on his dignity while letting others save theirs as well. Through a proper conflict resolution education we could improve the ability of the youth to communicate with each other to collaborate in problem solving, to manage and to youth to communicate with each other to collaborate in problem solving, to manage and to resolve their disagreement in a constructive and mutually satisfying (win/win) way. Self-efficiency and self-control are found to be significant predictors of conflict resolution styles learning scout competence to promote inter. Personal skills help integrate feelings, thinking and action in order to achieve specific socials miler personal goals. These skills include encoding and wiler pricing recreant social cues, anticipating consequences to an action and generating effective solutions to interpersonal problems. This attempt promotes and facilitate arbitration in disputes and an alternate approach to disputer resolution. They learn a safe construction way for persons in conflict to negotiate their differences by using problem solving techniques, referrals, conciliation techniques and mediation.

Objectives of Conflict Resolution Education for Youth

Learning to live and living to learn in the ever changing global environment is the true life long education. The increase in interpersonal conf–and conflict in the educational institutions has made it essential to resolve these differences for a peaceful coexistence and get along with each other.

Teaching youth the ways of managing conflict in a productive way help reduce the incidents of violent behaviour. Conflict resolution education is an important component of violence prevention and interventions programmes in the educational institutions, communities nation and the globe. It helps both the parties, recognise that even in the conflict situation, people can learn new skills to reduce conflicts in non-violent ways. Conflict Resolution education also helps to promote problem solving, decision making, effective communications critical and creative thinking, personal responsibilities towards peaceful cohesive society and self discipline. Understanding that peaceful education atmosphere promotes a climate that challenges youths and adults to believe and act on the belief that a diverse non-violence society should be the goal to be achieved. When the students are empowered with conflict resolution skills and strategy to regulate and control their own behaviour, they learn to accept differences and learn to articulate their feelings with greater self-control. This will help them to receive positive life skills and acquire positive behaviours to carry with them throughout their lives by learning to control their anger and react in a non-confrontational manner to defuse at tense situation which results in a satisfying experience in their lives. What is learnt in the educational institutions will go a long way while enhancing quality of life at home school and the community by reducing the disputes and violence in the educational institutions, the chronic absentees due to fear of violence, disciplinary actions and suspensions are reduced. This leads to self discipline, self esteem, self respect and personal responsibilities among the youths. Youths learn to handle disagreements with each other without letting their anger, and come out of control without using violence. The youth who learn to control their emotions and behave non-violently make friends more easily and become role models for others. Ultimately conflict resolution programme leads to a faith and commitment to peace and nonviolence prevents youths from inflicting violence, injury and damage to persons or properties. They are prevented from projecting their hatred upon others. When this hatred between the two groups takes the attitude reciprocally, the seeds of conflicts are sown. If understood positively and tolerated conflict situation is avoided.

Key Practices in Conflict Resolution

The following stragies could be the positive way of dealing with the conflicts among the youths and exposing them to conflict resolution techniques.

1. Make the youths distinguish between the position and interests. This includes understanding, individual positions in the issues leading to conflict. This may be relating to one's security and the well-being of her family. Every individual wants to achieve the positions, which he/she deserves.

2. Respect each other and face problems together. This implies that it is possible to help people shift their energies to focus on common concerns rather than seeing this as the problem.

3. Listen to understand each others. It is important that the focus on our attention on someone with the deep concern for improving and understanding rather than winning an argument. This procedure helps to mutual problem solving.

4. Youths are to be helped to choose approach–Peace is generated by the moment through some choices will help in solving the problem of conflict.

5. Make long term commitment to the conflict resolution which will be sustainable.

6. Use an integrated approach to resolve conflict–This implies that we need to apply many techniques simultaneously to drive away the conflict situations.

7. Be social entrepreneurs. Those who are socially conscious become creative thinkers, have a positive vision and develop achievable goals.

8. Become aware of local cultures. Success in conflict resolution is possible when we understand the culture of the individuals and communities and become partners with local people in conflict resolution.

9. Support and advance peace processes Participate with the local people by supporting them in peace making process and help them in decision making.

10. Take as many efforts as possible to reduce conflicting situations in the local communities.

11. Shifting attitudes and building foundation for peace. Understand the attitude and mind set of the youth and communities before initiating conflict resolution programme. This will become the foundation for peace education.

12. Equip communities to prevent and resolve conflicts by improving their skills and interest in decision making. This will prevent and resolve conflicts.

Strategies of Conflict Resolution

In all human relationships there are disagreements over resource allocations, roles and rights. In some we can arrive at acceptable compromises and adjustments. This is mostly in sharing the materials and in the social relationships. In these cases the traditional means of settlements – power bargaining, negotiations, mediation and arbitrations are followed. These methods could be utilised when there are disagreements over the resource allocations, roles and rights.

There are other cases where there cannot be compromises. Such as values, goals, groups identity and personal identities. Here we should understand that people are not able to sacrifice their identities and want to protect their territories. It is because of their struggle for recognition as persons from a particular ethnic group. These disputes and the conflicts which arise due to the personal and community identity are to be analysed for settlements. Disputes are those confrontations that could be settled by traditional means of negotiation or arbitrations whiles conflict are to be resolved by analytical processes.

Conflict analysis and resolution is a decision making process which avoids the necessity to rest on power on enforcement by getting into the source of problems and resolving them to satisfy all parties. Conflict analysis and resolution – describe a major shift in decision-making theory and practice from power theory to problem solving. This conflict resolution provides to have a holistic approach. Conflicts arising out of issues in economics can deal with the problem of unemployment as a means of inflation control law can focus on sources of problem; politics can redefine democracy and psychology can examine the consequences for individual structural violence.

Components of Conflict Resolution Education: It is identified that there are four general approaches to conflict resolution education – process curriculum, mediation, peaceable classroom, and peaceable school. These Strategies of conflict resolution education concentrates on what should be the principles and process of conflict resolution, education, and curriculum construction, the programme of negotiation for youth, staff and administrators. It tries to promote the skill among the peer group for mediation and thus creates a peaceable classroom and peaceable school.

Though conflict resolution concepts can be introduced as early as the preprimary level an intensive education programme as part of curriculum for youth at the higher education will be of great benefits to have a peaceful world by reducing disagreements, and arguments among different people and groups. As youth are getting ready to shoulder their responsibilities of nation building and decision-making knowledge of conflict resolution and social competence skills will promote a world without war.

"A Prayer for World Peace" by the Venerable Master Hsiung Yun, the Founder of Fokuangshan Buddhist order and Buddha's Light International Association says:

"The rumbling of war between nations,

The squabble of bickering between people,

The roar of greed in the rapids of craving,

The growl of hatred among races

The disagreement among different people,

Have caused so many arguments,

The discrimination among different races

Has caused so many disasters,

The intolerance between different religions,

Has caused so many misfortunes."

The conflict of interests among different nations through out the globe. As it is quoted we need to move towards a world where has caused so many chaos and upheaval, in the minds of human being.

"There be no jealousy, only admiration;
There be no hatred, only harmony;
There be no greed, only generosity;
There be no affliction, only fulfillment;
Let people of different ages live in harmony,
Let people of different social stations have mutual respect,
Let people of different professions work in cooperation,
Let people of different religions practice with tolerance,
The wisdom to close the distance between self and others,
The selflessness to eliminate all of our attachments;
The truth to resolve the confrontations between races;
The compassion to reconcile the conflicts between nations."

Bibliography

1. Agrawal Shaping India of our Dreams 2003. New Delhi, Knowledge Books Inc.

2. Alphonce 2007 Globalisation, Education and Development: Ideas, Actors and Dynamics.

3. Bharatan Kumarappa, (ed.) Towards New Education. Ahmedabad: Navjivan, 1953.

4. Bhanumathy K.P. Candid Conversations with towering persons. 2007. New Delhi, National Book Trust. India.

5. Beyerlin, Ulrich. Sustainable Development, Max Planck Encyclopedia of Public International Law.

6. Dhokalia, R.P. Eternal Human Values and World Religions. New Delhi: National Council of Educational Research and Training, 2001.

7. Gandhi, M.K., Hind Swaraj, Ahmedabad Navjeevan 1944, p. 24.

8. Gandhi, M.K. Basic Education. Bharatan Kumarappa, ed. Ahmedabad: Navjivan, 1951

9. Gandhi, M.K., An Autobiography (Ahmedabad Navjeevan, 1948, p. 408.

10. Gay. L.R. Educational Research. Competencies for analysis and Application. London. 1987, Merrill Publishing Company.

11. Glenside, PA: Pennsylvania Council on International Education, 7-20.

12. Jeanette Rhedding-Jones, Evaluation and Ethics in Teacher Education: English (in Norway) and Globalisation. Australian Association for Research in Education, Adelaide Australia, November–December 1998.

13. Jose Joaquin Brunner. Investing in Knowledge,1991, Canada.

14. Li, Rita Yi Man. [1], "Building Our Sustainable Cities" Illinois, Published by Common Ground Publishing.

15. Obul Reddy etal. Quantitative Techniques-I. 2003. Mumbai. Himalaya Pulishing House.

16. Pauline V. Young. Scientific Social Surveys and Research 1984. New Delhi. Prentice –Hall of India Private Limited.

17. Pezzey, J; M. Toman (January 2002). "The Economics of Sustainability: A Review of Journal Articles". Resources for the Future DP 02-03: 1–36. http://www.rff.org/documents/RFF-DP-02-03.pdf. Retrieved 2009-06-16.

18. Powar (ED), Internationalisation of Indian Higher Education, 2001, New Delhi, Association Indian Universities, AIU House.

19. Powar (ED), 2009. Quality Assurance in Distance Higher Education. New Delhi, Association Indian Universities, AIU House.

20. Powar (ED), 1995. Higher Education in India-In Search of Quality. New Delhi, Association Indian Universities, AIU House.

21. Prabhth S.V. (Ed) Perspectives on Naitalim, 2010, New Delhi, Serials Publications.

22. Prabhth S.V. (Ed), Youth and Rural India, 2011, New Delhi, Global Research Publications.

23. Radhakrishnan, S. (ed.), Mahatma Gandhi, Essays and Reflections.

24. Robert Davison and Ned Kock. Professional Ethics in ethics-l@listserv.gmd.de is a general list for the discussion of ethics in computing.

25. Roberts, J. (2005) 'Millennium Development Goals' are international targets now more.

26. Credible?', Journal of International Development, 17(1): 113-129.

27. Robertson, R. (1983) 'Interpreting globality' in World Realities and International Studies Today, Sam Pitroda, Advisor to Prime Minister of India, Advisor to Prime Minister of India. We have discussed a lot, now it's time to act, India Education Review.

28. Siddhartha Thulasi. Sadhana Deepika, 2001, Chennai, Sarada Publications.

29. Sudhir M.A., and M. Alankara Masilamani. Environmental Issues. 2003, New Delhi Reliance Publishing House.

30. Varkey, C.J., The Wardha Scheme of Education: An Exposition and Examination.

31. Varma V.P.,—Political Philosophy Mahatma Gandhi and Sarvodaya p. 100.

32. Vinoba Bhave,—Thoughts on Education (Varanasi; Sarva Seva Sangh) Prakashan, 1964).

Journals, Papers, Reports and Web Sites

1. http://www.classifieds.amlaan.com/|http://www.zahie.com/thisismyindia.com

2. http://www.spectator.sk/articles/view/37603/12/winning_essays_of_the_mahatma_gandhi_competition.html

3. ethcse-l@listserv.utk.edu hosts the discussion of ethical issues in software engineering.

4. Education in India 1992, and Selected Educational Statistics, 1997-98. Department of Education.

5. Interview with Ela Gandhi,The Gandhian View on Sustainable Development, Johannesburg, South Africa.

6. Annual report 1999-2000 Ministry of Human Resource Development.

7. Conflict Resolution for Kindergarten through Grade 3. Chapel Hill, North Carolina: Mediation Network of North Carolina, 1998.

8. Benchmark statements. benchmarking@qaa.ac.uk

9. India Education Review. News. Higher education to get additional 500 crore during 2013-14.18 Jan. 2013.

10. "National Curriculum Framework Review 2005. Peace." New Delhi: National Council of Educational Research and Training, 2005.

11. New Era Development Institute. Peace Education Activities for Children: A Teacher's Guide. Panchgani, India: New Era Development Institute, 2002.

12. National Knowledge Commission.Report to the Nation, 2007.

13. Interdisciplinary Research Collaborations between the Social Sciences and STEM. by Dr James Roberts [PDF: 612KB]

14. Summary of Proceedings National Symposium on Farm Credit for Inclusive Growth, Jointly Organised by CAB and NABARD at CAB, Pune-January 12 & 13, 2007.

15. Towards Meeting A Commitment. Status Paper on Achievement of Education for All, 1995, Department of Education, MHRD. Government of India.

16. United Nations. 1987. "Report of the World Commission on Environment and Development." General Assembly Resolution 42/187, 11 December 1987, Retrieved: 2007-04-12.

17. United Cites and Local Governments, "Culture: Fourth Pillar of Sustainable Development".

18. UN Decade of Education for Sustainable Development (DESD). UNESCO.

19. UNESCO (2003) EFA Global Monitoring Report 2003/4: Gender and Education for all: the Leap to Equality, Paris: UNESCO.

20. UNESCO (2005 a) Towards Knowledge Societies, Paris: UNESCO.

21. UNESCO (2005 b) Education for All: The Quality Imperative.

22. Institutional Accreditation. 2007. NAAC, Bangalore.

23. Infusing Dynamism in Teacher Education through ICT Integration. Learnings from India. 2008. NAAC, Bangalore.

24. 12th Five Year Plan. Draft Report of the Working Group on Rural Development, 2012.

25. Wikipadia, the free encyclopedia.

26. 500 million skilled manpower by 2022: Still a long way to go? Indian Education Review.

Index

S

T

U

V